The Virgil Michel Series

Virgil Michel, O.S.B., a monk of Saint John's Abbey in Collegeville, Minnesota, was a founder of the Liturgical Movement in the United States in the 1920s and fostered its development until his death in 1938. Michel's writing, editing, teaching, and preaching centered on the relationship between liturgy and the life of the faithful—the Body of Christ.

The Pueblo Books imprint of The Liturgical Press honors Virgil Michel's life and work with a monograph series named for him. The Virgil Michel Series will offer studies that examine the connections between liturgy and life in particular communities, as well as works exploring the relationship of liturgy to theology, ethics, and social sciences. The Virgil Michel Series will be ecumenical in breadth and international in scope, recognizing that liturgy embodies yet transcends cultures and denominations.

Series Editor: Don E. Saliers

Don E. Saliers, who teaches regularly at St. John's University in the summer program, is William R. Cannon Distinguished Professor of Theology and Worship at Emory University, Atlanta, Georgia.

E. Byron Anderson

Worship and Christian Identity

Practicing Ourselves

Virgil Michel Series
Don E. Saliers, Editor

A PUEBLO BOOK

The Liturgical Press Collegeville, Minnesota

www.litpress.org

A Pueblo Book published by The Liturgical Press

Design by Frank Kacmarcik, Obl.S.B.

Library of Congress Cataloging-in-Publication Data

Anderson, E. Byron.
  Worship and Christian identity : Practicing ourselves / E. Byron Anderson.
     p. cm.
  "A Pueblo book."
  Includes bibliographical references and index.
  ISBN 0-8146-6192-0 (alk. paper)
    1. Liturgics. 2. Public worship. I. Title.

BV176.3 .A53 2003
264—dc21   2002026712

Contents

Preface

In 1740 John and Charles Wesley published portions of Charles's hymn "The Means of Grace" in *Hymns and Sacred Poems*. It provided the Wesleys' response to the "stillness" of the Moravians. This hymn and the hymn "Still for thy loving kindness, Lord," which follows in the 1780 hymnal, outline the Wesleys' understandings of the use of the means of grace.[1] In these hymns, as in their sermons, the Wesleys were careful not to confuse the "outward" means of grace with the inner experience of the graced life. Nevertheless, they were clear that God provides, even "appoints," the outward means with which Christian people are called to practice the Christian faith.

In our own day, we are confronted by a church and culture that are more than ready to pick and choose among the most comfortable and comforting of Christian doctrines and practices, often yielding to a non-Christian culture the power to define the shape, character, and practice of Christian life. Somewhere and somehow Methodist people have lost sight of the evangelical, doctrinal, and practical method at the heart of our tradition. This book offers one response to this context, joining itself with the Wesleys to argue that there is something yet in God's appointed ways that remains a gift to the church and to the lives of Christian people.

That gift and task are perhaps best described in the first two stanzas of "The Means of Grace" (1740):

---

[1] "Still for thy loving kindness, Lord" was also entitled "The Means of Grace" in *Hymns and Spiritual Songs*, 1753. *The Works of John Wesley*, vol. 7: *A Collection of Hymns for the use of the People called Methodists*, ed. Franz Hildebrandt and Oliver A. Beckerlegge (Oxford: Clarendon Press, 1983) 188, 190.

Long have I seemed to serve thee, Lord,
With unavailing pain;
Fasted, and prayed, and read thy Word,
And heard it preached—in vain.
Oft did I with th'assembly join,
And near thy altar drew;
A form of godliness was mine—
The power I never knew.[2]

At the head of the chapters that follow, verses from Charles Wesley's hymns provide a theological starting point for exploring these questions. Verses from the two hymns on the means of grace head the first four chapters. Verses from other Wesley hymns serve a similar purpose at the head of the second four chapters. These hymn verses also invite us to explore how the sacramental and evangelical balance sought, if not realized, by the Wesleys might appropriately serve our churches today.

There is something at stake for the life of the church in the way and the language with which it worships. There is a power that we do not know or that we at best ignore. What is at stake? What is this power?

There are many to whom acknowledgment is due: the United Methodist congregations and pastors that permitted my questioning presence, friends who have watched this manuscript develop, and teachers who initially helped shape the questions. I am particularly grateful to Bruce Morrill and Michael Cartwright for the ways in which they have supported and encouraged this theological conversation; to Karen-Marie Yust for her theological insight and clear editorial hand; and to Ron Allen, who has been quietly and steadfastly a supportive and wise senior colleague.

I must also acknowledge the cooperation of those who published earlier versions of several chapters or sections of this book and permitted their use here. Part of Chapter 1 was published as "Worship and Belief: Liturgical Practice as a Contextual Theology" in *Worship* 75:4 (September 2001) 432–452; part of Chapter 3 was published in "Liturgical Catechesis: Congregational Practice as Formation," *Religious Education* 92:3 (Summer 1997) 349–362; part

---

[2] Ibid., 188–189.

of Chapter 4 in "Performance, Practice and Meaning in Christian Baptism," *Worship* 69:6 (November 1995) 482–504; portions of Chapters 5 and 6 in "A Constructive Task in Religious Education: Making Christian Selves," *Religious Education* 98:2 (Spring 1998) 173–188 and "The Trinitarian Grammar of the Liturgy and the Liturgical Practice of the Self," *Wesleyan Theological Journal* 34:2 (Fall 1999) 152–174; and a portion of Chapter 8 as "O for a heart to praise my God" in E. Byron Anderson and Bruce T. Morrill, S.J., eds., *Liturgy and the Moral Self* (Collegeville: The Liturgical Press, Pueblo Books, 1998).

Chapter One

Introduction

A form of godliness was mine—
The power I never knew.[1]

When the *United Methodist Hymnal* was introduced in 1989, followed by the *Book of Worship* in 1992, the church believed it had in hand resources that celebrated what the church had been and anticipated what the church might become.[2] Many in the church believed that these two books provided resources that both represented and would enrich the various traditions brought together in the 1968 merger of the Methodist and Evangelical United Brethren Churches. The church once again sought to reclaim the historical importance of the hymnal and the worship book as primary theological and devotional resources for United Methodist individuals and communities. As these books also brought together the pastoral, ecumenical, and scholarly liturgical work of the previous twenty years, many believed that they would serve the renewal of the sacramental and liturgical life of the church and support that life for some time to come. Little did the church know that it was

---

[1] Hymn 88, "Long have I seemed to serve thee, Lord," stanza 2 in *The Works of John Wesley*, vol. 7: *A Collection of Hymns for the use of the People called Methodists*, ed. Franz Hildebrandt and Oliver Beckerlegge (Oxford: Clarendon Press; New York: Oxford University Press, 1983) 189.

[2] *The United Methodist Hymnal* (Nashville: The United Methodist Publishing House, 1989) vi.

1

on the edge of significant changes in the expectations about Christian worship, the structures for it, and the resources to be used in it.

Since the introduction of these resources, questions of sacramental practice, inclusive or transformative language, and the renewal of congregational hymnody have been largely displaced by marketing questions and conflicts between "traditional" and "contemporary" worship. What has often been described as the most (racially) segregated hour of the week is now subdivided into increasingly specialized "target audiences" of singles, seekers, boomers, and Generation X-ers, with worship carefully packaged as "traditional" or "contemporary."[3] What at various points in Methodist history has been understood as a "means of grace" is now seen primarily as a "means of numerical growth" that largely borrows from the liturgical pragmatism articulated so clearly in Charles Finney's mid-nineteenth-century *Lectures on Revival*.[4]

Although risking overstatement, missing in both this pragmatic turn and in the conflict between "traditional" and "contemporary" worship is significant discussion of what is at stake for the identity of Christian persons and communities in the shape and practice of worship as a United Methodist Church. Perhaps more surprising, discussion of the theological shape and practice of worship also has been absent from recent church debates concerning theological standards in the United Methodist Church. These absences suggest that for many in the church today, worship has little to do with the shape and character of that belief; it is only a means for expressing the community's belief. In the midst of the worship wars it is time to "step back and ask some tough questions . . . about the purpose

---

[3] For a review of these issues, see Frank Senn, "'Worship Alive': An Analysis and Critique of 'Alternative Worship,'" *Worship* 69:3 (May 1995) 194–224, and Lester Ruth, "Lex Agendi, Lex Orandi: Toward an Understanding of Seeker Services as a New Kind of Liturgy," *Worship* 70:5 (September 1996) 386–405. Ruth argues that this market-conscious approach to Christian worship results in a new liturgical pragmatism: "What must be done (lex agendi) establishes new rules for how the church should pray (lex orandi) " (386–387).

[4] Reprint (Minneapolis: Bethany House Publishing, 1988). See Karen Westerfield Tucker's discussion of the influence of the revival and camp meeting on Sunday worship in *American Methodist Worship* (New York: Oxford University Press, 2001) 81.

of worship, about the character of God who is worshipped, and about the character-forming power of the community that strives to worship this God with integrity and purpose."[5]

Among the questions we must ask ourselves as a church are these: What is the relationship between communal prayer and belief? Between prayer and the formation of Christian persons and communities? Between prayer and our knowledge of self, world, and God? These questions point to a more fundamental question: What is at stake for the Christian community in the reform and renewal of liturgical sacramental practice?

These questions have occupied my attention, in one form or another, for almost twenty years. The question of the relationship between prayer and belief has its roots in my own theological education, which coincided with the publication of the "convergence" document *Baptism, Eucharist and Ministry* in 1982.[6] This document articulated an ecumenical vision that increasingly saw a church united in prayer and, through prayer, in belief. My theological education also coincided with a blossoming, even explosive, awareness about the power of language and image in our worship. Battle lines were drawn: how dare we continue to pray in ways that are experienced as patriarchal, exclusive, discriminatory? Yet, day in and day out my seminary community gathered to pray, to proclaim God's word, to share bread and wine at the Lord's table. However fragile the bond, our struggles to become a community in prayer enabled us to remain a community in the midst of theological difference and struggle.

The second and third questions concerning the relationships between prayer, Christian formation, and knowledge of God have their roots in my work as a parish pastor, musician, and educator. In large and small congregations alike, I encountered people hungry for the life of prayer and sacrament, for explicit formation in the Christian life, for an understanding of community as gathered in God's name and nurtured at the Lord's table. At the same time, in the same communities, I encountered a clash of traditions—in hymns known and loved, in suspicion or love of sacramental and

---

[5] Philip D. Kenneson, "Worship Wars and Rumors of Worship Wars," *Reviews in Religion and Theology* (May 1996) 74.

[6] Geneva: World Council of Churches, 1982.

3

liturgical practices, in the willingness or hesitancy to dig deeply into the Christian story. In these communities I also encountered children and youth absent from, and unable to participate in, the liturgical life of the community. For the sake of expediency, children and youth were sent off to Sunday school, while the adults gathered for worship. Excluded from corporate worship as children, youth absented themselves from worship except for the occasional "Youth Sunday" and disappeared completely as high school graduation approached and passed. (They learned their lessons well.) Excluded from "adult worship," they created their own forms, many of which seem to be returning in the guise of "alternative" worship today.

The fourth question—what is at stake for us as a Christian community—came to life in the process of a year's work teaching about and introducing the then new denominational hymnal and its accompanying revised liturgical resources at the local and statewide level. Here, even as I met a willingness to learn, I was confronted by the question "Why?" "Why should we care about these new things?" "Why should we learn new hymns?" "Why should we pray differently?" Why, indeed?

The questions and battles continue today, although the dividing lines have shifted. On the one hand, this market-conscious context makes any attempt to make normative, constitutive, and catechetical or formational claims about the liturgy appear foolish or anachronistic. On the other hand, it is precisely this context that requires that we explore what is at stake for us as a church in the patterns and practices of Christian worship. This context also requires that we begin to develop not only a liturgical theology but also a theory of sacramental practice as liturgical catechesis,[7] of liturgical practices as a central means by which the church shapes the faith, character, and consciousness of its members. In doing so, we may begin to see the practical implications of reclaiming the centrality of what John Wesley called the "ordinary means of grace" and what Henry Knight, in his study of the Wesleyan means of grace, calls a "necessary pattern of activity for the Christian life." As

[7] Throughout the book I will use the term "liturgical catechesis" to refer to the ways in which worship teaches, instructs, and forms us in the Christian faith.

4

Knight argues, the mutually interdependent means of grace "provide the context within which an ongoing relationship with God is sustained over time, and the Christian life is correspondingly enabled to grow in love."[8]

Knight's as well as Randy Maddox's readings of Wesley's understanding of the "means of grace" help frame the discussion of liturgical practice that I develop in this book. Knight claims, first, that "grace, for Wesley, is relational: grace both enables and invites us to participate in an ongoing relationship with God."[9] Second, "there is a pattern of means of grace which is essential to the maintenance and growth of that relationship."[10] Third, for Wesley "the means of grace form an interrelated context within which the Christian life is lived and through which relationships with God and one's neighbor are maintained."[11] Further, "the means of grace provide the context within which an ongoing relationship with God is sustained over time, and the Christian life is correspondingly enabled to grow in love."[12] In these, Knight suggests the constituting nature of sacramental practices: they invite, enable, and maintain patterns of relatedness to God and to neighbor. Such practices are normative, not only because they are essential to the constituting work but also because they provide the "normal" context in which Christian life is lived.[13]

As for Maddox's work, three statements are important here. First, Maddox suggests that Wesley's understanding of the work of sanctification undertaken in and by the power of the Holy Spirit "was a process of character formation that is made possible by a restored participation of fallen humanity in the Divine life and power."[14] Second, he suggests that Wesley "took for granted a virtue psychology that emphasizes the role of habituated affections in motivating and guiding authentic human actions."[15] Finally,

[8] *The Presence of God in the Christian Life: John Wesley and the Means of Grace* (Metuchen, N.J.: Scarecrow Press, 1992) 13, 15.

[9] Ibid., 8.

[10] Ibid.

[11] Ibid., 2.

[12] Ibid., 14.

[13] This has consequences for the shape of our liturgical and sacramental practice, especially for eucharistic praying, as we will see in Chapter 6.

[14] *Responsible Grace* (Nashville: Abingdon Press, Kingswood Books, 1994) 122.

[15] Ibid., 132.

Maddox argues that, for Wesley, "proper worship helps structure the formation of Christian character, while openness to the Spirit's witness provides access to the empowerment for this formation."[16] The first statement points us toward Wesley's theological anthropology. The restoration of humanity to the image of God in which it was created is a restoration of humanity in the image and holiness of the Trinity.[17] The second and third statements point to the role of regular and repeated practice of the means of grace in the formation of Christian persons.

What do these statements signal for a discussion about liturgical practice? First, our participation in the means of grace, the practices of liturgy and sacrament, names and shapes a Trinitarian context and pattern of living. This is particularly true in the prayer texts that accompany and interpret these practices. Faith is enacted as doxology, not merely assented to. Second, this Trinitarian context and pattern require the development and sustaining of relationships between persons and God, as well as persons and communities, that are dynamic rather than static ways of being in the world. It is in such relationships that we grow in love of God and neighbor and are restored to the likeness of God. This understanding of sacramental practice permits an understanding of the Christian life as a pattern or complex of patterns ever forming, transforming, and emerging through regular participation in the "means of grace."

WORSHIP AND BELIEF
IN TWO UNITED METHODIST CONGREGATIONS

Over the past several years I have used these assumptions and questions to shape a series of interviews concerning the formative role of liturgical practice in four United Methodist congregations.[18]

[16] Ibid., 140.

[17] See Barry Bryant's discussion of this in regard to the hymns. Barry E. Bryant, "Trinity and Hymnody: The Doctrine of the Trinity in the Hymns of Charles Wesley," *Wesleyan Theological Journal* 25:2 (Fall 1990) 68–69.

[18] This research was supported by a grant from the Wabash Center for Teaching and Learning in the summer of 1999. In the third congregation, attention was focused on the weekly use of the Affirmation of Faith of the United Church of Canada, as found in *The United Methodist Hymnal*, p. 883. In the fourth, attention focused on the "bracketing" of the weekly liturgy by the

In what follows, I summarize the work with two of the four congregations as a way to explore these assumptions and questions. These two congregations in particular offer a distinctive opportunity for comparisons between practice, theology, and context. They also provide an opportunity to explore the ways in which the practice of the local church questions and challenges official denominational theologies.

These two congregations share several characteristics. Each is self-identified within the United Methodist Church as a "reconciling congregation" intentionally committed to welcoming and ministering with homosexual persons. Both congregations have a clearly articulated missional purpose that commits them to ministry in difficult urban contexts. Both focus their ministries with those persons marginalized by church and society. Both congregations celebrate the eucharist on a weekly basis. This distinguishes them from most United Methodist churches, in which monthly celebration of eucharist is common.

EUMC

The EUMC congregation was founded in 1966, in the midst of social racial conflict, with the hope that it could provide a reconciling presence between African-American and Anglo-American people. It is situated on the margin between a low-income neighborhood, a thriving and expanding university, and an expanding two-billion-dollar-a-year industry that encroaches upon the residential community.

With the exception of a brief period in the early 1970s when eucharist was celebrated monthly, EUMC has celebrated eucharist on a weekly basis since its founding in 1966. For the most part, EUMC uses the basic service of Word and Table as currently found in *The United Methodist Hymnal* and *The United Methodist Book of Worship*.[19] The congregation has reviewed this practice at several points in its history as it sought to discern the shape of its mission and ministry. As noted above, this long-term practice of weekly eucharist is in many ways an exception to worship practice among United Methodists today.

---

exchange of peace. In all four congregations, two questions were predominant: How has this weekly practice shaped you as a Christian person? How has this practice shaped this particular congregation's self-understanding?

[19] Nashville: The United Methodist Publishing House, 1989, 1992.

In my interviews in the congregation I asked each person two questions: How has the weekly celebration of communion shaped you as a Christian person? How has this weekly celebration shaped the life of this congregation?[20] The way in which the individual and communal interact at EUMC makes the answers to these questions difficult to separate. Nevertheless, the answers I received to these questions were thoughtful and rich, sometimes even surprising.

Two important qualifiers also shaped the answers. First, the service of the table at EUMC is clearly more than the sharing of the bread and cup. It begins with the exchange of peace and the movement into a circle and the joining of hands. It continues with an invitation to the table, the great thanksgiving, and the sharing of bread and cup as it is passed around the circle, each person serving the next. It concludes with intercessory prayer for the church and the world and with the singing of "Shalom."[21]

This point leads to the second qualifier: not everyone gives the same weight to weekly eucharist, that is, there are portions of the service of the table other than the sharing of the bread and cup that are more important for some. Even so, there is a clearly expressed understanding that these other portions are important parts of the service of the table as practiced at EUMC and do not stand on their own. As part of the eucharistic practice at EUMC, the meaning found in each component part contributes to the overall eucharistic theology of the congregation. The ways in which people give value

---

[20] I ask these questions believing that even when lay people lack the ability to use "official" theological language to speak about their experience, they are nevertheless able to offer explicitly theological interpretations of that experience when invited to do so. As Joyce Ann Zimmerman writes, ". . . we may never forget that members of a liturgical assembly are called upon to interpret the liturgical text (celebration) both in terms of an assessment of the liturgical action itself as well as the appropriation of the meaning of that action in their own daily living. We might want to distinguish this latter as an 'informal' or 'subconscious' interpretation, but it is interpretation nonetheless. If interpretation of liturgical texts is only the work of experts, then the liturgical celebration itself is diminished in power and meaning." Joyce Ann Zimmerman, *Liturgy and Hermeneutics* (Collegeville, Minn.: The Liturgical Press, 1999) 48–49.

[21] Set to a traditional Israeli melody, as found in *The United Methodist Hymnal*, 667.

to each component part in the service also help to frame two common themes in the interviews: hospitality and communion.

Hospitality. In many ways individual and congregational meaning is defined by the congregation's response to the invitation to the table: "Everyone has a place at this table." Although this value has always been an intentional part of the congregation's life for many years, the ritual character of this response has emerged only over the past three years. It has provided a way to clearly identify the congregation's identity in a time of transition in pastoral and lay leadership marked by the retirement of the congregation's founding pastor and the death of an important lay leader. "Everyone has a place at this table" functions as both a weekly affirmation of the faith of the congregation and "a challenge to practice . . . radical hospitality."[22]

Hearing this invitation and response weekly "is an affirmation and a good reminder to everyone in the church as to one of the fundamental reasons why EUMC exists." In responses to the questions about both individual and congregational life, there was a clear sense of the radical character of this invitation "in a society that almost by default marginalizes . . . some people and says you are not welcome." This sense of radical hospitality at the table permits an understanding common among those interviewed that "we come to the table broken, estranged at times, not of one accord on every issue on the table, but we come to the table and we share the one loaf and the cup." Hospitality extends to meals that are shared in members' homes as well as to meals provided for neighborhood children through the summer months.

For some, this sense of welcome remains focused on the invitation; for others, it is on the gathering in the circle, the serving of the bread and cup to one another, or on the intercessory prayers after the sharing of the bread and cup. As one person stated, "Here we . . . deliberately think about things a little more and have different ideas about them. And what is meaningful for the one person is not necessarily meaningful to another. But what is meaningful to that other begins

---

[22] This and subsequent quotations in this discussion and in the discussion of the second congregation, unless otherwise indicated, are from the taped interviews with members of the congregations and their pastoral leaders.

to be understandable and take on meaning that was not there before." One person recounted serving the bread and cup to another person in one worship service. "I can remember how people looked at you with such seriousness as you were going to give them the bread, and I remember being very surprised at the first few people and I thought, 'Well, you think that this is such a holy thing, why would it be very different if you were standing on the other side?'"

Perhaps one of the strongest summaries of the importance of the invitation at the individual level is in the following statement. It reflects what was a common experience for many persons victimized or marginalized by the institutional church in other places. It also seems to reflect the congregation's clear awareness of this experience of marginalization.

"The blessing for me is that 'everyone has a place at this table' and I would go 'yea, but what about me, because you know this has so much pain, how can I have a place at your table? Why should I be at this table when I don't even know what is going on inside of me?' But you know, after a while it kind of grows on you and . . . somehow my place has been made that whatever it is that is going on with me or whatever pain I am carrying, there is a place for me too."

Another person stated, "There is just no doubt in my mind that I am welcome. I just sense that. Not just from that statement but it's symbolic of everything that's done. That you're truly welcome and the expectations of you participating are no less either, that all of us are expected to incorporate the Jesus story in our own lives because we are participating in this." A third person, for whom weekly sharing of bread and cup is not important, also argued that this invitation and sense of welcome reaffirmed her belief that "all people should be welcome at the table. It instills in me my belief that God accepts everybody and that Jesus did not shed his blood just for a few, that he shed his blood for everybody." As another person summarizes, "It is a teaching . . . that sinks down, I think, and that's a place where worship informs behavior . . . that can work a transformation on getting us past racism, sexism, homophobia, 'trackism' based on income, 'beliefism' based on others' education."

Communion. Part of the transformation that happens within this congregation is the movement from being welcomed to being embraced, even by strangers to the community. This embrace begins in the sharing of the peace. And while no one denied the importance of the invitation to the table, some focused their reflections on the actions of joining hands in the circle, the sharing of the bread and cup there, and the intercessions that concluded the service.

For some, the circle provides the physical and visual confirmation of the truth of the invitation. "To be able to look around [the circle] and see the different kinds of people, the different dress, the different nationalities, the different races, the different ages, the different conditions . . . It's real here. We really believe in diversity." Another said, "A circle brings more closeness . . . [it] feels more like being a part of the whole event." In the circle you are "connecting with the person that's next to you . . . you're looking at that person, you're saying something to that person." As another person said, "When we stand around the table and look at each other and know a great many of our stories and see our differences, the variety that is here and the affirmation that is here in a tangible way . . . we see one another face to face, and we partake of God's grace that is dispensed in these elements, and we can say, not only do we belong here but that everyone else that wants to belong, belongs here." With this understanding comes a shift from understanding eucharist as a means or sign of personal salvation to understanding it as a sign of the salvation of the whole community.

For some, the unbroken circle around the table takes on eschatological significance: meeting face to face becomes a reminder or sign of the heavenly banquet, of God's tremendous creativity in humanity, and of the extravagance of coming to the feast each week. It also provides a hope of remembrance of participating in this community of faith. "One day I won't be in the circle, but I'll be remembered as being in the circle, so passing the bread and cup—I think this goes into the memory, the consciousness of who we are."

What of the sharing of the bread and cup itself? Several responses echoed the following statement:

"No matter how far afield, no matter how much this simply neighborhood stuff, urban renewal stuff, suffering stuff, no matter how much that had been heard, the Lord's Supper always brought us back to the primary fact of our faith: that our life is the gift of grace and the Lord's Supper dramatizes that and does that for us."

As another person describes it, "If I had any notion that my faith is elsewhere or my attention elsewhere, I get focused again, brought back into that framework. What the eucharist does for me is to really focus the faith experience on Jesus . . . on that person and that experience and that peculiar and awful presence of God in human form." Even those for whom the invitation, the circle, or the intercessions carry more personal weight acknowledge that it is the sharing of the bread and cup that provides the motivation for the circle. "The sharing of the bread and cup are part of why the circle is there and part of why we make the circle." The sharing of the bread and cup are part of the "Jesus story alive and how it translates this Sunday in our lives." It is "a sharing of the ways it has come together, all of humanity in the bread and the wine." And for another person it has become an ordinary part of her life: "I celebrate not only here but every time I break bread and I drink. It's a reminder that this is daily."

Finally, some place more weight on the concluding actions around the table—the intercessions and the singing of "Shalom." The communion enacted in sharing the bread and cup continues in the communion of suffering and celebration as these are shared in prayer. Yet, as one person suggested, to separate the prayers from the sharing of bread and cup "would be just standing around in a circle, talking about needs or sharing. [It] wouldn't have the same kind of worship benefits that come when communion is also served. A lot of groups could talk about, support groups could talk about what kinds of needs do you have and we're there behind you and give you hugs." Here it is a clear sense of the connection between or the combination of the bread and cup with the prayers that provide the weight or importance for the person. As we heard earlier, even when some people do not experience sharing the bread and cup as the most important part of the service, the bread and cup provide the center around which hospitality and communion become possible.

Throughout these comments we hear ways in which individual meaning and congregational meaning are linked with each other.

What communion or eucharist or the Lord's Supper (all three names were used) means at the individual level is directly linked to what the individual believes it means for the life of the congregation. The place of welcome, care, intimacy, and prayer provides "a sense of the fellowship of faith and the sense of the communion of people with one another and with God." "It's really in holy communion that the sense of being again a part of the community of faith, in every way . . . has been affirmed for me." "We meet there around the same core of belief, however we affirm and understand it, and we meet there accepting one another, loving one another, caring about one another, being cared for. . . ." Another person, reflecting on the history of the congregation, observed that "I think from the beginning we sensed, although we were to grow in this conviction in time, I think we sensed that the Lord's Supper dramatized the grace of God in a unique way for us."

As this last statement indicates and as we heard earlier, the weekly celebration of eucharist has shaped and is shaping the belief and identity of EUMC. Those interviewed express a clear sense of the relationship between what is practiced in worship and the congregation's self-identity in witness and mission in the neighborhood and city. A weekly celebration in which hospitality and communion are enacted has been a means of nurture and support for the values of welcome and inclusiveness that are core to the congregation's identity throughout its ministry. But weekly celebration of the eucharist also provides an opportunity to the congregation to continue to test and be tested by its commitments. As one person commented, in saying "everybody has a place at this table,"

"we are not just simply mouthing the phrase, but we are participating in something that shapes over and over and over again our commitments to the gospel and to what the gospel represents. . . . the eucharist informs our congregation every time we come together. That is our focus. And I think that has a sound effect on shaping the commitment we have here at EUMC to actually try to do what Jesus says he wants us to do."

Finally, there is a clear sense, especially among those who have been in the congregation for an extended period of time, that the intentionality of congregational reflection on, as well as education about, the meaning and importance of weekly communion at various points in the congregation's history has permitted a depth of theological reflection not often found in many congregations. As we will hear, the depth of hospitality and communion expressed by EUMC and the intentionality of its reflection provide distinct contrasts with the second congregation, PUMC.

PUMC

PUMC , although sharing several initial characteristics with EUMC, is distinguished from EUMC in a number of ways. First and foremost, at the time of the interviews PUMC had been in existence as a congregation for only eighteen months. Second, whereas EUMC began life in a house, PUMC began its life meeting in the basement of a restaurant/bar. Several months prior to the research, it had moved to a coffee shop situated at the intersection of industrial, residential, and university neighborhoods. Although the pastor has an office in a local church, the congregation had made a conscious, missional decision not to meet in any church or churchlike building. It has gone where it believes its (potential) congregation is; it has also consciously placed itself in a public setting that is familiar to those it seeks to address. Third, where EUMC has been and continues to be a multi-generational community, PUMC was formed as an attempt to connect with Generation X and other marginalized seekers. Its members are predominantly in their twenties and early thirties, most are unmarried, some are in committed relationships. Finally, where EUMC consciously uses the official liturgical resources of the United Methodist Church, PUMC uses what might be called a "bare outline" of the pattern of Word and Table as represented in the United Methodist resources.[23]

It was perhaps too early in PUMC's life to ask questions concerning the formative power of liturgical practice over time that were at the heart of the interview project because they had not had the time together as a community that permits reflection on long-term practice. At the same time, it was not too early to be asking questions of identity and experience as PUMC begins doing a (self-described) "new thing" in the context of new congregation development and outreach to communities of persons disenfranchised or alienated, for a variety of reasons, from the traditional life of the

[23] See, for example, *The United Methodist Hymnal*, 2.

14

church. This is especially important because of its decision to put eucharistic practice at the center of its life together in a time when many church-growth experts discourage such attention to sacramental practice.[24]

PUMC describes itself as gathering "for coffee around tables, sharing ancient and new stories and talking about issues that affect our lives and our relationship with God and one another. Then we gather around another table, and we remember our connection with God in the simple gifts of bread and drink through the story of Jesus sharing bread with his friends." As a basic statement of what they do as a worshiping community, this is a very precise description. As people arrive at the coffee shop for the service, they purchase coffee or other beverages and pastries. They gather at tables of various sizes and shapes. One table has been prepared as a "liturgical center" with candles, bread, grape juice, baskets, and other items. Simple songs, some drawn from Taizé resources and others composed by members of the leadership team, along with informal words of welcome, are used to gather people. A biblical text and other non-biblical materials are read, often selected to focus on a particular theme or image. The pastor does not preach but invites each table to converse about the readings and the theme. Some talk, others do not, some gather materials to draw or to write responses. The pastor leads a concluding conversation, and the musicians (often with simple instruments such as guitar, drum, and flute) lead another song. An invitation to the table, drawing upon the themes of the conversation and paraphrasing the institution narrative, is offered to all. Some individuals come to the table, serving themselves bread and wine. Others come to the table placing prayer requests in one of the baskets on the table. Others remain quietly at their tables. The service concludes with more song, a brief blessing, and dismissal. Some linger for brief conversation after the service, but most leave immediately.

As they answered the questions concerning the relationship between worship and belief asked of the other congregations,

---

[24] This is also a concern as a number of congregations have invited or drawn upon PUMC to provide a model "alternative liturgy." By nature, PUMC is not likely to grow as a single worshiping community, but by creating other small communities.

members of PUMC tended to focus on several specific concerns that may typify their generational focus: authority, access, hospitality, and community. It is difficult to separate these from one another because many of the comments about one are linked to comments about the other.

Authority. There were several clear statements suggesting that one of the problems for Gen-Xers and others drawn to the table at PUMC is the way in which authority is practiced and manifested in "traditional" congregational life. The experience of authority as "authoritarian" (the imposition of rule) in contrast to "authoritative" (the rightful but always questioned claims about life together made by tradition, leadership, and community) has resulted in a sense of rejection of both the authoritarian and the authoritative. This rejection comes, in part, as a response to an experience of church as manipulative and barrier-producing. It also includes, contrary to much recent literature on "contemporary" or "seeker" worship, a rejection of the highly performative and technological means of communication that are being used in the consumer-oriented, suburban church-growth movement. Authority is experienced as that which moves people against their current needs or desires and as that which keeps people out. Rejection of such barrier-producing authority was important to everyone I interviewed, and especially to those who have experienced rejection, hurt, or alienation by the church as gay/lesbian persons.

The rejection of the authoritative was expressed in several different ways, but especially in the tension expressed by some members with being explicitly religious Christian people who can and do talk about Jesus. It also appeared in the intentional rejection of communal prayer forms. Prayer, while in community, occurs privately and individually. (Individuals may place written prayer concerns in a basket on the table during the table service, but these are never read or used for prayer by the whole community.) Although PUMC has been clear to claim the Christian Scriptures as important for the community, there is a relativizing of these texts as they are placed alongside other texts from a variety of traditions.

Access. Perhaps the clearest place in which distrust of authority appeared was in the concern all expressed about "access" to the table. As one person said, "The way PUMC had set up their communion service . . . really tells people that 'you have direct access to God, you don't need an intermediary, you are welcome at this table. This table is set for you.'" And as another said, "There is nobody between me and the bread, no one to say 'you can't come.'" Perhaps more telling is the comment made by another person that [communion at PUMC] is "very different from communion at home, where I am on my knees and with my hands like this [cupped and waiting]—very different. I'm not asking for it, I'm answering an invitation at PUMC, as opposed to begging for something or asking for something."

The importance of access is also expressed in the concern to provide for several different levels of participation—people may come to the table for the bread and cup, to light candles, or to place prayer requests in the prayer baskets, or they may choose not to come at all. In this, worshipers themselves determine "when and how much and how they share" at the table.

Hospitality. The concern for access by all at whatever level of participation is comfortable is also expressed in the concern by the design team to provide a place of table hospitality. This is expressed by pastoral leaders identifying themselves as "hosts" rather than as "authorities." As host, the leader sets and arranges the tables, the bread and cup, the candles, and other worship resources for that day, then "backs away" so that worship can happen. As the host, she can "depend on the fact that the people will be there and that God will be there and I don't have to be in charge of that."

The concern for hospitality and access is also expressed in the predominant image used to describe the table practice at PUMC. It is like a buffet table at a party, where everything has been prepared for you. You can approach it if and when you are hungry, and no one will say, "You can't eat that or that." "The host prepares the table and makes sure you're welcome to go and take what you need." As the congregation says in its own material, "Openness to all is important to us; we remember the stories of Jesus inviting all sorts of folks to parties and dinners, and we believe God's table is open to everyone. The table is set. There's room for you."

Although the concern for access and hospitality is undisputed among those interviewed, there was some concern expressed about the tension between the Christian tradition/norm of serving one's neighbor and the "self-serve" character of what happens at the table. Even so, the unmediated access to the table takes on additional importance in inviting a form of personal responsibility:

"The embodied element is very essential for me . . . to have that ritual every week of getting up and going to the table and having the responsibility being upon me to listen to what I hear at that moment. And then to be responsible for making it what I need it to be or what I want it to be."

This person seems to be suggesting that the character of hospitality provided by PUMC both permits and invites response and responsibility; there is an expectation of engagement at some level.

Community. When one is invited to a party with a buffet table at which individuals determine when, how, or if they will share in the food, how does PUMC talk about community or communion? They acknowledge that the character of the host, the sense of invitation and welcome, and the permissive playfulness of the service all provide individual worshipers a place of entry into the community.

Second, they acknowledge that entry alone does not create the community. Several of those interviewed talked about the table(s) as the focal point for the sense of community, differentiating these from other church experiences. The tables place persons, even if unknown to one another, in a context where conversation may and often does happen. One person described the importance of providing a space "in which to be not only creative in how you practice and talk about your faith but also where you can be heard every week." Several people also described a sense of connection to people in *watching* others participate at the table—taking bread and cup, lighting candles, placing prayer concerns in the prayer baskets. "It binds us together. There's a closeness that comes with watching someone take it [communion]." "It's almost an intimate activity to watch someone take communion."

Third, as one person described PUMC, there was a sense that it provided small-group, social-fellowship, and Bible-study experiences all at the same time.

What can we say about the relationship between worship and belief at PUMC? First, it is clear that the character and practice of hospitality at PUMC are providing a number of persons formerly alienated from the church access to an experience of Christian community. This has been important from the beginning of the design process, even though gathering about the table for sharing of the bread and cup was not part of the original plan. The use of the word "communion" to describe what PUMC does in/as worship is the most commonly used description of what they are doing. The character of prayer at the table (or its absence) prevents it from being heard or experienced as "eucharist" or thanksgiving. And although they generally recount the Upper Room narrative as part of the story at the table, this narrative does not seem to carry more important weight than other table stories. In this sense "the Lord's Supper" also is not the primary name to use for what they are doing.

Perhaps the comments from some describing a feeling that communion at PUMC "must have been like the early church's experience" suggests language no more complex than that found in Acts 2. That is, in this community there is a sharing that could be described as (neither more nor less than) "breaking the loaf." It is perhaps remarkable to note that the decision to celebrate "communion" weekly was not prompted by the pastoral leadership but by an unchurched member of the congregational design team who argued that even if he could not personally participate in the sharing of the bread and cup, this was something the congregation needed to do each week.

Second, as one person talked about the tension created for him by the "self-service" nature of the communion service, he noted that it also felt natural in this context. This has to do, at least in part, with the character of hospitality provided throughout the service. In spite of the "naturalness" of the service, the distrust of authoritative traditions within the wider church seems to prevent the leadership from drawing on the richness of these traditions. One wonders if there is a way in which the rich tradition of prayer might permit a growing understanding of the table as communion *and* Lord's Supper *and* eucharist that would also preserve the simplicity, connectedness, and naturalness of what PUMC is doing. This tension leads more explicitly to a question not only about the relationship between worship and belief but also of the relationship between the local and the universal in faith and practice.[25] As a response to marginalized seekers, PUMC seems, as Robert Wuthnow has recently suggested, at risk of creating yet another form of spiritual dabbling rather than a tradition of spiritual depth.[26]

CONCLUSIONS

What, then, might we say about the relationship between worship and belief from these two examples? Certainly it is difficult to insist on a specific cause and effect relationship. With both EUMC and PUMC it is as possible to argue that particular beliefs have come first in the lives of these congregations and subsequently shaped their liturgical practices. We do hear, however, several relationships between the congregations' liturgical practices and their belief systems. The ongoing liturgical practices in both these communities function to embody and express the particular theological and social commitments of each community. The reflections of each community on its eucharistic practice provides a partial statement of the community's operative "local" theology.

Hospitality and Communion. Although both congregations articulate and practice forms of hospitality and communion, we have heard several contrasting understandings that are present in their liturgical practice as well.

Eucharistic practice at EUMC is not just about sharing the bread and cup but an expression of who is invited to the table. The con-

---

[25] Gordon Lathrop rightly notes that "universal validity" is not an accurate measuring stick for liturgical celebration. One needs rather to ask about the wholeness and integrity of the signs of water, bread, wine, assembly, leadership as these things appropriately correspond to both biblical meaning and local culture. *Holy People: A Liturgical Ecclesiology* (Minneapolis: Fortress Press, 1999) 65. I am aware that some will see in the description of PUMC neither validity nor integrity of the signs.

[26] Wuthnow writes, "If a spirituality of seeking is suited to the complexities of American society, it nevertheless results in a transient spiritual exercise characterized more often by dabbling than by depth." *After Heaven: Spirituality in America Since the 1950s* (Berkeley: University of California Press, 1998) 168. Wuthnow, like Lathrop, argues that "practice requires integrity, a commitment to the internal logic and rules of the practice itself; it generates a basis from which to make judgments that are internally consistent." Ibid., 185. These are questions with which PUMC will have to wrestle as it matures as a congregation and as it seeks to take its place within the wider church.

gregation's commitment to welcome everyone at the Lord's table grew out of their initial decision when the church was founded during the civil rights movement to create a place that welcomed people of all races. That commitment, enacted at the table, has expanded as the church has been confronted by and wrestled with the issues of the feminist as well as the gay/lesbian movements. This commitment resulted in the emergence of the ritualized invitation/proclamation "Everyone has a place at this table." The invitation and practice combine to make even those who wonder about their own place feel that they do, in fact, have a place at the table.

EUMC continues to struggle with various manifestations of human diversity and attempts to create means of reconciliation within this diversity. Although not all are of one mind about the meaning of their eucharistic practice, they know that by gathering about the Lord's table week in and week out they are being shaped as a community. They also know that in this weekly face-to-face encounter with one another they are called again to responsibility for those in the houses, apartments, and neighborhoods that surround them. It is the center from which they offer resistance to the neighboring industry that would further displace people from their homes. In this congregation we see a congregation "becoming habituated to the practice to the point that one can exercise wisdom when new situations necessitate making difficult judgments."[27]

At PUMC we also find a theology and practice of hospitality. In contrast to EUMC, the welcome extended here is less about creating a community of difference than about providing space in which strangers may encounter one another, perhaps hear one another, but in which they are not required or expected to take responsibility for one another. The weekly celebration means whatever each person wants it to mean. Eating the bread and drinking the cup (or choosing not to do so) becomes whatever one wants it to be. The commitment to "access" that shapes the congregation's liturgical practice leads to a celebration that is less about creating community than setting out to create a context in which a person has access to the holy on one's own terms.

[27] Ibid., 184.

Although both congregations express a concern for hospitality and the creation of community, we find in their liturgical practices and their reflections on these practices important differences. EUMC enacts a hospitality that invites participation in the life of the community, even at some risk to one's self-understanding. EUMC's circle of hospitality continues to grow as it is confronted with new forms of human difference. PUMC's welcome bears more resemblance to the coffee shop in which they meet. Just as everyone can choose one's own beverage at the counter, so too everyone has "access" to what the gathering provides. Nothing, however, invites relationship or commitment. At EUMC the embrace of peace, holding hands through the prayers, serving one another the bread and cup, and praying for one another face to face invite and practice an intimacy that is recognizable as "communion." The table around which PUMC gathers resembles a buffet table at which participants can watch one another but are not expected to have any contact with one another. It offers only the "intimacy" of watching from a distance. Worshipers may talk to one another around the tables, but they do not eat together, pray for one another, or in any way touch one another.

Authority. Another striking contrast between the two congregations is their relationship to the official eucharistic practice and theology of the church. On the one hand, EUMC makes direct and conscious use of the United Methodist Church's eucharistic liturgy. It is guided by the shape and theology of this liturgy as well as by the discipline of the church in its practice, even as it pushes against the boundaries of this discipline. It has found a way to invite participation in regular conversation with the tradition of the wider church. PUMC minimizes its denominational relationships,[28] makes no use of the authorized liturgical materials, and makes minimal use of other ecumenical expectations concerning prayer and practice at the Lord's table. Its resistance to tradition, it insists, is the means by which it provides access to church or to the holy.

On the other hand, both congregations practice a form of "open communion" increasingly common in United Methodist churches, although by no means authorized, in which all present, baptized or

[28] In spite of my use of the identifier PUMC, the congregation does not use "United Methodist Church" in its name.

unbaptized, are invited to participate in the meal. Behind this inclusivism at PUMC is the desire to provide access for all, a commitment to exclude no one. While this is also true at EUMC, EUMC also articulates an understanding of table practice that expresses a gracious generosity of God that seeks to draw those so welcomed into the fullness of the community's life.[29]

Margaret Mary Kelleher notes that "liturgical action discloses the beliefs, values, commitments, relationships, memories, and hopes that are constitutive of the church as a community. Included in this disclosure are those meanings that have already been crystallized and those that are in the process of being brought to birth."[30] As we have heard in their reflections on their eucharistic practices, the regular weekly liturgical practices of these communities, even as the practices express the particular commitments of each community, are the means by which these communities continue to be constituted as communities. We see in each community an interaction between their social commitments and liturgical practices that is shaping the normative claims each community is willing to make. We hear in each "This is how we pray and therefore what we believe and how we should live" as well as "This is how we live and what we believe and therefore how we should pray." And we hear in each a challenge to the traditional boundaries of eucharistic practice in the church. In EUMC we especially hear the consequences of these interactions over an extended period of time. It will be interesting to see how PUMC will be shaped and to hear what normative claims it will permit itself to make over the same amount of time.

---

[29] David Ford addresses the "ethics of exclusion" at the eucharistic feast at the close of *Self and Salvation*: "The feast of the Kingdom of God is described (and acted out) by [Jesus] as generously inclusive beyond anyone's wildest dreams. That is the main point: the free, surprising love of a God who can be utterly trusted to judge truthfully and then decide far more compassionately than any of the rest of us. There is also a sharp note of exclusion, but it is one that follows from the inclusiveness. The excluded are those who cannot bear God's generosity and will not imitate it." *Self and Salvation: Being Transformed* (New York: Cambridge University Press, 1999) 269. The implications of Ford's conclusions, as well as of the eucharistic practices at EUMC and PUMC, require further exploration than possible here.

[30] "Liturgy: An Ecclesial Act of Meaning," *Worship* 59:6 (November 1985) 491.

Thus, even as liturgical practices express the "functional" theology of a congregation, that expression is shaping the ways in which the community comes to think about itself theologically. Table hospitality can be practiced in ways that invite recognition of, commitment to, and communion with another. It can also be practiced in a way that maintains a safe distance from the other. Engagement with the symbolic richness of eucharistic tradition and intentional reflection on that tradition may encourage, even though it does not guarantee, an openness and plurality of readings and interpretations of that tradition that do not exclude the possibility of shared meaning.[31] While this engagement with a tradition is always conditioned by the historical and cultural location of particular communities, we need to ask whether engagement with a "bare outline" of a tradition permits the same interpretive richness or whether it will leave us captive to the spirit of the age, waiting to "have it our way."

At the end we may still be longing for an *orthodoxia* that results in *orthodoxy*. But it may be that we are unable to bear God's generosity and close ourselves off from the very transformation we seek. The truth and reality that are performed, disclosed, and interpreted in Christian liturgical practice do intend a way of life with one another and with God. As the tensive, mutually causative relationship between worship and belief continues, we continue to be invited to ask how these practices teach us to intend all things to God. The remainder of the book will lead us more fully into this question.

THE RULE OF PRAYER: *LEX ORANDI LEX CREDENDI*

The preceding questions concerning the means of grace, as well as those posed by the exploration of these two congregations, anchor my personal involvement with this project. The theoretical anchor, however, lies in the now familiar, often cited, and generally misap-

---

[31] It also suggests, as Craig Dykstra and Wuthnow both argue, the need for instruction in and about Christian liturgical practices to support the interpretive work of the congregation. [See Craig Dykstra, *Growing in the Life of Faith: Education and Christian Practices* (Louisville: Geneva Press, 1999) 44, and Wuthnow, *After Heaven*, 184.] Where EUMC has undertaken such instruction and reflection on a regular basis throughout its history, such work has yet to begin at PUMC.

propriated and misquoted ancient motto *lex supplicandi statuat lex credendi,* usually translated "the law of prayer constitutes the law of belief." Among liturgical theologians it appears most frequently in an abbreviated form as *lex orandi lex credendi.* This motto invites questions about the relationship between communal prayer (more broadly, liturgy) and belief, between practice and theology, between theory and praxis.

Paul De Clerck has provided an analysis of the origin and problems associated with the history of this now familiar motto.[32] The motto first appeared in the *Capitula Coelestini,* an anthology of the declarations of Popes Innocent I (401–417) and Zozime (417–418) and of the Council of Carthage of 418, edited by Prosper of Aquitain, who, around 435, became secretary to Leo the Great. The motto appeared there as part of Prosper's defense of the Augustinian arguments for the necessity of grace prior to faith. Prosper claimed that the church's ongoing prayer to God for the gift of faith—the "law of prayer"—argues for the "law of belief" that faith is dependent on God's grace. The law of prayer is that for which the church prays; the law of belief is that which is contained within and expressed by those prayers.

In his attempt to conclude the controversy over grace, Prosper based his appeal to the prayer of the church on two assumptions about the church's prayer, which he later developed in *De vocatione omnium gentium.* First, the church's prayer is theologically normative, because Scripture commands that we pray for all humanity. Here Prosper appeals to 1 Timothy 2:1-6.[33] Second, the church's

---

[32] "'Lex orandi lex credendi.' Sens original et avatars historiques d'un adage equivoque," *Questions Liturgiques* 59 (1978) 193–212, and "La prière universelle, expression de la foi," in *La liturgia, expression de la foi,* Conférence Saint-Serge, XXV Semaine d'études liturgiques, ed. A. M. Triacca and A. Pistoia (Rome: Edizioni Liturgiche, 1979) 129–146. De Clerck provides the most comprehensive contextual reading of Prosper's use of the *lex orandi.* Geoffrey Wainwright also provides a review of the use of *lex orandi,* including its use among the ante-Nicene fathers.

[33] The text reads: "First of all, then, I urge that supplications, prayers, intercessions, and thanksgivings be made for everyone, for kings and all who are in high positions, so that we may lead a quiet and peaceable life in all godliness and dignity. This is right and is acceptable in the sight of God our Savior, who desires everyone to be saved and to come to the knowledge of the truth. For

prayer represents the living tradition of the church. Thus, while arguing for the normative status of the church's prayer, Prosper is also arguing that this prayer is further normed by Scripture and Tradition. De Clerck concludes that in our own appeal to this motto we are questioning the normative status of the practice of the church. He also concludes that while liturgical texts are always formulated within the context of particular cultures and thus necessarily reflect particular theologies, the primary purpose of these texts is the expression and celebration of Christian faith.

Contemporary liturgical theologians from a variety of liturgical traditions have attempted to clarify the relationship between *lex orandi* (or *lex supplicandi,* the law of supplication) and *lex credendi* with varying results. Liturgical theologians Alexander Schmemann (Orthodox) and Aidan Kavanagh (Roman Catholic) were among the first of the recent generation to explore this relationship. Kavanagh makes three points about this relationship. First, "the verb *statuat* subordinates the law of belief to the law of worship in just the same way . . . as our reception of God's word is subordinated to the presentation of that Word to us in the act of its being revealed and proclaimed to us."[34] With Alexander Schmemann, this subordination permits Kavanagh to locate theology "within the Church," "as a witness to the eschatological fullness of the Church."[35] Second, Kavanagh argues that expressions of the *credendi*—creeds, theories, texts—emerge in a "dialectical process of change and adjustment" to the changes the community experiences in the liturgically defined encounters "with the living God in its own faithful life." Third, the *lex supplicandi* is not to be equated with "some broad notion" of the practice of the church but refers in a limited way to the law of supplicatory prayer, "prayer which petitions God for the whole range of human needs in specific." In this third point, Kavanagh most clearly draws on Prosper's initial argument.

---

there is one God; there is also one mediator between God and humankind, Christ Jesus, himself human, who gave himself a ransom for all—this was attested at the right time" (NRSV).

[34] *On Liturgical Theology* (New York: Pueblo Publishing Co., 1984) 91, 92, 134.

[35] See Alexander Schmemann, "Theology and Liturgical Tradition," in *Liturgy and Tradition,* ed. Thomas Fisch (Crestwood, N.Y.: St. Vladimir's Seminary Press, 1990) 18.

Edward Kilmartin was less willing to subordinate belief to worship. Although he agreed with Kavanagh that a dialectical relationship must exist between the two, he argued for a more fully "mutually critical" relationship:

"On the one hand, the law of prayer implies a comprehensive, and, in some measure a pre-reflective, perception of the life of faith. On the other hand, the law of belief must be introduced because the question of the value of a particular liturgical tradition requires the employment of theoretical discourse. One must reckon with the limits of the liturgy as lived practice of the faith."[36]

Geoffrey Wainwright seems to argue for a similar position. He notes that the ambiguity created by the reversibility of prayer and belief in Prosper's motto "corresponds to a material interplay which in fact takes place in Christian practice: worship influences doctrine, and doctrine worship."[37]

Kevin Irwin's response to these limits of liturgy as lived practice of faith results in an expanded form of the motto: *lex orandi, lex credendi, lex vivendi* (the law of living). United Methodist Don Saliers has articulated a similar position, adding the phrase *lex agendi*, the law of ethical action.[38] Saliers and Irwin argue that not only is there a relationship between prayer and belief, but also

[36] *Christian Liturgy: Theology and Practice* (Kansas City: Sheed and Ward, 1988) 97.

[37] *Doxology: The Praise of God in Worship, Doctrine, and Life* (New York: Oxford University Press, 1980) 218. Wainwright also notes the tendency of Roman Catholic theologians to move from past and present liturgical practice to justify their doctrinal positions and for Protestants to extend a "critical primacy of doctrine in relation to liturgy" (ibid., 219). A question we may need to ask later is whether or not this description still holds in light of recent Roman Catholic statements reasserting their doctrinal authority over the liturgy and in mainline Protestant developments that seem, for pragmatic reasons, to set doctrine aside.

[38] Kevin Irwin, *Context and Text: Method in Liturgical Theology* (Collegeville, Minn.: The Liturgical Press, Pueblo Books, 1994) 55–56. Don E. Saliers, "Liturgy and Ethics: Some New Beginnings," *Journal of Religious Ethics* 7:2 (1979) 173–189. Here Saliers argues that when *lex orandi lex credendi* is properly considered, "there is an internal, conceptual link between liturgy and ethics" (174). In his recent work *Worship as Theology: Foretaste of Glory Divine* (Nashville: Abingdon Press, 1994), Saliers argues, "Unless the liturgy has become hopelessly idolatrous—a possibility in every age—it will be ethically normative in some sense" (172).

between prayer, belief, and living. While throughout the church's history Christian prayer and theology have variously influenced each other, they have become a "churchly" practice disconnected from worldly action. Saliers and Irwin press us, in a way that supports the method of this study (although beyond its scope), to see the connection between the practices of prayer, belief, and ethical action. If liturgical sacramental practice is constitutive and normative for the nature and identity of Christian persons and communities, then it is oriented toward the life of such persons and communities in and with the world.

Lex orandi statuat lex credendi. The law of prayer establishes the law of belief. Whether we quote and use Prosper's phrase accurately or inaccurately is not the point.[39] Rather, we find in the use of the phrase a practical summary with which to name and to explore the relationship between worship and belief in the Christian community and a means to begin exploring the functional theology of particular Christian communities.

The relationship between prayer and belief as named by Prosper and his heirs points us to yet another series of questions: What is the relationship between the ecclesial practices and the official theology of a Christian community? In what ways do particular ecclesial practices both shape and express the theology of a particular community or congregation? In what ways might we speak about liturgical practices as carrying both normative and constitutive weight in such communities? This last question is increasingly important in Protestant communities like the United Methodist Church. As we seek to capture the attention of the unchurched, there is a growing tendency to dispose of or hide our often unexplored liturgical and sacramental traditions. Replacing these traditions are patterns and practices that more readily express the unfaith of the seeker than an invitation to the particular ethical way of God in Jesus Christ. We ourselves ask, as Christians must in every place and time, how our liturgical practices do more than express the spirit of the age. We ask

[39] Michael G. L. Church has recently challenged liturgists who, he contends, use this phrase inaccurately to attend more clearly to its original intent and, in doing so, to recover an ethic of "just conflict among Christians." See Michael G. L. Church, "The Law of Begging: Prosper at the End of the Day, *Worship* 73:5 (September 1999) 442–453.

how our practices invite the transformation of heart and life that, over time, teaches us "to refer all things to God, and to learn how to intend our lives and the world to God."[40]

Behind these questions lie several assumptions that I am making: Christian worship is a cluster of practices[41] in which persons and communities are formed intentionally and unintentionally in particular understandings of self and church. Second, Christian worship provides a "grammar" of the self through which we interpret our relationships to God and neighbor. And, implicitly or explicitly, Christian worship remains a means through which we express these relationships.

In making these claims, it is tempting to claim also a cause and effect relationship between worship and belief. We want to believe that if only we can worship rightly, we will believe and/or act rightly, that *orthodoxia* will yield *orthodoxy*, right praise will yield right opinions. Yet, as we have seen in the preceding discussion, the relationship between the two has more often been "mutually causative," an ongoing interaction between practice and belief. In such a mutually causative relationship, we begin to discover ways in which liturgical practice does have normative and constitutive consequences in the life of the church. We also discover the ways in which our life together reshapes liturgical practice. In the end we are left with a more modest claim. If we cannot claim that this particular practice produces that particular belief, we can at least argue for and hope that "engagement in the church's practices puts us in a position where we may recognize and participate in the work of God's grace in the world."[42]

[40] Saliers, *Worship as Theology,* 148.

[41] Although I will develop the concept of practice more fully in Chapter 3, let me provide a working definition of "practice" here. A practice is a pattern of action that we do repeatedly, over time, with particular intent. Christian practices include such actions as providing hospitality, intercessory prayer, hymn singing, celebrating the church year, preaching, and others. One recent exploration of Christian faith practices is Dorothy Bass, ed., *Practicing Our Faith* (San Francisco: Jossey-Bass, 1997).

[42] Dykstra, *Growing in the Life of Faith,* 41. Dykstra is among those who deny the causative role of practices for Christian life. He writes: "[Practices] are not, finally, activities we do to make something spiritual happen in our lives. Nor are they duties we undertake to be obedient to God. Rather, they are patterns

THE SHAPE OF THE BOOK

All our liturgical practices are open to what hermeneutical theorists call a "pluralism of readings." Not only are our interpretations multiple, but the very tools we use to create these interpretations are also multiple. In the remainder of this book, you are invited into what may feel like a conversation with all too many different voices and approaches. Nevertheless, these different voices will help us construct what we might call a "critical hermeneutical conversation." In the chapters that follow, we will borrow from and explore the contributions that ritual theory, social-relational psychology, and Trinitarian theology make to this conversation. Each will lead us into a deeper understanding of what it is we do before God, to ourselves, and to the communities in which we worship when we engage in the worship of God.

The book develops in two parts. In the first part our attention focuses on issues raised by the concepts of ritual and sacramental practice. The second part focuses on the self in relationship to God that is "practiced" in liturgical sacramental practice. The chapter following this introduction addresses the constitutive and normative claims made about and in sacramental liturgical practice. It begins with reflection on selected interviews that focus our attention on the meaning and importance of sacramental liturgical practice in the parish. This reflection builds a series of progressively wider circles, examining the comparative reading of the claims made about worship in the church-growth movement, in feminist liturgical theology, and in the liturgical theologies represented by Don Saliers and James White. The chapter argues that worship is not only the expression of a community's beliefs but also a means by which communities shape the way they think about themselves theologically.

In the third chapter our attention turns to a discussion of ritual and ritualization in contemporary life. The chapter begins with a

---

of communal action that create openings in our lives where the grace, mercy, and presence of God may be made known to us. They are places where the power of God is experienced. In the end, they are not ultimately our practices but forms of participation in the practice of God" (66). Dykstra seems to miss, however, the possibility that activities we do "to make something happen" or "to be obedient" can be steps toward such openings in persons' lives.

brief review of the functions of ritual in human life. This review, while perhaps a detour from the main argument of the book, is important because of the ongoing Protestant suspicion of ritual, habit, and repetition. And this review will provide a foundation for an exploration of ritual practice as a way of knowing. The fourth chapter focuses more explicitly on ritual practice in Christian life and faith. After an extended discussion of ritual as process, performance, and practice, I explore a threefold model of sacramental practice as a form of strategic action that carries a particular orientation toward past, present, and future. These chapters help us answer the question "What are we doing when we worship?"

The second section of this book focuses on the question of the self that is constituted or practiced in liturgical sacramental practice: Who are we becoming in relationship to God? In the fifth chapter we explore some of the ways in which worship provides a grammar for our faith, with particular attention to the ways in which this liturgical grammar lends itself to a Trinitarian theological framework and an intersubjective, social, relational psychological framework. In the sixth chapter we look at several liturgical examples of this grammar. Together, these explorations suggest a definition of the Christian person as a *theonomous* self, a self that is neither wholly self-determined (the *autonomous* self) nor wholly other-determined (the *heteronomous* self).

The seventh chapter draws on a comparative discussion of John Wesley's understandings of sanctification, his understanding of "the means of grace" as converting and transforming practices, and the Eastern Orthodox concept of theosis. This exploration contributes a final theme, the eschatological nature of the liturgy and thus of the theonomous self. The final chapter offers a case study of the liturgically constituted self. Having arrived at the "end" *(telos)* of the self, we begin to see the consequences of our liturgical practice for the shaping of the Christian person. At the end we will see that what we do in worship as Christian people is practice "who we are becoming" and, in doing so, engage in a variety of practices that are constitutive of and normative for the identity of Christian persons and communities.

Chapter Two

Making Claims About Worship

But I of means have made my boast[1]

How does the liturgy of the church, especially in all of the diverse forms present within the United Methodist Church, provide an ideal image of the Christian life for persons and communities? Beyond offering this ideal image, how and what do our liturgical practices contribute to the formation of Christian identity? What influence should the liturgy and sacramental life of the church have on the life and mission of Christian communities and persons? We have yet again rewritten the patterns and texts for Christian worship. So what?

As Mark Searle has asked, What connection is to be found between the reform of liturgical books and the renewal of Christian life, given the explosion of liturgical reform during the past thirty years and the promulgation of revised liturgies and hymnals throughout Protestant and Catholic communions?[2] What does it mean for us to speak about liturgical sacramental practices as normative and constitutive for the identity of Christian persons and

---

[1] Hymn 88, "Long have I seemed to serve thee, Lord," stanza 6 in *The Works of John Wesley,* vol. 7: *A Collection of Hymns for the use of the People called Methodists,* ed. Franz Hildebrandt and Oliver Beckerlegge (Oxford: Clarendon Press; New York: Oxford University Press, 1983) 189.

[2] "New Tasks, New Methods: The Emergence of Pastoral Liturgical Studies," *Worship* 57:4 (July 1983) 293.

communities? The normative question asks: How do liturgical sacramental practices establish and maintain particular standards for the Christian life? The constitutive question asks: How do these practices function to organize or construct Christian identity both individually and communally?[3]

These are the questions that will occupy our attention in this chapter. They push us to explore the appropriateness of making normative and constitutive claims about our liturgical practice as well as the consequences of making such claims.

MAKING CLAIMS IN THE LOCAL CHURCH

In a study of how United Methodist congregations responded to the liturgical and musical revisions represented in the *United Methodist Hymnal* (1989), members of several congregations were asked about the influence of the Lord's Supper and baptism on the fellowship and mission of the congregation.[4] In response to ques-

---

[3] Geoffrey Wainwright poses similar questions in his discussion of the relationship between worship and belief: "What gives to the Church's worship any authority which it carries in matters of doctrine?" "Is the worship practice of the Church equally authoritative throughout, or are there rather internal gradations in its values as a doctrinal locus?" Wainwright concludes that it is hard "to see how absolute certainty could attach to any doctrinal conclusion drawn from the worship of the Church." Yet he argues that such authority is possible only "in so far as [worship] is the place in which God makes himself known to humanity in saving encounter" and in so far as worship reflects dominical origin, universality in practice, and produces the fruit of holiness. *Doxology: The Praise of God in Worship, Doctrine, and Life* (New York: Oxford University Press, 1980) 242–243, 250.

Similarly, in a discussion of theology as church practice, Reinhard Hütter argues that the learning of Christian faith can be understood as "entry into the praxis of faith by way of paradigmatically acquired configurations of language and action," and as "the ever new learning of faith through engagement with a theological interpretive practice which itself inheres in the praxis of the Christian faith." *Suffering Divine Things: Theology as Church Practice*, trans. Doug Stott (Grand Rapids, Mich.: Wm. Eerdmans Publishing Co., 2000) 51.

[4] These interviews were gathered as part of the study "The Faith and Practices of Christian Congregations," Thomas E. Frank, project director. The study included 2065 surveys from fourteen Protestant churches or church circuits in Georgia, South Carolina, and Minnesota. The interviews from which the following quotes are drawn were elicited in a part of the project that focused on the reception and use of *The United Methodist Hymnal* (Nashville: The United Methodist Publishing House, 1989) under the direction of Don E. Saliers. The interviews quoted were gathered at church #11.

tions about the influence of the Lord's Supper, one person responded by saying, "I can't see why it would [have any influence]." A second person, a bit uncertain about the relationship, offered the hope that "communion is becoming something that is very alive in the minds and hearts of the people, that they are realizing how important this sacrament is and are able to accept it as forgiveness so that they can go out as free people, not weighted down by guilt and self beating up." A third remarked that communion was the most meaningful part of worship because "it helps me remember who I am and where I belong."

These three responses express a range of claims about worship, extending from a perceived lack of connection between sacramental practice and congregational life, to a hope for connection between sacrament and life, to a statement of that practice as important for personal identity. Confronted, on the one hand, with a complete separation between liturgy and life, we might argue that sacramental practice is something we do in church, perhaps for ourselves, perhaps for no understandable reason. On the other hand, at least one response indicates that sacramental practice is, in some way, normative and constitutive of Christian identity, naming who we are and where we belong. At the least, the sacrament is understood as doing something important for one's sense of self—naming the individual as a forgiven person. More provocatively, the interviews reveal a sense that the sacrament speaks in a certain way about who Christian people are individually and in community. But these interviews also raise the question of what claims we can or should make about the role of liturgical practice in congregational life.

Similar questions about the influence and understanding of baptism prompted equally diverse responses. The most concise statement was that baptism means that "you have become a Christian. Baptism is baptism . . . it wouldn't be the same congregation without it." Another person tried to articulate the relationship between baptism and conversion in one of the more theologically sophisticated, yet (for many people) sacramentally problematic responses given in the interviews. In response to the question "What does baptism mean to your faith?" she reflected

"that I have died to this world, I was buried in the water that covered my past life and that I arose from the water a new creature. I was rebaptized when I became, when I committed myself to Christianity and so for me, that was very important. The full submersion baptism was what I did because it was a public statement of my Christian beliefs. I do feel [it is] something that is important to do with full knowledge, I mean, I believe in infant baptism. I think it is very important, but as an adult, when you totally accept Christ back in your life, I think you should make another public statement about your belief through getting rebaptized. Not that they have to, but . . . that was my choice."

A more common response to the questions about baptism is reflected in this statement:

"Well, it certainly wasn't meaningful to me when I was baptized. But, increasingly, it is meaningful to me to be part of the congregation and participate in others' baptisms. I see it as a symbol of hope more than actual practice as part of the congregation; we commit to nurturing this individual."

The themes of hope and commitment were echoed in a fourth interview. Significant here is the suggested need for pre-baptismal counseling, a suggestion that seemed to amaze the interviewer:

"Baptism to me is almost, it's more of a commitment on the part of the parents, that it is a commitment or a ritual that you should act out for the sake of the family obviously and that is something that . . . maybe people take a little too lightly and I would, I think it might be good, even, when you get married, you have counseling courses before marriage that I don't know what the procedure is here, but, I hope that when it is our turn [to have a child baptized] that there is some type of counseling or something that is there, even if it is for two or three nights where you can go and talk about the commitment you are about to make. *Q:* For baptism? *A:* For baptism."

Picking up on the parallel to marriage preparation, another person offered the following:

"I'm not sure that we always know what kind of pledge that it [baptism] is. In a way, if we were all taking it seriously, we would be standing in a line to teach Sunday school. As for me personally, it meant that I took a very serious vow, as serious as my marriage vows, that I would live my life as a Christian."

These last two statements express an understanding of baptism focusing on the commitment of parents and congregation to the Christian nurture of a child. In the first of these, we hear that "something" is wrong, that people do not understand what it is that they are doing or are about to do on behalf of their child. The second suggests that neither parents nor the church take these commitments seriously.

Scholars and pastors who have undertaken the work of liturgical and sacramental reform over the past thirty years may welcome the confirmation of the need for their work in the identification that something might be "wrong" in the church's sacramental practice. A similar confirmation may be heard in the expressed need for some type of pre-baptismal catechesis. It is hard to hear, and harder to give credence to, liturgical criticism such as the following:

"I think the baptismal service the church is using now is just terrible. To have the people stand up there and have to go through the Apostles' Creed and all the rigmarole that's this long service in there I think is terrible. . . . I like a simple, to-the-point baptismal service that's meaningful to the parents and never mind the Apostles' Creed at that point. That's crazy to put that in the baptismal service . . . and all the stuff about their sins and whatnot. I don't like that at all."

The fact that this person finds the service uncomfortable in its naming of sin, focused on the faith of the church, somehow disconnected from the personal meaning of the parents, and ritualistic rigmarole betrays the lack of liturgical and theological education provided by many of our congregations.

Again, what claims can we make about liturgical and sacramental practice? Several of the responses to the questions about baptism and eucharist express shared hopes for connections between sacramental practice and congregational life and between sacramental life and identity. For instance, in the first response, baptism is claimed as a constitutive element or practice of the church, perhaps even the sine qua non of the church: ". . . it wouldn't be the same congregation." In the second response, baptism is named as a practice important to the expression of individual experience and identity: ". . . when I committed myself to Christianity . . . . it was a public statement of my Christian beliefs." At the least, this response offers a way to speak of "who we are" if not "where we belong," as one person suggests about one's experience of the eucharist. While clearly rooted in the death and resurrection imagery of Romans 6, this comment focuses on what individuals do in response to the experience of (re-)awakened faith. It also raises the question of what the church does with these individuals: How do we celebrate this re-awakened faith communally and liturgically?

The responses about baptism also point to several problems the church continues to encounter in its baptismal practice and, therefore, with the claims the church makes about its practice. Two problems in particular arise as a consequence of the tension between the revised rites for baptism and the church's ongoing practice of infant baptism. One problem is a tendency to see baptism solely as an act of dedication or commitment on behalf of the parents, perhaps also hinting at congregational engagement in some form of Christian nurture: ". . . we commit to nurturing this individual," ". . . it's more of a commitment on the part of the parents." The effect is to reduce baptism to a quaint rite neither more nor less important than enrolling one's child for kindergarten; it is simply something one does with one's child.

A second problem focuses specifically on the consequences of using a rite designed for adults on and with children. This results in comments like that offered in the final quote: "To have the people stand up there and have to go through the Apostles' Creed and all the rigmarole . . . I think is terrible." Why do we, why should we, ask such questions about sin and evil, about faith in Jesus Christ when speaking to and of infants? Why is it that the person raising these questions also finds the Creed, which has its roots in the baptismal liturgy, so problematic? What claims are we making in and about this sacramental practice?

ASSUMPTIONS AND CAUTIONS

Something *is* at stake for both Christian persons and communities in the renewal and reform of liturgy, especially in the reform of sacramental practice. There is a connection between the reform of liturgical texts and books and the renewal of Christian life. More importantly, however, this connection pushes beyond liturgical texts and books to the question of the embodied practices toward which these reformed texts lead us. This connection between liturgical reform and reformation of life articulates an expectation that goes beyond the concern for individual feeling and the increase in church membership desired by the church-growth movement. A "revitalized" and "accessible" liturgy may make people feel better about themselves and contribute to church growth, but it tends to do so by sacrificing the theological content of the liturgy and by discarding the historical voice of the church as found in Scripture and tradition. What good is a church that can neither critique nor console the world? While liturgical renewal and reform may result in some form of "revitalization" or "accessibility," the reform and renewal of worship in the church is about a renewal and revitalization of the life and mission of the church and Christian persons in and for the world.

As a result of the liturgical, catechetical, and ecumenical movements of the past century, the liturgical reforms proposed, published, and enacted over the past thirty years have helped the church move toward a liturgical goal originally set forth in a Roman Catholic document, the first published from the Second Vatican Council, the Constitution on the Sacred Liturgy (*Sacrosanctum Concilium*, Dec. 4, 1963). Each member of the Body of Christ within the worshiping community is called to "full, conscious, and active participation in liturgical celebrations."[5] Clearly, the expectation has been that the reform of texts will renew the way in which a community worships and experiences those acts of worship.

Yet, as Craig Erickson reminds us, the "purpose of liturgical participation is not liturgical participation. The purpose of liturgical participation is the glorification of God and the equipping of Christians with power, to carry out the mission of the church in the world. The two are inseparable."[6] The reform of liturgical life pushes beyond the confines of the walls of the church. The connection between the renewal of the liturgy and the renewal of the Christian life requires more than "an updated liturgical choreography." It requires "fundamental changes in the way each person

[5] Vatican Council II, *The Conciliar and Post Conciliar Documents,* ed. Austin Flannery, O.P., new rev. ed. (Collegeville, Minn.: The Liturgical Press, 1992) p. 7, no. 14.

[6] "Liturgical Participation and the Renewal of the Church," *Worship* 59:4 (May 1985) 232.

conceives of self as an agent in an agent-full assembly."[7] Thus the continuing post-conciliar and ecumenical expectations of liturgical reform are that our liturgical practices not only should make a person and community feel a certain way but should transform or convert that person and community as well.

This set of assumptions requires that we clarify what we do in worship (a question that I will address in a definition and discussion of ritual practice in Chapter 4) and how worship may be more fully *leitourgia,* the church's "public work." In part, the assumption that worship is a public work provides an initial answer to the question of what we do in worship. We could even say that worship is the place or event in which the church "transacts" its business.

I. H. Dalmais argues that an analysis of the term "liturgy" reveals that it is first and foremost "an operation or action *(ergon)*" rather than a form of discourse *(logos)* or a way of knowing.[8] By emphasizing the action or work-like character of the liturgy, Dalmais reminds us that the liturgy is something the church *does* rather than *thinks.* This is not to say that the liturgy is a "thoughtless" enterprise, as the fear often expressed by those who resist the ritual character of the liturgy supposes. Rather, as Aidan Kavanagh argues, it is a way in which the church enacts and, therefore, expresses itself: "a church's worship does not merely reflect or express its repertoire of faith. It transacts the church's faith in God under the condition of God's real presence in both church and world."[9] It is in this "public work" or transaction that the church makes itself known. But this

[7] Michael Warren, "Speaking and Learning in the Local Church: A Look at the Material Conditions," *Worship* 69:1 (January 1995) 41.

[8] Irénée Henri Dalmais, "Theology of the Liturgical Celebration," in *The Church at Prayer*, vol. 1: *Principles of the Liturgy*, ed. A. G. Martimort, trans. Matthew J. O'Connell (Collegeville, Minn.: The Liturgical Press, 1987) 229, 259. His observation raises two further issues. First, if liturgy is primarily action rather than discourse, we must challenge the tendency for worship to be named only as an expressive enterprise—in effect, arguing that individual belief alone determines how one should pray and worship—to the detriment of its formative and transformative powers. Second, we must critically examine the implications of Dalmais's argument about the connections between doing and knowing, between action and discourse in the liturgical practice of the church. Has he set the two in opposition to one another or offered a sequential reordering of liturgy's functions?

[9] *On Liturgical Theology* (New York: Pueblo Publishing Co., 1984) 8.

very disclosure or self-expression is secondary to the transaction of the church's faith. Stephen Happel further qualifies the nature of this liturgical transaction, holding together what Dalmais separates, the work or action from the discourse or knowing:

"Worship is not politically, economically, or aesthetically naive; it argues, persuades, and embodies various schemes of social recurrence. Through its visions of the future, it redirects common desire, not in such a way that the community feels guilty for not living up to an ideal but by transforming the communion of believers, however incrementally, in the present. Through the sacraments we are enabled to love and established to complete a common work."[10]

Note how Happel describes this work: the liturgy argues, persuades, embodies, redirects, transforms, enables, and establishes. Liturgy is active. But is this action not also thoughtful? Is it not also a way of knowing?

Yet, in Dalmais's attempt to reclaim the active character of the liturgy and to restore liturgy's expressive function to its proper secondary place, he loses sight of the intrinsic relationships between action and discourse, action and knowing, as well as the normative and constitutive capabilities of the liturgy. The need for Christian worship to be offered as our response to experiencing God's presence in our lives, which is liturgy's expressive function, must be held in critical tension with the need for Christian worship to be offered as a normative and constitutive practice of "who we are and where we belong." When expression and transformation are held together in a such critical tension, we can affirm the claim that "[l]iturgical celebration is the Christian community's symbolic expression of the Christian kerygma and its response to that teaching."[11] At the same time, this critical relationship enables us to affirm the equally determinative claim that "[b]ecause the liturgy offers a world of meaning for appropriation, it has the potential to transform the lives of its participants."[12]

[10] "Speaking from Experience: Worship and the Social Sciences," in *Alternative Futures for Worship*, vol. 2: *Baptism and Confirmation*, ed. Mark Searle (Collegeville, Minn.: The Liturgical Press, 1987) 179.

[11] Catherine Vincie, "The Cry for Justice and the Eucharist," *Worship* 68:3 (May 1994) 200.

[12] Ibid., 210. See Walter Brueggemann's discussion of the "the constitutive power of praise" in *Israel's Praise: Doxology Against Idolatry and Ideology*

This chapter began with an admittedly selective conversation with the local church. The questions generated by this conversation, the aforementioned cautions against the reduction of liturgical practice to the either/or of expression and transformation, and the cautions against the separation of doing and knowing now permit us to focus on the more specific normative and constitutive claims in liturgical sacramental practice and theology.

THE CLAIM OF THE CLASSIC

One way to approach normative and constitutive claims about liturgical and sacramental practices is to argue that such practices, even if not universal in text or interpretation, function as "classic" practices of the church (or, in the language of the Wesleyan tradition, as "ordinary means of grace"). David Tracy develops the use and function of the "classic" in his work on the method of systematic theology. Although Tracy focuses on the "classic" event and person of Jesus Christ, he suggests that religious classics also include texts, events, images, rituals, symbols, and persons. Each may be considered a "classic" by the normative claim it exercises on individuals and communities and by the willingness of those individuals and communities "to be provoked by its claim to attention"[13] to some form of interpretive engagement. Texts, rituals, and symbols acquire status as classics sometimes by means of the authority that supports such status, but more often by the manner in or extent

---

(Philadelphia: Fortress Press, 1988) 6–11. Through an analysis of various psalm texts, Brueggemann argues that "in public worship Israel is engaged in constructing a world in which Israel can viably, joyously, and obediently live" (6). Further, "To the extent that praise, and worship more generally, is constitutive, awareness of this constitutive element will permit greater intentionality and will permit the agents of the liturgical drama—priests and pastors—to be more knowingly critical of what they themselves do" (7). Teresa Berger concludes her study of the relationship of doxology and theology in a similar fashion: "doxology is the bearer of a very specific and unique worldview (or, more concretely, of a particular interpretation of religious existence), which, in the final analysis, only has meaning for those who make doxological speech their own." *Theology in Hymns?* trans. Timothy E. Kimbrough (Nashville: Abingdon Press, Kingswood Books, 1995) 162.

[13] David Tracy, *The Analogical Imagination* (New York: Crossroad Publishing Co., 1981) 102.

to which the text, ritual, or symbol is enacted and by the ways in which the liturgy itself acts upon individuals and communities.

Although the normative claim of the religious classic may initially depend on an external authority granting it such status, its normative power is dependent upon the interpretive engagement of individuals and communities with the classic. This engagement tends to be an interactive and, therefore, mutually critical process. Tracy argues that the classic must not only claim attention in some form but must also prompt recognition of

"nothing less than the disclosure of a reality we cannot but name truth . . . some disclosure of reality in a moment that must be called one of 'recognition' which surprises, provokes, challenges, shocks and eventually transforms us; an experience that upsets conventional opinions and expands the sense of the possible; indeed a realized experience of that which is essential, that which endures."[14]

Further, "the kind of claim to attention that a religious classic, *as religious,* provokes is a claim that discloses to the interpreter some realized experience bearing some sense of recognition into the objectively awe-some reality of the otherness of the whole as a radical mystery."[15]

The recognition of the normative claim of the classic, coupled with the tentativeness of Tracy's claims—"some realized experience," "some sense of recognition"—leads neither to the necessary reification of the status quo nor to the closure of interpretation. Tracy offers the possibility that recognition of and interpretive engagement with a religious classic not only confirm its normative claim, tentative as it may be, but reveal the classic as offering a constitutive moment as well. Normatively, the classic unfolds as "cognitively disclosive of both meaning and truth."[16] At the same time, the classic contains "its own plurality and encourages a pluralism of readings"[17] as well as bearing "an excess and permanence of meaning"[18] that resists definitive interpretation. Such plurality and excess preserve a sense of openness and prevent the premature

14 Ibid., 108.
15 Ibid., 168–169.
16 Ibid., 132.
17 Ibid., 113.
18 David Tracy, *Plurality and Ambiguity* (San Franciso: Harper and Row, 1987) 12.

closure of interpretation. This openness also suggests that transformation of person and community is itself a normal, even normative, expectation. As such, it points toward a constitutive moment in which the classic unfolds as "ethically transformative of personal, social, and historical life."[19] The classic thus speaks of who we are individually and in relationship to one another.

YOUR CLASSIC IS NOT MY CLASSIC

Unfortunately, naming particular liturgical and sacramental practices as "classics" does not resolve challenges to their normative or constitutive status in the life of the church. We are still dependent on the increasingly relativized experience, recognition, and interpretation of individuals and communities. In a helpful article, Max Johnson explored the problem of relativism in liturgical practice and interpretation. He reviewed the ways in which contemporary liturgical scholarship approaches "classic" liturgical texts and practices and the claims made for such practices. Johnson noted the increasing uncertainty about claims to the "so-called 'unchanging' and 'divinely instituted' elements" of the church's liturgical traditions. As he explored the relationship between present experience and inherited tradition, he was compelled to ask, "*which* inherited tradition and from what *church* is that 'tradition'?"[20]

Johnson succinctly reviewed the ways in which the relationships between experience and tradition are developed in the work of Gordon Lathrop (Lutheran), James White (United Methodist), and Paul Bradshaw (Anglican). He placed Lathrop and White on opposing ends of the experience/tradition spectrum. Lathrop, he argued, provides "a model, vision, and a language by which the immense variety of Christian worship past and present might be evaluated along theological lines." Lathrop's *ordo* "provides a clear, historical, and ecumenically sensitive model for how some kind of liturgical normativity might still be advocated today."[21] White, on the other hand,

[19] Tracy, *Analogical Imagination*, 113.

[20] Maxwell E. Johnson, "Can We Avoid Relativism in Worship? Liturgical Norms in the Light of Contemporary Liturgical Scholarship," *Worship* 74:2 (March 2000) 136.

[21] Ibid., 139. In particular, see the ways in which Lathrop's reading of *ordo* has influenced the most recent ecumenical liturgical conversations and the documents produced from those conversations: *So We Believe, So We Pray,*

seems to emphasize present experience. White challenges the normative claims made by Lathrop and encourages liturgical theologians to be more descriptive and less prescriptive. White argues that there are no universal norms "other than, perhaps, particular tradition-based norms in and for *specific* churches themselves."[22] Bradshaw lands somewhere in the middle, finding Lathrop's argument promising but "too tidy" for the complex and difficult work of historical research; he notes that there are few "'deep structures' running through liturgy" to which we can apply a test of universal observance.[23]

United Methodist liturgical theologian Don Saliers also seems to land somewhere in the middle of this continuum. He does so, however, in a way that balances the concern for experience with the theologically normative claims of a life oriented to God. Saliers explores this tension in much of his work on prayer and the Christian affections. He is particularly careful to make a distinction between the "immediacy of feeling" and the "depth of emotion." Saliers challenges those who would reduce liturgical renewal to the question of how the liturgy makes us feel. "The question is not 'Am I feeling better?' or 'Do I really enjoy my prayer life?' but rather, 'Is the will of God being realized in my life and in the life of the community?'"[24] When the focus of the renewal and reform of the liturgy is transformative rather than expressive, the "liturgy well-celebrated should permit us, over time, to refer all things to God, and to learn how to intend our lives and the world to God."[25] The claims performed by and made of the liturgy reach beyond "feeling." They extend over time to the deep formation of persons in communities of prayer and sacrament.

Faith and Order Paper 71, ed. Thomas Best and Dagmar Heller (Geneva: World Council of Churches, 1995) and *Eucharistic Worship in Ecumenical Contexts*, ed. Thomas Best and Dagmar Heller (Geneva: World Council of Churches, 1998).

[22] Johnson, "Can We Avoid Relativism," 140, 141.

[23] Ibid., 142.

[24] *The Soul in Paraphrase: Prayer and the Religious Affections* (New York: The Seabury Press, 1980; rpt. Cleveland: OSL Publications, 1991) 91. See also *Worship as Theology: Foretaste of Glory Divine* (Nashville: Abingdon Press, 1994) 37, 147–148, 176–178, and "Liturgy and Ethics: Some New Beginnings," *Journal of Religious Ethics* 7:2 (Fall 1979) 178–179.

[25] Saliers, *Worship as Theology*, 148.

Johnson argues that they are *all* correct. There does seem to be an *ordo* which has survived and which serves as a norm for authentic Christian worship that transcends local diversity and variety. The history is not as tidy as a cursory reading of Justin Martyr suggests. And, as White argues, we must engage in more careful description, with particular attention to the diversity of liturgical experience in North America, and more explicitly name the theological criteria with which we evaluate such experience. But, as Saliers reminds us, neither present experience nor historical *ordo* is complete without its theological reference point.

Johnson answers the "so what" question by arguing that what is at stake for the Christian church is "not simply how we worship or how we think about worship, but the very identity and liturgical self-expression of classic orthodox Christianity itself."[26] What is at stake is our ability to make either normative or constitutive claims about liturgical texts and practices and their place in the shaping of Christian life. I am at much the same place that Johnson, with Saliers's qualifications, ends. There is, I believe, something at stake in and for the life of the Christian church in the way the church approaches questions of liturgical practice and reform.

Nevertheless, I want to call us back to the opening interviews as a means of using one tradition's present experience of liturgical reform to push Johnson's questions a bit further. What happens when one person's or a community's interpretive engagement with a liturgical or sacramental practice leads to the rejection or marginalization of such practices? Can such practices still be considered normative or constitutive? Although Johnson notes that the church-growth movement accepts the church's traditional liturgy as "merely one of several options," he does not look at the consequences of such a move or at the claims this movement makes about worship as a whole.[27] Nor does he review the extensive critical writing from feminist liturgical theologians. Although he asks *"which* inherited tradition?" and *"what* church?" he neglects to ask *"whose* experience?"

---

[26] "Can We Avoid Relativism," 155.
[27] Ibid., 136.

Given the rapid growth of literature about contemporary worship, published in books, church-growth newsletters, and online resources, and its increasing influence in local church conversations about worship, it is important for liturgists to explore the claims this movement both makes and rejects. As it is not my intent to review all of the literature at this point, I will focus on the work of one of its leading voices, William Easum, with particular attention to the claims he makes about worship. Given the significant influence his ideas about worship have had in discussions about the renewal of worship, some may be surprised to discover that the issue of liturgical reform and renewal does not occupy a more significant place in Easum's writing.

Easum's critiques of "traditional" worship have gained the attention of pastors, liturgists, church musicians, and judicatory personnel alike. So-called "traditional" worship, for Easum, is spiritless, emphasizes "elements of worship brought over from the old country," is "slow, linear, and predictable," "lifeless, dull, and boring," "filled with 'dead spots'—long, life-sucking periods of unplanned time . . . between segments."[28] He argues that "if your congregation still worships through long liturgies and stately hymns of earlier generations, the odds are your congregation is declining. . . . Effective worship today grows out of the culture of the area. The style and form is comfortable to those attending worship from the non-Christian world."[29]

Praise worship, which Easum estimates characterizes ninety percent of the growing churches in the United States, "never comes right out of the hymnal," never has "dead spots," and only makes use of "limited forms of recognizable liturgy from the past."[30] Easum has consistently emphasized that experience is more important than content, and transformation is more important than education. "The more practical the experience, the better."[31] His

[28] "What I Now See in Worship," reprinted from *Net Results*, retrieved August, 2001 <http://www.easum.com/netresul/Easum/oo-o6.htm>. Although many of us may not agree with his prescription, his diagnosis does seem to ring true to the worship life of many mainline Protestant churches today.

[29] *Dancing with Dinosaurs* (Nashville: Abingdon Press, 1993) 81.

[30] "What I Now See in Worship."

[31] *How to Reach Baby Boomers* (Nashville: Abingdon Press, 1991) 132.

"paradigm communities" are defined "more by their style of ministry than by their doctrine. How they minister is more important than what they teach."[32] The emphasis in worship is on helping people "meet God, not learn about God."[33] He encourages worship planners to "give up those sacred cow cultural styles, personal opinions, and denominational traditions that can get in the way of communicating the gospel."[34] Worship, he argues, should be a "corporate celebration rather than a time for somber reflection." It is the "responsibility of the worship leaders and members of the congregation to direct their praise to God. . . . The entire service becomes an offering to God."[35] "Worship is for the purpose of adoring and praising God for who God is and what God can do in our lives. Worship is vertical. Worship emphasizes the mystery and majesty of God."[36] Easum's criterion for music, which he argues "is the ritual of our time," also serves as the primary criterion for all of worship: "Does it bring people closer to God? The only acceptable music is that which conveys the message of new life. . . . No form is inherently better than another. Music is good if it conveys the gospel; it is bad if it does not."[37]

Clearly, Easum sees no tension between inherited tradition and present experience. He is not concerned with the claims "classic" practices make on persons and communities, because such practices are dead and should be buried. The present experience of the church requires that it set aside its inherited traditions as irrelevant to the cultural needs and concerns of non-Christian people in North America. The only normative criterion to be applied to worship is whether it fosters an experience of God. There are no other normative claims to be made by worship. Nor can we claim that

[32] *Dancing with Dinosaurs*, 88.

[33] "What I Now See in Worship." See also his "21st Century Worship," reprinted from *Net Results*, retrieved August, 2001 <http://www.easum.com./netresul/Easum/96-08.htm>.

[34] *How to Reach Baby Boomers*, 106. In *Dancing with Dinosaurs*, 14, he argues, "bureaucracies and traditional practices are the major cause of decline in most denominations in North America."

[35] *How to Teach Baby Boomers*, 114.

[36] *Dancing with Dinosaurs*, 82.

[37] Ibid., 85, 86. Frank Burch Brown provides a careful analysis of and challenge to Easum's arguments about music in worship in *Good Taste, Bad Taste, and Christian Taste* (New York: Oxford University Press, 2000) 233–251.

48

worship practices are constitutive of Christian communities; the present experience of the community is both normative and constitutive for the shape of its liturgical practices (if they may be described as such). *Lex vivendi statuat lex orandi:* the law of living establishes the law of prayer.[38] Note that Easum does not resist making prescriptive liturgical claims; there is acceptable music and unacceptable music; music and liturgy "never come right out of the hymnal." Note, too, that there is nothing in his theological claims about worship that would necessarily lead one to the conclusions he makes. Few Jewish or Christian liturgical theologians today would reject descriptions of worship as fostering the adoration, praise, and offering of the self to God; few Christian liturgical theologians would reject the claim that worship should be about communicating the gospel of Jesus Christ. Yet even in James White's resistance to prescriptive liturgical theology and his call for more attention to description of liturgical practices, he has continued to call our attention to the historical, liturgical, and pastoral norms of our various traditions and communities when we plan, reform, and renew our liturgical practices.

How might White's call for careful descriptive work and Bradshaw's call for attention to the messiness of liturgical history help "traditional" liturgists pay more careful attention to the present diversity of liturgical experience, even within our individual communities? How might such attention invite our consideration of the tensions between the "local" and "official" meanings of our reformed liturgies? And how might such attention provide a means by which we can respond to communities that the liturgical movement has either passed by or in which someone has decided that the church has already "outgrown" the movement?[39]

SUSPICIOUS CLASSICS

In perhaps unlikely ways, feminist liturgical theology shares a number of concerns with the church-growth movement, but it does

[38] See Lester Ruth's exploration of this pragmatic relationship in "Lex Agendi, Lex Orandi: Toward an Understanding of Seeker Services as a New Kind of Liturgy," *Worship* 70:5 (September 1996) 386–405.

[39] Geoffrey Wainwright poses these questions in "Renewing Worship: The Recovery of Classic Patterns" in *Worship with One Accord: Where Liturgy and Ecumenism Embrace* (New York: Oxford University Press, 1998) 139.

so in a way that provides a critical theological voice that may bridge the "traditional" and the "contemporary." First, the two movements share a concern for the renewal of worship (if not explicitly of liturgical practice) and the transformation of the church. This concern for the renewal of the church not only binds together the feminist and church growth movements but also, as Marjorie Procter-Smith observes, binds these movements with the more traditional liturgical movement. They have all been concerned, in some way, that "the church's liturgy was diminishing the church's ability to witness to the gospel in the world and distorting the church" and that "poor liturgy endangered the church's authentic relationship with God."[40]

Second, like the church-growth movement, the openness, flexibility, and localization of feminist liturgical practice have not produced any one set of liturgies or rites.

Third, where the church-growth movement rejects tradition as irrelevant, feminist liturgical theology and practice critique the tradition's perceived and experienced oppressive structures and practices, resulting in the development of guiding principles rather than specific texts, authorities, or traditions.

Fourth, like the church-growth movement, the feminist liturgical movement has been suspicious of past liturgical forms as traditionally interpreted, but unlike the church-growth movement, its suspicion is present because of the "silencing and marginalizing of women in the construction of tradition."

Finally, the feminist liturgical movement, like the church-growth movement, privileges present experience; unlike the church-growth movement, the feminist liturgical movement privileges women's experience and makes such experience normative for the development of ritual practices.[41]

In spite of these many similarities, the two movements differ in their understanding of the transformative potential of ritual ex-

[40] Marjorie Procter-Smith, *In Her Own Rite: Constructing Feminist Liturgical Tradition* (Nashville: Abingdon Press, 1990) 20. This work seems to be acquiring a "classic" status of its own. It continues to function as a basic introduction to feminist liturgical practice and as a model for what some might call a "mutually critical correlation" between the work of the liturgical movement and Christian feminist liturgical practice.

[41] Ibid., 27.

perience and the constitutive role liturgical practice plays in shaping a community's identity and faith. Where Easum leads us to worship as a "celebrative experience," many in the feminist liturgical movement lead us to worship as a communal practice of transformation that is critically engaged with Christian traditions. Where Easum invites personal experience of God, feminist liturgical practices invite forms of embodied relatedness that pursue and support justice, equality, and interdependence.[42] In significant ways over the course of a generation, feminist liturgists have treated liturgical classics with suspicion and have asked, "*Which* tradition and *whose* experience?"

Anne Carr describes the basic tensions between tradition and experience in feminist thought, as well as the tensions between feminist theology and other modern theological perspectives, this way:

"Thinkers debate whether Christian thought should, or necessarily does, accommodate itself to its particular cultural time and language while remaining faithful to the whole of Christian tradition or whether it should strive rather for faithful presentation of the grammar and narrative patterns of its originating sources in the Bible and the rules of classical doctrines."[43]

It is obvious that Christian thought and practice have accommodated themselves to the particular cultures, languages, and times within which they live. Less obvious is the fact that in some cases such accommodation has also sought to faithfully present the grammar and narrative patterns of the originating sources of Christianity. This accommodation itself raises questions, generally unasked in the church-growth movement, about its own limits and the criteria by which to define those limits. What criteria will determine which of the grammars and narratives are so corrupted by practices of oppression and domination that they need to be rewritten or dropped from the canon? Do practices of equality and liberation long subverted by patriarchy contain their own transformative, re-creative seeds?

[42] Janet Walton, *Feminist Liturgy: A Matter of Justice* (Collegeville, Minn.: The Liturgical Press, 2000) 36–37.

[43] "The New Vision of Feminist Theology," in *Freeing Theology: The Essentials of Theology in a Feminist Perspective*, ed. Catherine Mowry LaCugna (New York: HarperCollins Publishers, 1993) 7.

Mary Catherine Hilkert places these questions in the context of liturgical practice:

"Precisely because communal ritual celebration is recognized as central to the formation of a community of faith by feminists as well as other Christians, liturgy has become arguably the most divisive and painful reminder of the pervasive patriarchy within the Roman Catholic tradition. The church does indeed perpetuate itself in worship. . . . At the same time, an androcentric worldview and patriarchal control are also perpetuated in a male-dominated sacramental system that is legitimated in the name of Jesus and by the authority of God's will."[44]

Hilkert's critique of the patriarchy perpetuated in much Christian liturgical sacramental practice is not unexpected. Nevertheless, I call our attention to the claims she acknowledges for the formative power and function of these practices in spite of this critique. Where feminist theologians and liturgists are challenging the kinds of normative claims made for liturgical sacramental practice, they continue to acknowledge and build upon constitutive claims in order to call the church to more authentic gospel practice. The very acknowledgment of these constitutive claims encourages their ongoing liturgical experimentation and critique. But we are now asked if this sacramental economy can remain paradigmatic without the subversion of patriarchy. If the end product, an "androcentric worldview and patriarchal control" of the church, has truly reflected the means, a "male-dominated sacramental system," what changes are now required in that sacramental system in order to bring about a church based on radical equality and inclusion? Can a reformed sacramental system overcome that worldview and control, or must the system itself be discarded?

Unlike the response we see in William Easum's work, there is no simple answer to these questions. Feminist liturgical scholars are themselves divided in their relationship to the traditional sacramental system of the church. They caution readers and researchers that critical reflection on feminist liturgical practice is still in its

[44] "Experience and Tradition—Can the Center Hold?" in *Freeing Theology: The Essentials of Theology in a Feminist Perspective*, ed. Catherine Mowry LaCugna (New York: HarperCollins Publishers, 1993) 71.

early stages, building on the experimentation and ritualizing of feminist communities over the past twenty-five years.

Two feminist liturgical scholars who have most clearly identified the operative norms and principles within feminist liturgical practice are Mary Collins and Marjorie Procter-Smith. Collins names five principles that she believes are "basic to intentionally feminist liturgy." Feminist liturgies (1) "ritualize relationships that emancipate and empower women"; (2) are "the production of the community of worshippers, not of special experts or authorities"; (3) intentionally "critique patriarchal liturgies"; (4) seek to "develop a distinctive repertoire of ritual symbols and strategies"; and (5) "produce liturgical events, not liturgical texts."[45]

Procter-Smith supplements this list in several ways. Where Collins names a focus on the production of events rather than texts, Procter-Smith argues that this production is further characterized by commitments to process, in which the creation of the liturgical event is itself a form of catechesis for liturgy or a form of 'conscientization,' experimentation, and contextuality. Where Collins suggests that these events focus on relationships within the community and on a critique of patriarchal structures, Procter-Smith further argues for the explicit "rejection of hierarchical forms of liturgical leadership and a corresponding commitment to shared leadership."[46]

The intent in feminist liturgical or ritual practice to create new communities of equality and emancipation clearly speaks of the constitutive nature of liturgical practices. Procter-Smith affirms this when she describes "the conviction that liturgy is constitutive of a community's identity as well as its faith" as one area of potential common ground between the feminist and liturgical movements.[47] Even so, there is some question as to the extent to which feminist liturgists share this view. Describing some of the results of feminist liturgical practices, Janet Walton suggests that "[o]ver periods of time, patterns emerge. However, these patterns do not become

---

[45] "Principles of Feminist Liturgy," in *Women at Worship: Interpretations of North American Diversity*, ed. Marjorie Proctor-Smith and Janet Walton (Louisville: Westminster/John Knox Press, 1993) 11.

[46] *In Her Own Rite*, 21–23.

[47] Ibid., 30.

authoritative or normative; they are simply informative. They suggest helpful rhythms and methods for engagement."[48] In arguing that these patterns are only expressive/informative, Walton seems to suggest that they speak only about the present experience of a ritualizing community. While she does not explicitly challenge the constitutive claims of liturgical practice, she does seem to suggest that, with the clear concern to reject androcentric structures, practices, and tradition, it is no longer possible to continue to speak about liturgical sacramental practice as exercising any normative claim.

Such claims become even more problematic in the context of statements such as the following by Collins:

"Feminist consciousness is antithetical to the normative tradition of ritual worship to which 'liturgy' refers. When Christians and Jews take up the feminist liturgical project, they regularly critique the normative liturgical traditions of church or synagogue from their standpoint as insiders precisely by introducing the norm of feminist consciousness."[49]

In effect, Collins overturns Walton's rejection of the normative function of the liturgy by introducing "the norm of feminist consciousness." Ritual practices that enhance equality and are powerfully liberating are not only informative but also are the only practices received as authoritative or normative. In this way feminist liturgical communities offer the church a critical retrieval of the practices of those communities of radical equality and care as described in such idealistic and prototypic texts as Acts 2:42-45 or the *First Apology* of Justin Martyr, to which Lathrop, White, and Bradshaw give their attention.

If this critical retrieval is what is now occurring in the feminist liturgical movement, it pushes the liturgical movement beyond its attention to the historically diverse practices of the early church. In doing so, it requires openness on behalf of the liturgical movement to a liturgically constituted symbolic vision that judges all ecclesial

---

[48] "The Missing Element of Women's Experience," in *The Changing Face of Jewish and Christian Worship in North America*, ed. Paul F. Bradshaw and Lawrence A. Hoffman (Notre Dame: University of Notre Dame Press, 1991) 212.

[49] "Principles of Feminist Liturgy," 20.

life and institutions.[50] Collins, Procter-Smith, and Walton rightly call the church to a deep suspicion of traditional interpretations and structures of the church's liturgical sacramental practices, perhaps even of Christian tradition as a whole. Although I am cautious of Collins's claim that "[t]he ritual workings of feminists are strategic productions expressing an emerging new consciousness, a consciousness not to be found in *any* [my emphasis] existing liturgical order,"[51] what may be developing in this process of critical retrieval and liturgical experimentation is the re-emergence and reclaiming of a distinctive critical Christian consciousness normed and constituted by "classic" Christian liturgical practices.

Two points recall the discussion that opened this section. On the one hand, the norm of feminist consciousness requires that Christian liturgical practices and languages accommodate themselves to the present age while remaining both faithful to and critical of Christian tradition. This tends to support an argument for the expressive and constitutive nature of liturgical sacramental practice.

---

[50] Mary Collins, *Worship: Renewal to Practice* (Washington: The Pastoral Press, 1987) 178.

[51] "Principles of Feminist Liturgy," 24. Interestingly, Collins argues elsewhere that the "sources for ritual adaptation and development" are more likely to be found in the "'anti-structural' experience equivalent to communitas or the quest for it." See Collins, *Worship: Renewal to Practice*, 67. What Collins ignores in this conversation with Victor Turner is (a) the extent to which communitas is not so much sought as "given" or "performed" in a ritual context, and (b) the extent to which "anti-structural experience" is dependent on structured experience of and in the social institution. I suggest a parallel between Turner's and Collins's understandings of the anti-structural and Don Handelman's so-called "logic of composition," which he names "representation." Within this model or logic, ritual events are intended to do the work of social comparison and contrast, "offering propositions and counter-propositions" around and about the social order, putting the "social order to question." In contrast to the intent of feminist liturgical practices, Handelman understands this logic to function in some way as a form of social affirmation. That is, practices of social inversion, which function paradigmatically for representation, are both dependent upon the existing social order and offer "a discourse about its validity." Ritual social transformation occurs only when the inversion somehow exceeds the boundaries of its composition and/or severs its ties to the order it inverts. See Don Handelman, *Models and Mirrors* (Cambridge: Cambridge University Press, 1989) 49–53. Of course, this may be exactly Collins's point.

On the other hand, the critical claims of feminist practice point to a retrieval of the radically egalitarian and inclusive grammar and narratives of Christianity's originating sources. This offers the possibility that these practices are, at the least, provisionally normative for the community, to the extent that they are themselves normed by *orthodoxia* and *orthopraxis*. As Procter-Smith wrote more recently, "Christian identity is ritually created, not doctrinally defined, and at the center of Christian feminist praying is not finally words but objects and action, generating and extending emancipatory life beyond ritual into the political social world."[52]

THE CLAIMS WE MAKE

If we return to the interview comments that opened this conversation, we see that regardless of what we as liturgists claim about the normative and constitutive nature of liturgical and sacramental practice, the way in which these practices are interpreted and the weight they carry in Christian life vary widely. Within one congregation, sacramental practices are normative and constitutive for some and, at the same time, denied as such by others. For some people, the intent of liturgical reforms in baptismal and eucharistic practice has either escaped them, passed them by, or simply been neglected as a concern in adult Christian formation.

A second concern emerges out of recent critiques of Turner's theory of liminality, particularly its applicability to women's experiences. Turner's processual model describes a dramatic pattern moving successively from breach to crisis, redress, and reintegration. This pattern generally involves separation from the community or the reversal of social status. From the standpoint of women, however, the themes are less separation and reversal than continuity. "One either has to see the woman's religious stance as permanently liminal or as never quite becoming so." [Caroline Walker Bynum, "Women's Stories, Women's Symbols: A Critique of Victor Turner's Theory of Liminality" in *Fragmentation and Redemption: Essays in Gender and the Human Body in Medieval Religion* (New York: Zone Books, 1991) 32–33.] If women's religious stance is permanently liminal, their experiences of communitas are in continuity with their experiences of social marginality and therefore structural rather than the "anti-structural," as Collins argues. See Catherine Vincie, "Rethinking Initiation Rituals: Do Women and Men Do It the Same Way? *Proceedings of the North American Academy of Liturgy* (1995) 145–170.

[52] Marjorie Procter-Smith, *Praying with Our Eyes Open* (Nashville: Abingdon Press, 1995) 120.

It may be that the church's neglect or minimizing of the need to prepare people for participation in liturgy and sacrament, accompanied by a similar neglect of what liturgical participation itself does in the formation of personal and communal identity, works against the kind of claims ecumenical liturgical theologians make about Christian liturgy. Following James White's argument, we need to engage in a new kind of descriptive work that engages not only liturgies as practiced in churches but also the interpretive frameworks that are functioning in the lives of various congregations. And, following Johnson's argument, we also need to engage in, and continue to provide the resources for, critical theological reflection in the context of the local church.

Yet this is not enough. Johnson argued that the burden of proof for the claims made or rejected for Christian worship falls "on those who, for whatever reason, have chosen to separate themselves from that 'ecumenical or historical standard'" that survives in the form of the *ordo* as described by Gordon Lathrop and others.[53] Although I am not inclined to make the same leaps that Easum makes in rejecting the long tradition of the ecumenical church, I do believe, as we see in the work of Collins and Procter-Smith, a similar burden of proof also falls on the ecumenical liturgical movement. We do not and cannot stand outside of the standards of *orthodoxia* and *orthopraxis*. Orthodox texts properly and carefully performed cannot guarantee *orthodoxia* or *orthopraxis*, regardless of the claims we make for such texts and practices.[54]

It is not enough to argue that certain liturgies proclaim the gospel if they permit practices contrary to that gospel to continue. If we are to continue to make normative and constitutive claims about particular liturgical and sacramental practices, we must demonstrate how these practices contribute to the death-defying, life-giving, emancipating, egalitarian vision and practice of the church in and for the world.[55] This, too, requires that we undertake a far more

[53] Johnson, "Can We Avoid Relativism," 147.

[54] As noted earlier (n. 3), the claims of dominical origin and universality of practice, though necessary, are insufficient; the authority of our liturgical practices also depends on the character of life they produce. Do they lead us toward the fullness of the love of God and neighbor?

[55] These have been consistent themes not only in the work of feminist liturgical theologians such as reported here but also in the work of Gordon Lathrop,

engaged description of the practices of the churches and critical reflection on those practices with the churches than have been present in our work to date. We will need to account for those practices that continue by design or default to contribute to systems of oppression, denial, and disenfranchisement.

We can continue to make normative and constitutive claims about liturgical and sacramental practices, but such claims must be carefully qualified by the ongoing practice of the churches. In the tension between *orthodoxia* and *orthopraxis,* we come face to face with the fact that even as we "perform" liturgy, liturgy is also "performing" us. It is inscribing a form of the Christian faith in body, bone, and marrow as well as in mind and spirit. As Philip Pfatteicher notes, liturgy not only expresses our thoughts and feelings but also impresses them, giving them shape and form "by shaping and forming our attitudes so that they conform to those of Christ." This we might call "ritual knowledge," for we learn in it the process of liturgical participation. I will explore this in the next chapter. But Pfatteicher also reminds us that "because the liturgy does not always express what we think or feel it has the potential to transform those who share in it."[56] This becomes a question of liturgy as a "strategic ritual practice," which I will explore in the fourth chapter.

Don Saliers, Kevin Irwin, and Aidan Kavanagh. As each reports, the end of "classic" liturgical practice is neither the liturgy, nor a theological *ordo* (Lathrop), nor particular religious affections (Saliers), but participation in the mystery and life of God for the sake of the cosmos.

[56] *The School of the Church: Worship and Christian Formation* (Valley Forge, Pa.: Trinity Press International, 1995) 102, 105.

Chapter Three

Worship as Ritual Knowledge

What are outward things to Thee[1]

In the previous two chapters I explored, first, the relationship be-tween prayer and belief and, second, the claims we can make about worship. I have been particularly concerned to explore the ways in which the church today tends to limit our understanding of the role of Christian liturgy to that of a means for a community's ritual expression and, in doing so, obscures the normative and con-stitutive claims of the liturgy for that community. Once this limita-tion is firmly in place, an understanding of the formative power of liturgy becomes more difficult for the community to retrieve.

Where the explorations in the previous chapter primarily fo-cused on the normative claims we make about Christian worship, this chapter will focus on the constitutive claims we make about worship. How does faith get into our bodies? How does the church imprint upon its people the memory of who and whose it is, the memory of a life with God in Jesus Christ, the memory of the One whose passion, death, and resurrection Christians claim for our-selves? How, as I asked at the end of the previous chapter, does liturgy "perform" us?

---

[1] Hymn 88, "Long have I seemed to serve thee, Lord," stanza 4, in *The Works of John Wesley*, vol. 7: *A Collection of Hymns for the use of the People called Methodists*, ed. Franz Hildebrandt and Oliver Beckerlegge (Oxford: Clarendon Press; New York: Oxford University Press, 1983) 189.

To answer these questions, I want to pursue in this chapter, as well as the next, what it means to talk about "ritual knowledge" and "ritual practice." Ritual knowledge and practice are important issues because, whether we participate in "high" or "low" church worshiping communities,[2] we engage in ritual actions that work on and in us to form us as a particular Christian people. Two questions structure the work of this chapter: (1) What functions do ritual and ritualization serve psychologically, socially, and historically in the development of persons and communities? (2) Given these diverse functions, what then does it mean to speak about "ritual knowing"?

Some of the following discussion may seem to be a detour from our primary questions. Nevertheless, questions related to ritual and ritual knowledge are particularly important in an age and culture that is suspicious of habit, ritual, and tradition, and in a church context that increasingly lacks much visible commitment to common symbols and ritual actions. (One need only note how readily symbols of the faith, such as Bible, font, table, and cross disappear from settings designed for "seekers.") Cultural anthropologist Mary Douglas proleptically described this cultural shift over thirty years ago when she noted the social movement from contempt of external ritual forms to the private internalizing of religious experience to a generalized humanist philanthropy.[3] Douglas argued that

"alienation from the current social values usually takes a set form: a denunciation not only of irrelevant rituals, but ritualism as such; exaltation of the inner experience and denigration of its standardized expressions; preference for intuitive and instant forms of knowledge; and rejection of mediating institutions, rejection of any

---

[2] We sometimes forget that ritualized liturgical sacramental practices are not limited to "high church" forms. These practices are, in many ways, as diverse as the church itself. References to "high church" forms generally indicate eucharistic and initiatory rites, gestures such as kneeling, bowing, genuflecting, and making the sign of the cross. References to "low church" forms generally indicate hymn singing, testimonies, pastoral prayers, and preaching. Of course, the ritual practices of many churches cross back and forth between "high" and "low" patterns.

[3] *Natural Symbols: Explorations in Cosmology*, 2nd ed. (New York: Pantheon Books, 1982) 7.

tendency to allow habit to provide the basis of a new symbolic system."[4]

But Douglas also noted that once a community discovers a need for organization to sustain itself and a need for a "coherent system of expression," ritual practices re-emerge.[5] How is it that ritual maintains such a prominent place in our personal and communal lives? What does ritual do for us, even when we attempt to deny its power?

RITUAL AND RITUALIZATION

In what follows, I provide a brief review of the psychological, social, and historical functions of ritual and ritualization. My goal here is threefold: (1) to orient us to the diversity of perspectives about ritual present in our communities today; (2) to avoid limiting the discussion to the "idea" of ritual (or ritual as object); and (3) to encourage an understanding of ritual and ritualization as action, something not only "done" but done with intention by persons and communities.[6] In this section, therefore, I review seven different yet

[4] Ibid., 19.

[5] Ibid.

[6] As I begin this section, I offer three caveats: (1) Because the psychological and anthropological literature on ritual and ritualization is vast and continues to grow, the following discussion is necessarily condensed. In the following, building primarily but often indirectly on the work of Erik Erikson, I review the basic adaptive functions of ritual and ritualization. (2) Because I want to move from these understandings of liturgy as ritual toward an understanding of liturgy as ritual practice and strategic ecclesial practice, the question of ritual practice will receive more substantial treatment in the next chapter than ritual and ritualization receive here.(3) Finally, my intent to focus on ritual practice rather than on ritualization precludes the necessity of rehearsing the whole of Erikson's work on ritual and ritualization.

Erikson presents his theory of ritualization in three forms: "Ontogeny of Ritualization" in Rudolph Loewenstein, Lottie Newman, Max Schur, and Albert Solnit, eds., *Psychoanalysis—A General Psychology* (New York: International Universities Press, 1966) 601–621; *Toys and Reasons: Stages in the Ritualization of Experience* (New York: W. W. Norton, 1977); and *The Life Cycle Completed* (New York: W. W. Norton, 1985). Of these, the first provides the clearest statement of his theory and the last the best summary.

Erikson never speaks directly of liturgy or rite but of a developmental process of "ritualization" defined as "an interplay between at least two persons who repeat it at meaningful intervals and in recurring contexts; . . . this

interrelated functions that ritual and ritualization serve in the development of persons and communities.[7] These seven functions are:

1) to integrate external sources of anxiety into the human order;
2) to speak to the unconscious through symbol;
3) to give life sense and value;
4) to facilitate the expression and catharsis of feelings in individuals and groups;
5) to help address the unsettledness and unpredictability of life;
6) to reveal and enact the power and permanence of a group;
7) to mark the cycles and passages of human life.

The first function that ritual and ritualization serve is to integrate into the human order those cosmic, biological, and social experiences that often are a source of anxiety if they remain exterior to the human person. Ritual and ritualization "domesticate"[8] the

---

interplay should have adaptive value for the respective egos of both participants" ("Ontogeny," 602.) Although Erikson traces, and in some cases merely hints at, the developmental sequence of ritualization throughout the life cycle, the core of its development is completed by the end of childhood. This core includes four components: (1) the *numinous*, by which he means the affirming face of the transcendent other, particularly the mother; (2) the *judicious*, representing the boundaries between right and wrong, yes and no, the sacred and profane, the acceptable and the out of bounds; (3) the *dramatic*, the ability for imaginative play and, increasingly, for narrative, plot, and the projection of possible endings; and (4) the *formal*, as the structured consolidation of the previous stages into what would now be recognized as *ritual*. Paul Philibert argues that these four basic elements "together form a common potentiality to realize the power of symbol within ritual interaction. Symbols have the power to formulate experience, evoke urgency, summon an assembly, claim meaning, and situate shared experience." See Paul Philibert, "Readiness for Ritual: Psychological Aspects of Maturity in Christian Celebration," in *Alternative Futures for Worship*, vol. 1: *General Introduction*, ed. Regis A. Duffy (Collegeville, Minn.: The Liturgical Press, 1987) 91.

[7] Pierre Erny, in "Rites et education: Les grandes fonctions du rite," *Lumen Vitae* 2 (1992) 159–173, provides one of the clearer summaries of the functions of ritual in regard to ritual knowing and learning. The following discussion builds on Erny's basic outline.

[8] "Domestication," on the one hand, refers to a shift of responsibility for Christian formation from the church to the household, especially to the mother-child relationship. Here the term functions in a parallel, if not literal, fashion, bringing the cosmic, biological, and social into the interior "economy" of the person.

world, enabling person and community to mark the turning of the seasons, the biological changes that accompany the life cycle, as well as social events such as war and revolution, victory and liberation, even crisis and catastrophe. Through the repetition of particular actions, stories, and practices within the context of a community, we simplify and tame what might ordinarily be perceived as a dangerous complexity.[9] By taking the story into ourselves, it is no longer "other" than us; whether we are working with a story of success or of suffering, we work with the story to make meaning of it for ourselves and for our communities.

Second, ritual and ritualization speak to the unconscious through the language of symbol, touching all aspects of human life. Such arguments are common to Jungian psychoanalytic traditions.[10] In Erikson's terms, however, ritualization and the language of symbol hold up to awareness the importance of "reason as an organizing function," as well as the significance of the irrational as seen in "the arational and prerational way in which persons interdependent on each other create significant ritualizations."[11] On the one hand, we might bemoan, as some have, the loss of the sense of transcendence and mystery from Christian liturgy as a result of ongoing liturgical reform.[12] On the other hand, when we look at the arational and prerational ways in which persons create significant ritualizations, we may wonder at the emotional ties created and sustained by the gaze of mother or primary caregiver and child. In later development the ritualization of the "holy gaze" leads people of faith to sing "Let the light of your face shine on us" (Psalm 67:1) and to pray "May the light of God's countenance shine upon you and give you peace" (Numbers 6:26). So, too, we wonder at the

[9] George S. Worgul, Jr., *From Magic to Metaphor* (New York: Paulist Press, 1980) 57.

[10] In particular, see Carl G. Jung, "Transformation Symbolism in the Mass," in *Psyche and Symbol*, ed. Violet S. De Laszlo, trans. R. F. C. Hull, (Princeton: Princeton University Press, 1991), and Jolande Jacobi, *Complex/Archetype/Symbol in the Psychology of C. G. Jung*, trans. Ralph Manheim (Princeton: Princeton University Press, 1971).

[11] "Ontogeny of Ritualization," 621.

[12] Such arguments are found in the autobiographical work of Richard Rodriguez, *Hunger for Memory* (New York: Bantam Books, 1982), and in Victor Turner, "Ritual, Tribal and Catholic," *Worship* 50:6 (November 1976) 504–526.

relationship between seasonal depression and the loss of sunlight in the winter and the word of hope that resounds through Advent, Christmas, and Epiphany in expectation that darkness be defeated and light returned to the world.

Third, ritual and ritualization give life sense and value. Through ritual we make meaning about our lives and acquire a sense of orientation to why and where we are. We perform stories about ourselves and about those with whom we are in relationship. "Through ritual we organize our understandings and dramatize our fundamental conceptions, rearranging our fundamental assumptions in the course of rituals themselves."[13] In rites of confession and penance we name our failures of relatedness to God and one another. In renunciations and confessions of faith, such as the ones that introduce the United Methodist liturgies for baptism and baptismal reaffirmation, we name and rename ourselves within those relationships. In rites of initiation we are taken into a community and claimed as its own. These ritual practices of confession, renunciation, and initiation offer strategies and contexts for the self-expression of person and community. Yet they also result in the ongoing social and psychological "re-writing" of person and community. How? George Worgul, in his discussion of Erikson and ritualization, suggests that ritual and ritualization "secure[s] a consistent identification of one human generation with another" and "provide[s] a psychological foundation for 'ego' development which is essential for the eventual total personality integration in adulthood."[14] Socially and psychologically, the sharing of meaning enacted and constructed in the course of ritual identifies a person with (or outside of) a community even as it grounds that person's sense of self, rooting deeply "an orientation which can be drawn upon at a moment's notice, even unconsciously."[15] Initiation and,

---

[13] Barbara Myerhoff, "Rites of Passage: Process and Paradox," in *Celebration: Studies in Festivity and Ritual*, ed. Victor Turner (Washington: Smithsonian Institution Press, 1982) 128.

[14] *Magic to Metaphor*, 57.

[15] Paul J. Philibert, "Readiness for Ritual," 83. Philibert identifies *repetition*, *relationality*, and *reason* as three elements of what he believes Erikson means by ritualization. Repetition plants deeply an orientation in mind and body. Relationality is indicated by the fact that "rituals take place between persons who are vitally involved with one another." Reason is indicated by the sharing

with it, practices of renunciation and confession of faith are practices of naming, even performing, the boundaries of a community. They draw a person through or across those boundaries in a manner that results in an understanding by person and community that the person is now a member of that community.

Fourth, ritual and ritualization facilitate the expression and catharsis of individuals and groups. Even as they facilitate the expression of certain feelings, they also provide the means to channel, to contain, to rule, to submit to social constraints, and to impose models of respect. Here ritualization functions "to provide structure for social interactions. . . . It provides a model, normative form of interaction, yet allows for creative expression within that structure."[16] In regard to this expressive and cathartic function of ritual and ritualization, we need to think of things only appropriately said or done in certain circumstances and contexts. The mourning and weeping appropriate to a funeral are inappropriate at a wedding feast (although there is often a form of mourning and weeping that may occur there as well). Yet it is the rite and ritualization we recognize as a funeral that provide the means by which to both express and contain that mourning and weeping, even as it offers an opportunity for person and community to name who, why, and where one is, as the previous model suggests. At its best, such ritualization "represents a creative formalization which helps to avoid both impulsive excess and compulsive self-restriction,

---

of meaning within the context of this relationship as we find between mother and child.

[16] Randie Timpe, "Ritualizations and Ritualisms in Religious Development: A Psychosocial Perspective," *Journal of Psychology and Theology* 11:4 (1983) 312. Clifford Geertz, in *The Interpretation of Cultures* (New York: Basic Books, 1973), and Don Handelman, in *Models and Mirrors* (Cambridge: Cambridge University Press, 1989), more thoroughly address the question of ritual as model. Geertz distinguishes between models *of* and models *for*. Models *of* express structures in a synoptic form so as to render them apprehensible. A model *of* attempts to show or describe how reality *is*. A model *for* is a theory "under whose guidance physical relationships are organized," offering a blueprint for the structuring of behavior or relationships (Geertz, 92–95). Handelman takes up these distinctions, renaming the model *of* as "mirror." The mirror displays how things are while not acting directly on anything. It provides a means by which the social order can look at itself, putting the social order on display and "open to inspection" (Handelman, 41–47). The model behaves "as if it

both social anomie and moralistic coercion."[17] At its worst, such ritualization "may be perverted into social pathology, pseudo-ritualization, or ritualism."[18]

Fifth, ritual and ritualization help persons and communities address the unsettledness and unpredictability of life. Thus, while ritual and ritualization structure expression and catharsis, they have other ongoing structural functions for individuals and societies. Heije Faber writes: "Rituals arise in community and try to give direction to and set boundaries for the behavior of human beings."[19] Faber further suggests that these structural functions address three human needs. First, ritual addresses the human need "for life to be structured." No one is able to live in complete chaos. Second, ritual addresses the human need "for [the] sameness or coherence which forms a necessary basis for the growth of the concept of identity and the development of a self-consciousness." That is, we do not, perhaps cannot, know who we are individually or in community if there is no sense of "sameness" across time and experience. In this sense, ritual provides a place in which the sameness of our bodies over time (height, shape, gestures) interacts with the sameness of our internal selves. Third, ritual addresses the human need for safety "at points where life 'breaks through the walls of the person,' particularly where human beings are being confronted with the irrational and therefore threatening aspects of the numinous."[20] Imagine our lives are like rivers that, like the

---

were the world," setting up a schema by which transformative action may take place, has specific directions toward which it moves, and provides a "preview" of some hypothetical future (Handelman, 27–28). Timpe's use of "model" is consistent with Geertz's "model *for*" and Handelman's "model."

[17] Robert L. Browning and Roy A. Reed, *The Sacraments in Religious Education and Liturgy* (Birmingham: Religious Education Press, 1985) 90.

[18] Timpe, "Ritualizations and Ritualisms," 314. "Ritualism" is a category created by Erikson to speak about the maladaptive possibilities of ritualization. As Timpe indicates, ritualisms "take on the form of compulsive compliance, obsessions, or delusions" and are "essentially neurotic in form and origin." Erikson provides his clearest exploration of the maladaptive "ritualisms" that parallel adaptive ritualizations in *The Life Cycle Completed*, 55–83.

[19] "The Meaning of Ritual in the Liturgy," in *Current Studies in Ritual*, ed. Hans-Günter Heimbrock and H. Barbara Boudewijnse, (Amsterdam and Atlanta: Rodopi, 1990) 43.

[20] Ibid., 45.

Mississippi, can and do overflow their banks. This overflow in itself is destructive and carries with it thousands of other dangerous elements—uprooted trees and homes, the effluence of overrun sewage plants—that may cause harm. At the same time, these floods regenerate the flood plain, depositing new soil and providing needed nutrients that enrich the land. Here ritual and ritualization provide the barriers or channel markers that contain and direct that overflow, as well as something to cling to for support. While these images may suggest that ritual is only about managing crisis, we see that this management is also a source of renewal.

Sixth, even as ritual and ritualization mark, contain, and direct the flow of human life, they also reveal, convey, and enact the power and permanence of a group. We may focus on either the power of the group over the individual or how ritual and ritualization unify a generation. Ritual serves to break the individual out of isolation, attending to the human need to recognize, affirm, and maintain values, beliefs, and common sentiments that ground the unity of a group. Here we can think broadly about "tradition" as established usage or custom or as a return to the fundamental inspiration of a culture transmitted from generation to generation, indicating a permanence or continuity of identity. In this sense, ritual and ritualization provide the four walls of a home, an enclosed and clearly defined space that is both a place of shelter and a place of welcome and familiarity. Here, as in previously described functions, ritual offers a clear sense of *where* one belongs as well as *who* one is. Lest we romanticize such images, we should remember that the four walls of a home can also become the imprisoning walls of a cell. Think about the ways in which ritual practices reinforce particular political or ecclesiastical structures, such as the hierarchy of the priesthood, the power or powerlessness of the baptized community, or even the co-opting of Christian events by civil religious practices as found in Fourth of July or Memorial Day commemorations enacted by church congregations.

Finally, like the integrating, structuring, meaning-making, and identity-conferring functions described above, ritual and ritualization enable us to mark the cycles of human existence and to orchestrate or perform the grand passages of life. Ritualized structures mark passages from childhood to adulthood, as in confirmation or the receipt of car keys; from non-believer to Christian in baptism, chrismation (anointing), and eucharist; and from life to death in funerals and memorial services. New forms of ritual and ritualization (at least for North American Christians) seek to address the passages of women's lives, such as the onset of menarche or the giving of birth.[21]

As I believe is evident in this overview, ritual and ritualization do more than express the beliefs, traditions, or identity of persons and communities. Even as they provide such expression, they simultaneously provide the means by which communities and persons-in-community are constituted and normed. Boundaries are drawn and crossed, names given, stories told and acquired, lives reshaped. Within the web of these seven overlapping functions, we see ritual practices as simultaneously expressive, constitutive, and normative for persons and communities. Where and when the expressive character does rise to prominence, it is not the idiosyncratic expression of one person or community; rather, this expression is focused within and contained by the ritualized practice, the "tradition," of the larger community. As a ritualized event,

---

[21] Rites of passage and their tie to life-cycle events are an important form and function of ritualization. Nevertheless, it is unfortunate that this single form and function, particularly the threefold structure of separation, liminality, and reintegration, have come to dominate much of the discussion about ritualization and liturgical sacramental practice. This is due in large part to the influence of Victor Turner and his recovery of the ritual processes identified by Arnold van Gennep as *rites de passage*. Its dominance is perhaps most evident in discussions of baptism and Christian initiation. Following Turner and van Gennep, liturgical scholars have described baptism and its related rites as "rites of passage" or "rites of initiation" with its defined and discernible structures based on these categories. Perhaps because these processes and structures have been so accessible, especially Turner's concept of *liminality*, many ritual events are described as in some way *liminal* or threshold experiences. To the extent that the concept of liminality has directed our attention to the question of what and how baptism does what it does in the Christian community, such readings of Christian baptism have been helpful. Nonetheless, a focus on process and structure limits our understanding of what happens in events such as baptism. I will return to how it does so later in this chapter. See Victor Turner, "Passages, Margins, and Poverty: Religious Symbols of Communitas" in *Dramas, Fields, and Metaphors: Symbolic Action in Human Society* (Ithaca, N.Y.: Cornell University Press, 1974) 231–277; *The Ritual Process: Structure and Anti-Structure* (Ithaca, N.Y.: Cornell University Press, 1977) 94–125; and Arnold van Gennep, *The Rites of Passage*, trans. Monika B. Vizedom and Gabrielle L. Caffre (Chicago: University of Chicago Press, 1960) 1–14.

the repetitive character of ritual further binds this expression. At the same time, the expressive and creative nature of ritual enriches, challenges, and even transforms its constitutive and normative functions. In this tensive relationship between the expressive, constitutive, and normative functions, ritual and ritualization provide the means by which we come to know ourselves in a particular place and community, the means to "rewrite" this sense of self and community, and to "practice" this knowledge.

AN EXPRESSING AND CONSTITUTING RITUAL

We are not alone, we live in God's world.
We believe in God:
    who has created and is creating,
    who has come in Jesus, the Word made flesh,
    to reconcile and make new,
    who works in us and others by the Spirit.
We trust in God.
We are called to be the church:
    to celebrate God's presence,
    to love and serve others,
    to seek justice and resist evil,
    to proclaim Jesus, crucified and risen,
    our judge and our hope.
In life, in death, in life beyond,
    God is with us.
We are not alone.
Thanks be to God.[22]

For over ten years the TUMC congregation has recited this affirmation of faith as a weekly part of worship. I spent some time with them exploring the consequences of this ritual event. Among those church members interviewed—some had been members for five years, others for as long as twenty-five years—many had the feeling that this affirmation had always been a part of worship at TUMC. Certainly among the current population of children and youth this was true. Yet the use of this affirmation came through the intentional action of their pastor around the second year of his

[22] "A Statement of Faith of the United Church of Canada," *The United Methodist Hymnal* (Nashville: The United Methodist Publishing House, 1989) 883.

pastorate, after the current *United Methodist Hymnal* was published (1989). Prior to this, TUMC had been using a variety of creeds, affirmations, and statements of faith as part of its weekly worship service. The issues pastoral leaders were trying to address during a time of experimentation (prior to this particular pastorate and into the first two years of it) included a desire for congregational response that spoke in "fresh" language to the needs of the congregation and a desire to address the concern for inclusive language. Attempts to address the latter included altering the traditional Trinitarian language of the Apostles' Creed to include a naming of God as "father and mother." There was some awareness within the congregation of the inadequacy of this response.[23] The publication of the hymnal in 1989, with its inclusion of the statement of faith of the United Church of Canada, provided an opportunity to address these concerns in a way that has served the congregation well for the subsequent ten years. Among some middle-aged and older members interviewed, especially among those who had grown up either in the Methodist church or in the Roman Catholic church, there was a tendency to contrast this affirmation with the Apostles' Creed. Some talked about the familiarity of the Apostles' Creed and of their sense of connection with the historic faith and tradition of the church through it. Some contrasted the "esoteric" but timeless theological character of the Apostles' Creed with the "freshness" and "concreteness" of the language of the Canadian statement of faith. Others suggested that the Apostles' Creed was problematic because it "didn't seem to include all of us and address the greater concerns of a relationship to faith in the world and witness." Another person put it this way: Although the Apostles' Creed states the basics of the Christian faith and has the "roots" better, "it's easier to say the Apostles' Creed and not think about what's going on in the community, in the congregation, or in the world."

What, then, does it mean for this congregation to say, week in and week out, "We are not alone, we live in God's world"? This congregation was not immune to the "typical" Protestant resistance to the "rote" recitation of anything over a period of time—as one per-

---

[23] The sense that this response was inadequate focused primarily on dissatisfaction with and concern about altering this creed of the ecumenical church.

son observed, repetition risks loss of attention. Yet they found a way to hold this resistance in tension with the ongoing use of an affirmation that became "second nature" to the congregation. Its weekly repetition has brought a richness of meaning to many, though not to all.

Various members of TUMC were asked about the ways in which this affirmation shaped the way they think about themselves as a Christian people and how this affirmation had shaped the way the congregation thinks about itself as a Christian community. Some had never thought about these questions before and had difficulty beginning to answer these questions. Some suggested that they just did not connect to the affirmation outside of the context of worship. But when asked to think about which phrases of the affirmation first came to mind, most found that they somehow carried this statement with them in their daily lives.

For about half of the group interviewed, the first and last phrases stood out: "We are not alone." For some, this statement was important at the most personal level as a response to personal isolation, loneliness, and the "single" life. In the midst of a sense that "aloneness can be a real depleting kind of feeling," the affirmation provided a reminder that we are never by ourselves, that God is with us in everything—"in life, in death, in life beyond death." For others, the statement that "we are not alone" provided a reminder that the Christian community is more than the local congregation and that the "people of God" are more than the Christian community. In this, the sense of togetherness encouraged by the affirmation took on a sense of global connectedness. This sense of connectedness pushed some to claim the importance of the second phrase, "we live in God's world." Our connectedness in God's world provides a point of critique of and contrast with the values of North American culture. With some, the focus of reflection on "we are not alone" came on the "we" (in contrast to the "I" of the Apostles' Creed). In this, the affirmation provided a reminder that this statement is that of a community rather than of an individual. The connection not only is with God (or God with us) but also with one another, leading into life in the civic as well as church community.

Several responses focused on the phrase "in life, in death, in life beyond death." Although these responses eventually led back to the phrase "we are not alone," emphasizing a sense of personal connection with God and the community, the responses also described the ways in which this connection provided personal and communal comfort in the face of sorrow, loss, and death, and of the omnipresence of God in the midst of all of life and beyond (a reminder that "death is not the end of the story"). This sense of God's presence in the midst of struggle also became important in reflections on the way in which the affirmation served the congregation as a whole. (I will return to this below.)

Several responses highlighted the importance of the reminder that God "has created and is creating." For one person, this provided an opportunity to reflect on how a person in a healing profession can participate in God's ongoing work of creation and re-creation, becoming "a vehicle for God's Spirit" in the world. For another, this suggested God's continuing creative activity through the Spirit within us, a creating that does not happen in isolation from one another. Through shared experience in worship, and in recitation of the affirmation, God continues to strengthen and build a community of faith. For this person, the experience of love and care for her by the community provided an experience of God's continuing creative activity within the community.

One way in which several people summarized the personal effect of this affirmation was to say that, although they were not aware of it pushing them in a particular direction, the language of the affirmation provided a means of support for personal direction, work, and mission. In some cases the language of the affirmation provided a starting point for reflection on one's own relationship with God as well as a desire not to limit oneself to the words of the affirmation itself.

How, then, did this affirmation shape the life of TUMC? The answers to this question really cannot be separated from the responses about the shaping of individuals; there is a strong sense of connection between individual identity and life in the community. Nevertheless, there were several distinctive emphases. One emphasis was on the sense of "fit" between the affirmation and the life and ministry of the TUMC congregation. In this sense, the focus turned to the phrases "we are called to be the church" and "to seek justice and resist evil." As one person stated, "We are better at seeking justice than proclaiming Jesus crucified and risen." In this we hear a restatement of the claim that this affirmation gives more attention to life, witness, and mission in the world than does the Apostles' Creed.

The sense of the appropriateness and fit of this affirmation calls our attention to the way in which ritual action provides a means by which a community expresses who and whose it is. But appropriateness is not the only criterion. Several in this congregation noted the importance of being able to "say something together." This "saying together" reinforced the sense of community present in the congregation, both as a reminder and as a "push" toward communion with others. This "saying together" provided a concrete sense of "being the church together" as the congregation speaks "with one voice." Another person suggested that the weekly recitation of the affirmation was a weekly reinforcement providing "a broad, generalized statement that everybody can buy in to" and from which we can "sort of step back and regroup." Analogous to the place where a family plans to regroup should some get lost, the affirmation provided a place for congregational "regrouping." As one person noted, "You know, we kind of get lost and spread out. Let's go back and meet where we were all together, and then let's regroup and try to go from there in ministry."

This sense of "saying something together" provided not only a regrouping place for the congregation but also a safe center by which people remained in contact with the beliefs of the community even when the beliefs were not wholly their own. This is perhaps clearest in the following statements: "It's a bigger picture and allows us to be part of the bigger picture, even if you are struggling with some of [those] issues that are not quite clear in your own mind." "You say this as a member of a community, and it helps transcend places where you may be struggling. It helps you be able to say, 'We believe in this and I'm part of this community, and I may be struggling with parts of it but I believe in it.'. . . I believe in it [even] if I can't quite figure it out, or I'm not sure I'm real steady with it, but I have faith that I do believe in it."

This participation in the "bigger picture" also provided for some members a means of accountability to one another within the congregation. It was a reminder of the community's and the individual's responsibilities and identity from week to week. As one person said, "In the midst of everything we're bombarded with through the week, you need time to say 'This is who I am, this is who we are.'" Even those who had difficulty saying anything about the particular words of the affirmation found it important to have such a statement (the particular creed didn't matter to one person, the fact of a creed did) that pulled the congregation together. In this sense, the affirmation took on an importance for some as a resource that could serve the congregation through the time of transition it was then entering (the interviews were all conducted six weeks prior to a change in pastoral leadership). It provided a means by which the congregation could and did ask, "Who are we?" and say to itself as well as to new pastors, "This is who we are."

For many in this congregation, the affirmation of faith, while present week in and week out, is not necessarily a conscious part of daily life. Yet there was also a clear sense that when invited to reflection on the affirmation, there was a richness of belief that was reflected in and shaped by its use. There was a clear sense of the appropriateness or fit of this affirmation in the life and work of this congregation. The affirmation appeared in a Sunday school class struggling with a mission statement, in Lenten devotional reflections, and, sometimes intentionally, sometimes unintentionally, in the preaching.

Notice, then, how one small component in weekly worship addresses several ritual needs. For some it provided a place of stability in a time of anxiety and change, addressing the unsettledness and unpredictability of life. For many it provided a way to name the common values of the congregation and to carry those values with them. For others it provided a regular way to enact the continuation of the congregation, even for the congregation to "reestablish" itself week by week, thus revealing and enacting the power and permanence of the group. As the congregation gave voice to its identity, proclaiming "This is who we are," they were also being told in the midst of that proclamation "This is who you are." What they were enacting was also "enacting" them. The ritualization of their faith in this affirmation became one of the means by which this congregation expressed its faith and was constituted as a particular community of faith.

RITUAL KNOWING

This brings us to my second question. In light of this epistemological ritual function, how do we come to know ritually? Social anthropologist Paul Connerton and theologian Theodore Jennings address the question of ritual knowledge in ways that are helpful to this discussion. While Jennings focuses on ritual as a means for transmitting and gaining knowledge, Connerton moves away from the structural and functional concerns with which we began toward a concern for ritual as an embodied way of knowing. He facilitates this move, first by a critique of the psychoanalytic and sociological positions described above, and second by attention to social commemorative practices and habit.

In the case of the psychoanalytic position, Connerton challenges theoretical positions which focus on the conflict-laden nature of ritual and which argue that rituals are "freighted with strategies of denial." He also challenges sociological positions that suggest that in communicating shared values within a group, ritual reduces internal dissension and constitutes social stability and equilibrium.[24] Connerton's concern is twofold. First, the tendency to focus on the content rather than on the form of ritual suggests that there is some "hidden point" behind ritual symbolism that requires an act of translation or decoding. Rather, ritual performance specifies a relationship "between the performers of the ritual and what it is they are performing." Further, "liturgical language is a certain form of action and puts something into practice. It is not a verbal commentary on an action external to itself; in and of itself liturgical language is an action."[25] This last comment stands as an important critique of attempts to make liturgy "educational" by commenting on the liturgical action and texts throughout the liturgy. Such commentary is more appropriately the task of mystagogy—teaching about the Christian mystery—and has to do with a different kind of

[24] *How Societies Remember* (New York: Cambridge University Press, 1989) 48–50.

[25] Ibid., 53–57. Connerton's attention to the question of performance anticipates my own more detailed attention to the same question in the next chapter, where I will argue that theories of ritual performance provide a link between ritual structure and ritual practice. His attention to the performative character of language also echoes the work of John Austin, *How to Do Things with Words* (New York: Oxford University Press, 1962), and John Searle, *Speech*

knowing, a knowing "about" the liturgy. Connerton is arguing, as am I, for a kind of knowing intrinsic to the liturgy itself.

Through his discussion of commemorative ceremonies, Connerton describes the "tendency to ignore the pervasive importance in many cultures of actions which are explicitly represented as re-enactments of prior, prototypical actions."[26] It is this character of re-enactment that Connerton considers the distinctive mark of commemorative ceremonies. It is also this re-enactment that is of primary importance for the shaping of social memory. In describing the "rhetoric of re-enactment," Connerton names three components: (1) calendrical repetition; (2) verbal repetition, with some disjunction between sacred and profane language; and (3) gestural repetition.[27]

The eucharist provides one example. Calendrically, Christians celebrate it on a weekly (or monthly or quarterly) basis. Verbally, it is marked in most cases by a distinctive prayer. In its fullest, this prayer is a Trinitarian prayer of thanksgiving, remembering, and invocation. At the least, it is a remembering through the institution narrative. Gesturally, it is marked by the giving, receiving, and consuming of bread and wine, as well as by gestures of kneeling, standing, moving in procession, and singing. In some cases we are more aware of the rhetoric of ritual gesture when we are asked to change it or when we discover that other people or congregations enact worship with different gestures. Note, for example, the tension a congregation experiences if its tradition is to receive the Lord's Supper while seated, and they are asked to move to kneel at an altar rail. Or consider the tension that arises when those who are used to kneeling at the altar rail are asked to remain standing in order to receive the bread and cup at multiple points in the worship space. Don Saliers helpfully observes, "The more directly the body is involved, the more theological conflict there is likely to be between traditions. . . . The bodily signs carry theological convictions at a deeper cultural level than do rationally expressed beliefs."[28]

Acts: An Essay in the Philosophy of Language (Cambridge, Mass.: Cambridge University Press, 1969).

[26] Ibid., 61.

[27] Ibid., 65–68.

[28] *Worship as Theology: Foretaste of Glory Divine* (Nashville: Abingdon Press, 1994) 164. Saliers notes that Protestants tend to focus their attention on their

Connerton's point is that such ritual practices are not only about the telling of and reflecting on a master story but also about the en-actment of that story in ritual performance. The persuasiveness of these commemorations, therefore, is not based on some level of cognitive competence (instruction for the liturgy), but on what he calls "habituation" to the ritual performance.[29] We are "persuaded" by the liturgy to the extent that it enters into and becomes a part of who we are spiritually, cognitively, and, above all, physically in that liturgy.

Connerton's primary concern is with how people remember such prototypical stories and actions when commemorative cere-monies no longer function to convey that memory or when people no longer perform such ceremonies. This concern draws his atten-tion away from the specific prototypical actions and narratives commemorated in ritual cultic events and toward the question of bodily habit. He argues: "Commemorative ceremonies prove to be commemorative only in so far as they are performative; performa-tivity cannot be thought without a concept of habit; and habit can-not be thought without a notion of bodily automatisms."[30] Here he points to the heart of the question of this project. What is at stake in the renewal of the liturgical life of the church? Connerton sug-gests that in addition to the remembering of the prototypical events and stories of the community, liturgical renewal is about the cultivation of a form of ritual persuasion that locates Christian identity in the body as well as in the mind. We "know" ourselves and our beliefs in our bodies as well as in our minds.

For Connerton, social memory and cultic re-enactment lead be-yond social ceremony to a remembering located in the body. This

---

differences from Roman Catholics, such as the practices of genuflection or making the sign of the cross. But similar tensions arise between "mainline" and "charismatic" Protestant traditions around such gestures as raising the arms in praise and prayer, or between white congregations and African-American congregations around clapping, standing, and dancing. Bruce Morrill explores and responds to the liturgical tension between Roman Catholic and African-American Baptist practices in his essay "Initial Consideration: Theory and Practice of the Body in Liturgy Today," in *Bodies of Worship: Explorations in Theory and Practice* (Collegeville, Minn.: The Liturgical Press, 1999) 1–15.

[29] *How Societies Remember*, 71.

[30] Ibid., 6.

remembering occurs through the "sedimentation" of memory in the body by way of incorporating and inscribing practices. Incorporating practices are those which impart messages by means of the current bodily activity of the sender or senders, by performance. In the case of the eucharist, these messages are conveyed by the prayers, postures, and practices that define its celebration. Inscribing practices are those which preserve messages after a performance has ended, as in the recording of a performance or the writing of a liturgical text. Here the message of the eucharist is conveyed as a printed text. Inscribing practices, unlike "live performances," tend to bring closure to meaning and practice; "improvisation becomes increasingly difficult and innovation is institutionalized."[31] It was just such innovation that was slowed, if not halted, when liturgical texts were fixed in sacramentaries. It was attempts to counter improvisation and innovation that led to the formulation of the creeds.[32]

Connerton's description of incorporating and inscribing practices provides two basic insights into the questions concerning liturgical renewal, the function of ritual within that renewal, and the kind of knowing resulting from that renewal. First, liturgical renewal has focused necessarily on the revision and rewriting of texts and rubrics. Such revision enabled the church to clear away some of the clutter accumulated over the centuries and to respond to the linguistic and cultural changes of our time. But textual revision has also done just what Connerton suggested it would do: it has brought closure to meaning and the institutionalization of innovation. Second, given the focus on the rewriting of texts, the incorporating practices of the community at worship remain largely unaddressed. The words are different, but the actions are the same. While Protestant and Catholic Christians recover the language of

---

[31] Ibid., 75.

[32] On the one hand, the growth of the church beyond its Mediterranean roots and the challenges presented to it by heresies and new cultures required the fixing of liturgical texts. On the other hand, once texts have become fixed, they tend to be treated like museum pieces that must be protected and preserved at all cost. The challenge today, as throughout church history, is to find an appropriate balance between preservation and change, tradition and enculturation. See James White, *Protestant Worship* (Louisville: Westminster/John Knox Press, 1989) 214–216, for a development of this argument.

thanksgiving in the eucharistic prayer, in most cases their bowed heads and kneeling bodies continue to speak the language of penitence. Here we deny with our bodies what we speak with our mouths. As Connerton reminds us, "It is precisely because what is performed is something to which the performers are habituated that the cognitive content of what the group remembers in common exercises such persuasive and persistent force."[33] Ritual and ritualization, then, are ways of knowing self and other, person and community in the world that is both other and more than a cognitive knowing. Ritual knowing is affective and physical, imaginal and embodied.

An example from a congregation I served underscores this point. Each Advent the church hosted a musical production that involved the construction of a stage and set that covered the altar rail as well as the platform for the pulpit. As the timing of this event coincided with the congregation's monthly celebration of the eucharist, the event required that the congregation change its ritual practice. The congregation's normal practice was to come forward to kneel at the altar rail, receiving the bread and wine by intinction. Although the pulpit and table were moved onto the stage, the presence of the stage obscured the altar rail and prevented this action. Consequently, on this one Sunday each person received the bread and wine by intinction as usual but, prevented from kneeling at the rail, did so standing in a processional line. Reflecting on this change, one person suggested that the worship committee consider rescheduling the eucharist to another Sunday in the month because reception in this form did not mean the same thing. The bread and wine, the prayer texts, and the community were all the same, but the change of physical action changed the meaning of the event. How we use our bodies in worship influences the meaning we attribute to our liturgical action.

Even as ritual and ritualization offer ways by which to narrate "who we are" and "where we belong," orient persons and communities in relation to one another, orchestrate passages through human existence, and integrate the human and cosmic, biological,

---

[33] *How Societies Remember*, 88. Connerton later writes, "Habit is a knowledge and a remembering in the hands and in the body and in the cultivation of habit, it is our body which 'understands'" (ibid., 95).

and social orders, ritual and ritualization construct an argument for a way of being and for knowing ourselves in the world. Ritual and ritualization locate this argument in body and mind. Ritual and ritualization offer, therefore, a way of knowing *that* or *what*—either in the recounting of personal and social histories or in the meaning of narratives and events—and a way of knowing, or re-membering, *how*. I learn *what* it means to be a Christian as, year in, year out, I hear and tell the stories and traditions of that commu-nity. I learn *how* to be a Christian by enacting those stories and tra-ditions in the ritual actions of the Christian community, in the dying and rising experienced in baptism, in the grateful reception of bread and wine, in kneeling, bowing or standing for prayer. In the example above, the implied conclusion is that *how* we are Christian, how we are in relationship to God and one another, is different whether we stand or kneel to receive the eucharistic bread and wine.

Theodore Jennings provides a framework for this distinction be-tween ritual "knowing what" and ritual "knowing how." Arguing that ritual is "one of the ways in which human beings construe and construct their world," Jennings describes what he calls "three 'moments' in the noetic [the knowing or thinking] function of ritual."[34] First, ritual is a mode of inquiry and discovery, a way of gaining knowledge. This "noetic moment" focuses on what the ritual participant does. Inquiry and discovery suggest cognitive ac-tions. Yet Jennings argues, as does Connerton, that this knowledge is "primarily corporeal rather than cerebral, primarily active rather than contemplative, primarily transformative rather than specula-tive." Ritual knowledge is "gained by and through the body"; it is gained through action and is "identical with doing or acting, with a bodily doing or acting," through engagement rather than detach-ment.[35] We gain liturgical ritual knowledge through active partici-

[34] "On Ritual Knowledge," *The Journal of Religion* 62:2 (1982) 112. The first two of these modes are of importance to this discussion. In Jennings's third noetic moment, ritual performance displays itself to participants and observers who reflect on its structures and meanings. This type of ritual knowledge, knowledge *about* ritual, is represented primarily by the reports, books, and ar-ticles written by anthropologists and ritual theorists. This discussion, perhaps even this whole book, is itself a form of this particular noetic moment.

[35] Ibid., 115, 116.

pation in and the performance of the liturgy rather than by instruction or education.

Not only do we act to gain knowledge but, as Jennings argues in his second "noetic moment," ritual also acts to transmit knowledge. In this moment, the focus lies on what the ritual action itself does. Through engagement in ritual action, ritual transmits and focuses "a way of being and acting in the world."[36] Like Connerton, Jennings argues that ritual knowledge is not primarily about seeing differently but about acting differently.[37] Acting differently leads us to see and to know differently. As we saw above, standing rather than kneeling for the eucharist changes its meaning.

Throughout this discussion I have been attempting to explore how faith "gets into our bodies," even how the liturgy "performs" us. When we deny or ignore the ritual character of Christian worship, we make it difficult to attend to the ways in which what we do in worship acts upon us. Yet, when we do attend to the ways in which a kind of knowledge about the Christian life is gained and transmitted in ritual action, it becomes possible for us to turn our focus away from the liturgy itself to that liturgy we call the Christian life.[38] What we are doing in worship, then, is not "talking about" our life together, although this does happen in the context of our praying for one another and in preaching, but "doing" our life together as Christian people. The performance of the liturgy is not a discussion about the liturgy, but an enactment of meaning, the practice of our story as God's people, a strategy by which we come to know that God is present and we are graced disciples. As Jennings demonstrates, worship provides several ways in which we come to know God and ourselves. And as Connerton has shown, our repeated participation in worship becomes the means by which the liturgy "writes" its meaning in and on our bodies. What, then, might it mean to talk about liturgy as a form of ritual performance and practice and, as such, a primary means by which we learn and live the Christian life? It is to these themes that we turn in the next chapter.

[36] Ibid., 112.

[37] Ibid., 117.

[38] Gilbert Ostdiek, *Catechesis for Liturgy* (Washington: The Pastoral Press, 1986) 9.

Chapter Four

Worship as Ritual Practice

Here in thine own appointed ways[1]

In order to understand the ways in which worship forms us as Christian people and provides a context in which we "practice ourselves," as I indicated at the end of the previous chapter, we will need to further expand the ways in which we think about ritual. In particular, we need to move beyond the language and problems of structure and process so prevalent in psychological, sociological, and liturgical discussions of ritual and ritualization to an understanding of worship as ritual practice. In doing so, we will discover a different way to see that what we do in worship has consequences beyond what is immediately visible on any Sunday morning.

FROM RITUAL PERFORMANCE TO RITUAL PRACTICE

Recent work in ritual studies suggests two post-structuralist frameworks that help us understand more clearly how ritual functions in a community and why it is important in the shaping of a community. A shift in ritual studies to consider ritual as performance was, as we saw in the previous chapter, anticipated by Connerton in his attention to the ways in which liturgical language is a form of

[1] Hymn 89, "Still for thy loving kindness, Lord," stanza 2, in *The Works of John Wesley*, vol. 7: *A Collection of Hymns for the use of the People called Methodists*, ed. Franz Hildebrandt and Oliver Beckerlegge (Oxford: Clarendon Press; New York: Oxford University Press, 1983) 190.

action that puts something into practice.[2] Performance, then, provides the first framework for our exploration. The work of Stanley Tambiah, Bruce Kapferer, and Richard Bauman, as well as Victor Turner's later work, represents this shift more thoroughly. Within this, I will give particular attention to the taxonomy of ritual performance as proposed by Tambiah.

Catherine Bell's proposal for a consideration of ritual as practice provides, in part, the second framework for our discussion.[3] The move to ritual practice is made necessary by the inherent limitations of the performance framework for the interpretation of ritual events. Here recent discussions of practice in practical philosophy and liturgical theology will assist us. Building on these frameworks of performance and practice, I propose a model by which to speak about ritual knowing, sacramental meaning, and, finally, retrieving a term I introduced earlier, liturgical catechesis as strategic ecclesial practice. Throughout this discussion I will use Christian baptism as a specific case to provide a reference point in liturgical practice.

RITUAL AS PERFORMANCE

Although I have already referred to our "performing" liturgy, what do I intend when I speak of ritual as "performance"? An initial answer suggests a context that involves a performer and an audience.

---

[2] Paul Connerton, *How Societies Remember* (New York: Cambridge University Press, 1989) 53–57. Connerton also suggests that attention to ritual performance focuses on the relationship between a performer and that which is performed.

[3] I have used the term "practice" numerous times throughout the discussion to this point but have intentionally left it ambiguous. I am aware of the multiple and conflicting uses of the terms "practice" and "praxis" as well as the tendency to use them interchangeably. In the following discussion "practice" will take on a more specific meaning. While I will offer a fuller definition of "practice" in my discussion of Bell's work, Rebecca Chopp provides a useful definition which parallels Erikson's definition of ritualization as explored in the previous chapter (as an "adaptive repeated interplay between two or more individuals") and which offers a preliminary starting point: practices are "socially shared forms of behavior that mediate between what are often called subjective and objective dimensions. A practice is a pattern of meaning and action that is both culturally constructed and individually instantiated." See *Saving Work* (Philadelphia: Westminster John Knox, 1995) 15.

This answer focuses on places and persons, drawing our attention to a particular kind of relationship between an observer and that which is observed. But what of the event itself? Richard Bauman attends to the event, defining performance as "a mode of communicative behavior and a type of communicative event" suggesting "an aesthetically marked and heightened mode of communication, framed in a special way and put on display for an audience."[4] To perform is thus a particular way of communicating, somehow different from everyday communication between persons in that it is "marked," "heightened," and "put on display." Stanley Tambiah accents the "marked and heightened" nature of performance when he suggests that ritual performance is "an ordering or procedure that structures [festivals, cosmic rituals, and rites of passage] a sense of collective or communal enactment that is purposive (devoted to the achievement of a particular objective)."[5] He, too, notes that performances are somehow different from "ordinary" everyday events.

Victor Turner, continuing his concern for structure and process, tells us that ritual performances are the "performance of a complex sequence of symbolic acts," a "transformative performance revealing major classifications, categories, and contradictions of cultural processes."[6] These complex sequences are, nonetheless, "never amorphous or openended" but defined by a "diachronic structure, a beginning, a sequence of overlapping but isolable phases, and an end," a structure "generated out of the dialectical oppositions of processes and of levels of process."[7] Turner sees, then, that performances are somehow closed events; the generation of meaning in and of the performance takes on some clearly discernible pattern that is fixed by the performance itself.

To summarize: We may say that a ritual performance is a communicative event marked by certain forms of language, differentiated

---

[4] "Performance," in *Folklore, Cultural Performances, and Popular Entertainments*, ed. Richard Bauman (New York: Oxford University Press, 1992) 41.

[5] "A Performative Approach to Ritual," *Proceedings of the British Academy* 65 (1979) 116–117.

[6] "The Anthropology of Performance," in *The Anthropology of Performance* (New York: PAJ Publications, 1987) 75.

[7] Ibid., 80.

from the everyday, situated in a special context, and defined by a particular structure that somehow prevents ambivalence of meaning and interpretation. The United Methodist baptismal liturgy provides an example of such a ritual performance. It is marked, first, by particular prayers over the water and for the one being baptized, as well as by proclamations, renunciations, and affirmations. Second, while the use of water bears some similarity to a bath or shower, the amount used is generally considerably less (unless the baptism is by submersion), the person being baptized is usually clothed, and the baptism occurs in a public space and meeting. Third, the ritual structure of renunciation, affirmation, commitment, confession, thanksgiving, water rite, and congregational welcome layers baptism with meanings not associated with other everyday events, certainly not with a daily shower.

Stanley Tambiah's work suggests that a definition of ritual performance does not end here. Tambiah further distinguishes three senses in which ritual action is performative and provides a taxonomy with which to expand a definition of ritual performance. The first sense of ritual action as performance follows the Austinian sense of the performative "wherein saying something is also doing something as a conventional act"[8] and where "the saying of the speech act is the 'doing of an action' subject to both regulative and constitutive rules."[9] In contrast to Austin's primary focus on speech acts and the means by which they succeed or fail, Tambiah pushes the meaning of the performative beyond the immediate context of a textual "saying" to the fuller social and ideological context. Tambiah continues:

"If ritual events are performative acts (in a much stronger sense than ordinary speech acts which also do something with words), then the connections between the unit acts and utterances of the ritual, the logic of the rules of obligatory sequences of the ritual acts per se, cannot be fully understood without realizing that they are the clothing for social actions; and these social actions cannot in

[8] Tambiah, "A Performative Approach," 119. Tambiah is drawing here on John Austin, *How to Do Things with Words* (New York: Oxford University Press, 1962), and John Searle, *Speech Acts: An Essay in the Philosophy of Language* (Cambridge, Mass.: Cambridge University Press, 1969).

[9] Ibid., 127.

turn be understood except in relation to the cosmological presuppositions and the social interactional norms of the actors."[10]

We have only recently begun to heed the reminder that the interpretation of an event, ritual or otherwise, requires contextualization not only in the immediate context of a congregation but also in the larger context of Christian faith and practice.

Charles Briggs expands on the relationship between the social, ideological, and cosmological presuppositions in performances named by Tambiah. He writes: "In performance, an individual assumes responsibility for invoking the tradition itself, not just pointing to its existence . . . . Performance involves 'an assumption of accountability to an audience for the way in which communication is carried out.'"[11] Perhaps this is to say no more than that there are rules by which the "saying," whether it occurs within a ritual event or not, must be said for it to function communicatively.[12] At this level it is most easy to attend to the ritual event as a text. The audience is aware, we hope, of the difference between "You are baptized in the name of the Holy Trinity (Father, Son, and Holy Spirit)" and "I christen you *name.*" We recognize the first as an invocation of the tradition of Christian baptism, the second as the naming of battleships or luxury liners. We find in Luke 4 one of the more familiar biblical texts that offer an example of this definition of performance. After reading from Isaiah, Jesus announces, "These words are fulfilled in your hearing." The "saying" is the "doing." The response Jesus receives to that announcement, however, indicates that some were not in agreement with this saying/doing and that this "saying" had in some way violated the rules for the "performance" of Scripture in synagogue.

In terms of baptism, one of the questions this raises is that of the relationship between the saying and the doing. For example, what does it mean when the saying or doing is altered, incomplete, or

[10] Ibid., 139.

[11] *Competence in Performance* (Philadelphia: University of Pennsylvania Press, 1988) 8.

[12] In this regard and for further exploration of the application of the Austinian model of the performative to ritual events, see Ronald L. Grimes, "Infelicitous Performance and Ritual Criticism," in *Ritual Criticism* (Columbia, S.C.: University of South Carolina, 1990).

inconsistent from one context to the next? Three examples will suffice, the first two having more to do with the saying than the action of baptism itself. First, recent discussion about altering the Trinitarian formula to some construction other than "Father, Son and Holy Spirit," such as "Creator, Redeemer, and Sustainer," serves as an example of the change of meaning by alteration.[13] Second, those who with biblical warrant baptize only "in the name of Jesus" suggest a change in meaning by an altered or incomplete saying.[14] By way of the question of inconsistency, I point to the practice I have observed in many Protestant congregations of a single sprinkling, minimalizing the sacramental sign to the point of insignificance, while invoking the threefold name of the Trinity. In each case we may ask how the variation in saying and doing changes the meaning of "baptism."

The second sense in which ritual action is performative that Tambiah identifies is that of a "staged performance that uses multiple media by which the participants experience the event intensively."[15] The set of definitions which were provided at the beginning of this section and which defined ritual action as an "aesthetically marked and heightened mode of communication"[16] that is "open to view by an audience and to collective participa-

[13] This alteration in the naming of the Trinity shifts from a naming based on relationship to a naming based on function (even though in contemporary Western culture "father" is often more about a function than about a relationship) or mode of action. Although I will return to this issue in the next chapter in a discussion of the relational nature of the Christian Trinitarian God, it is important to note that for the ecumenical church, baptism in the name of "Creator, Redeemer, Sustainer" is not Christian baptism. Responses to this particular question are found in Catherine LaCugna, "The Baptismal Formula, Feminist Objections, and Trinitarian Theology," *Journal of Ecumenical Studies* 26:2 (Spring 1989) 235–250, and in Marjorie Procter-Smith, *In Her Own Rite: Constructing Feminist Liturgical Tradition* (Nashville: Abingdon Press, 1990) 107–111.

[14] While there is New Testament warrant for this language (Acts 10:44-48), its use to address the problematic perceived (and practiced) patriarchy of the language of "Father, Son, and Holy Spirit" results (a) in a loss of the specific relational character of Christian faith, (b) in a reduction of that faith to a Christological monotheism, and (c) in a separation from the ecumenical consensus on the Trinitarian baptismal faith of the church.

[15] "A Performative Approach," 119.

[16] Bauman, "Performance," 41.

tion"[17] suggests this sense of ritual action as performative. Here the emphasis is upon those characteristics of the ritual event that separate it from everyday modes of discourse. These characteristics include marking by "special codes," a "heightened use of figurative language," the marked use of repetition, and particular "features of prosody, styles of delivery, uses of gesture, [and] body motion."[18] The results of such communicative ritual events include "the submission of persons to a compelling 'constraint,'" "their transportation into a supra-normal, transcendental 'antistructural,' 'numinous' or 'altered' state of consciousness, or as a euphoric communion with one's fellow beings," initiating or leaving sacred time and entering or leaving supranormal states.[19]

This second sense of performance draws us more specifically from the ritual event as "text" with particular rules for saying and doing to the interrelationship of text and context. We are drawn to the liturgical text for baptism as it is "situated, enacted, and rendered meaningful within [a] socially defined situational context,"[20] within a context of stylized or symbolic language forms. Thus baptism occurs in a baptistry, at the river, or in the far corner of the church (each place carrying its own theological meaning), involves water as opposed to a bottle of champagne, and is presided over by particular people—priests, pastors, and deacons rather than mayors, admirals, or presidents. We are also drawn to the way in which our experience and interpretation of a particular ritual event are different from those of other similar events. It is thus that we distinguish baptism from our morning shower or a Saturday night bath, even as it retains a relationship both in meaning and practice with them. It is the stylized and language forms that were protested when we heard, "To have the people stand up there and have to go through the Apostles' Creed and all the rigmarole . . . I think is terrible" (see p. 37).

The third sense of performance that Tambiah names is that of "indexical values . . . being attached to and inferred by actors during the performance."[21] In this sense of performance, parts of a

---

[17] Ibid., 46.
[18] Briggs, *Competence in Performance*, 9.
[19] Tambiah, "A Performative Approach," 141–142.
[20] Bauman, "Performance," 46.
[21] Tambiah, "A Performative Approach," 119.

ritual enactment are "existentially or indexically related to participants in the ritual, creating, affirming, or legitimating their social
positions and powers."[22] Perhaps this is only to say that there is
more to a ritual event than persons see and hear, but it is also to
say that, as a social event, ritual plays an often unrecognized role
in the ordering of society. It is this third sense that suggests the
possibilities or problems of considering liturgy as a "strategic"
practice. It is the sense of reordering of personal life that was reported earlier (see p. 35): Baptism means "that I have died to this
world, I was buried in the water that covered my past life and that
I arose a new creature."

Bruce Kapferer's phenomenological approach to ritual study
provides one model by which to attend to the indexical values of
ritual performance. Kapferer offers an "approach to ritual which
attends to its social and political context, to the logic of ideas which
are incorporated and organized within ritual performance, and to
ritual performance as the modus operandi of these ideas and of
their transformation."[23] The performance of the ritual event as performance is therefore more than an invocation of the tradition; it is
an enactment of the living nature of that tradition and of its inherent social, political, and cosmological relationships. Kapferer argues that it "is in performance that ritual gains its efficacy, and . . .
reveals itself as essentially the 'hermeneutic' of culture—a method
whereby culture analyzes itself."[24] Ritual performance, then, is an
event of social self-reflexivity, offering both cultural expression and
cultural interpretation. Kapferer further argues that in ritual
events, seen as artistic forms, "art is turned to the practical purpose
of acting upon the problems which affect the lives of human beings
in a mundane world." Art no longer exists for itself, but for its use-
fulness in and to the world. The primary concern is no longer aesthetic but pragmatic. Further, "individual experience and the
meaningful interpretation of it is a possibility of the way the context of action and experience is moulded and mediated in artistic
form,"[25] that is, the "art" of ritual acts both to shape and to mediate

[22] Ibid., 154.
[23] *A Celebration of Demons: Exorcism and the Aesthetics of Healing in Sri Lanka*
(Providence, R.I.: Berg; Washington: Smithsonian Institution Press, 1991) 2.
[24] Ibid., 244.
[25] Ibid., 245.

social life. In Kapferer's work we see a shift from a primary focus on text and context to the additional concern for the existential relationships of position and power, as well as to text and context situated, programmed, and coordinated within a network of social relationships.

Returning to the question of baptism, Kapferer's focus calls us to attend to questions such as: Who baptizes and why? Who is authorized or qualified to baptize? Who is qualified to be baptized? What is the relationship of the community of faith and the baptized to the ritual event? Is the community even present? Within this possibility for social reflexivity we also see an opening for a ritual event to speak critically both of and to the tradition as well as to those in various relationships of position and power. This opening provides part of the impetus for my proposal to consider ritual events as practices.

Kapferer makes two sets of statements that I believe provide links between theorists dealing with ritual as performance and those who focus on ritual as practice. He argues that "ritual is a social practice where ideas are produced in a determinant and dominant relation to action, and it is a practice where action is continually structured to the idea."[26] He encourages us to move from an understanding of performance as the enactment of a text, which reduces all cultural action to some concept of "text,"[27] toward " performance as a structure in its own right, a structure of practice" whereby "a 'text' takes its form and shape through performance and is inseparable from it."[28] In this first set of statements, Kapferer draws our attention to the circular relationship between idea/text and action, between theory and practice. He encourages an understanding of practice in which ideas seem to take precedence over or are determinative for action. He also pushes us to see not only the integral relationship between action and text but also the possibility of action as determinative or conditioning for the interpretation of the text. (I will return to this concept later.) Kapferer also reminds us that because the text can no longer be "objectified" as

[26] Ibid., 3.

[27] Such as Paul Ricoeur proposes in his essay "The Model of the Text: Meaningful Action Considered as a Text," *Social Research* 38 (Autumn 1971) 529–562.

[28] *Celebration of Demons*, 9.

such and because there is no position in relationship to that text that permits an observer to be "unbiased," we can no longer base ritual meaning on some textual object abstracted by an unbiased observer. "A 'text' abstracted from performance creates an object devoid of key dimensions of its structure, a structure through which it achieves its meaning for cultural members."[29]

Kapferer offers a second statement that I believe pushes us even further toward the consideration of ritual event as practice. Although an extended quote, it provides both a summary of my discussion of performance to this point and further markers for the discussion of practice that will follow.

"Ritual performance is a structure of practice emergent in a context which itself is ordered through the process of performance. It is in the structure of practices which comprise a ritual performance that meaning and the world of its experience is constituted. The meaning of [the ritual event] is progressively disclosed in its performance, and it is the engagement of participants in the progress of this disclosure which is central to an understanding of how a ritual communicates its meaning and also to an understanding of how it may achieve its transformational purpose as this is realized by the participants. What ritual communicates, and the transformations it may effect as these are revealed to participants, occurs on at least two planes: that of experience, the immediately felt individual subjective encountering of a context of meaning and action, and that of the conscious reflective grasping of this experience in terms of idea constructs and typifications of the culturally objectified world."[30]

The first part of this statement draws our attention to a notion of performance itself as a structure of situated or contextualized practices, a structure that arises out of the performance itself. In fact, we begin to see a way in which we may have a hierarchy of practices, from practice itself, to performance as a structuring or ordering of practices, and finally to ritual process as a "meta-structure" of practice. We also begin to see how practice itself becomes constitutive for performance and process: practices, as strategies of action, give rise to performance from the bottom up, as it were.

[29] Ibid.
[30] Ibid., 248.

In the second part of this statement, we see that ritual communicates at two levels. First, ritual communicates at the level of what Aidan Kavanagh and others following him call "primary theology"—the immediately felt experience of a practice as it is performed. This experience is, in many ways, pre-reflective; the feeling is somehow present, but we have not stopped to analyze it, to say "this makes me feel this way." Second, ritual communicates at the level of what Kavanagh calls "secondary theology," where those involved are able to distance themselves from the experience for the sake of conscious reflection on the practice.[31] Not only do I know how I am feeling, but I also have some understanding of why I feel this way. "This did *this* to me."

Kapferer also provides some indication of what I believe to be a multi-layered model for understanding the function of ritual practice, a model that bears similarity to and incorporates the three modes of performance offered by Tambiah. Although I will develop this model below, let me suggest at this point the three modes of ritual practice that my reading of Kapferer suggests: (1) Ritual performance is a communicative event that discloses, or perhaps manifests, a particular complex of meanings and relationships. Ritual makes something—some meaning, some form of relationship—present to us. (2) Ritual performance is experienced in the present and as such has a "pre-reflective" meaning. We do not know what or why we experience something; we are "in" the experience. (3) Ritual performance offers the possibility for the transformation or construction of meanings, relationships, and ways of being. Because ritual performance is an experience of the present, even as it is connected to a history and future, it draws us into its own meaning now and, in doing so, requires that we set aside our conscious connections to that past and future.

To this point I have argued that we need to move beyond ritual structure and process to performance and to questions of ritual

---

[31] *On Liturgical Theology* (New York: Pueblo Publishing Co., 1984) 77–83. John Macmurray makes a similar argument for a distinction between primary and secondary knowledge. He argues that "primary knowledge is the knowledge that arises in action, apart from any theoretical intention. It is this knowledge to which we sometimes refer when we use . . . the term 'experience.'" John Macmurray, *The Self as Agent* (London: Faber and Faber, 1957) 101.

practice. It is not my intent, however, to negate or neglect Victor Turner's contribution to this discussion. In fact, a more thorough review of Kapferer's work than provided here would reveal his debt to Turner as well as the extent to which his phenomenological approach to ritual performance builds on what Turner could only point toward. It would also reveal that Turner's later work on the anthropology of performance, much of it published posthumously, was not far from these themes.

What possibilities did Turner see within a post-structuralist perspective that now provide additional links with the turn to practice? First, Turner was aware of the need to move away from a perspective that divided "the world into observing subject and alien material objects."[32] Neither anthropologists nor liturgical theologians can continue to place themselves outside the ritual events of which they are in fact participants as well as observers. Second, he recognized that ritual performances revealed the "major classifications, categories, and contradictions of cultural processes."[33] To the extent that he would include issues of position and power within these classifications, he is in line both with Tambiah's notion of performance as indexical and Kapferer's phenomenological approach. Third, Turner acknowledged that the focus of postmodern theory on the "flaws, hesitations, personal factors, incomplete, elliptical, context-dependent, situational components of performance" provided "clues to the very nature of human process itself." This focus enables one to perceive that genuine novelty and creativeness were "able to emerge from the freedom of the performance situation."[34] Attention by postmodern theorists to the Austinian "performative" and to Austin and Searle's attempts to account for "performance failure" may have anticipated, in part, this change of focus. It may also have been anticipated by the move away from text-based considerations of ritual performance, a move we now take.

RITUAL AS PRACTICE
If the work of Kapferer and Turner prepares the way for a transition from performance to practice, then the recent work of

---

[32] *Anthropology of Performance*, 73.
[33] Ibid., 75.
[34] Ibid., 77.

Catherine Bell provides the theoretical framework for such a shift. Her work offers a critique of the performance approach and a proposal for understanding ritual event as "practice." While I suggested a provisional definition of practice earlier in this chapter, a more substantive definition will become evident in the following review of Bell's work.

Bell summarizes and critiques the various performance models discussed above.[35] She moves to the proposition that those studying ritual events focus instead on "'ritualization' as a strategic way of acting," such that "acting ritually emerges as a particular cultural strategy of differentiation linked to particular social effects and rooted in a distinctive interplay of a socialized body and the environment it structures."[36] In her attention to the "distinctive interplay of a socialized body," Bell seems to be pushing at the second sense of performance as identified by Tambiah. Even so, her focus builds more clearly on Tambiah's third, indexical sense. Thus she writes that "ritualization is a strategy for the construction of a limited and limiting power relationship."[37]

Bell's main difficulty with the performance approach to ritual study is that such an approach provides a "theoretical framework

[35] In her comprehensive overview of ritual in all of its dimensions, *Ritual: Perspectives and Dimensions* (New York: Oxford University Press, 1997), Bell provides a clear and concise review of each of these models, noting their relationship to one another.

[36] *Ritual Theory, Ritual Practice* (New York: Oxford University Press, 1992), 7. I note here the parallels between Bell's attention to the question of ritualization and Erik Erikson's psychological exploration of the ontogeny of ritualization. Bell argues that ritualization is "a particular cultural strategy of differentiation linked to particular social effects and rooted in a distinctive interplay of a socialized body and the environment it structures" (8). Erikson argues that this distinctive interplay "should have adaptive value for the respective egos of both participants." [Erik Erikson, "Ontogeny of Ritualization," in Rudolph Loewenstein, Lottie Newman, Max Schur, and Albert Solnit, eds., *Psychoanalysis—A General Psychology* (New York: International Universities Press, Inc., 1966) 602.] Bell uses "ritualization" to "draw attention to the way in which certain social actions strategically distinguish themselves in relation to other actions" (*Ritual Theory*, 74). Erikson treats ritualization as "a special form of everyday behavior" (Erikson, "Ontogeny," 603). Bell works toward a social-political construction, Erikson toward a social-psychological construction.

[37] *Ritual Theory*, 8.

in which activity is seen as dramatizing or enacting prior conceptual entities in order to reaffirm or reexperience them."[38] As I read this statement, her concerns echo those of Kapferer: Our attention to ritual performance/practice tends to focus on the means by which ritual action conforms to or is structured by particular ideas, whether those ideas are located within the culture being observed or in the observing theorist. The critique that Kapferer and Bell offer recapitulates some of the recent conversation about "practice" and its relationship to theory: Does theory drive practice, does practice drive theory, or are they co-determinative? Here it may be helpful to recall the circular relationship described by Kapferer above: Ritual performance both structures and interprets "text" even as the "text" structures the performance. Bell, I believe, is pushing theoretically at the priority of ritual practice for the development of theory.

Bell provides three additional criticisms of the performance approach. First, when seen as a performance, ritual events tend to be seen as symbolic acts "specifically meant to have an impact on an audience" that entreats "their interpretative appropriation."[39] One way to read this statement is to say that one measure of ritual performance is its emotive impact on the audience, such as we see among those concerned for the (emotional) "quality" of a "worship experience." While this is a helpful critique, it also seems to be based on a limited reading of those working with the performance model, and particularly ignores the work of Kapferer. Second, "a model of ritual activity provides the criteria for what is or is not ritual."[40] That is, performance becomes a primary criterion for determining the nature of ritual practice. We could level this critique, as well, against those who work with models of "practice," including Bell and this writer. Finally, Bell argues that "insofar as performance is broadly used for a vast spectrum of activities, there is no basis to differentiate among ways of performing."[41] It is finally in this third critique that I find the most constructive potential, especially as we move with and from Kapferer's work as cited above.

[38] Ibid., 38.
[39] Ibid., 42.
[40] Ibid., 42.
[41] Ibid., 42.

Where Kapferer could speak of ritual performance as a structure of practices "ordered through the process of performance,"[42] Bell focuses on the ways in which those practices are particular, strategic ways of acting. It is not clear to me if we are, in fact, simply comparing different levels of interpretation, as might be the case if the hierarchical relationship between process, performance, and practice suggested above were true. Even if this is the case, Bell's concern for practice pushes us to a new level for the interpretation of ritual events.

In turning to practice, Bell suggests that ritual practice has four features. First, ritual practice is *situational:* "much of what is important to it cannot be grasped outside the specific context in which it occurs."[43] Like a now misunderstood joke, you had to have been there to understand. With baptism, its Christian meaning is dependent on its situatedness in the church or Christian community. Within the Christian community, its meaning is dependent on who is baptized— infant or adult—as well as the particular context and practices of that community. Outside the Christian community, it shares some meanings—cleansing, bathing, purification—but means something else.

Second, ritual practice is *strategic:* "a ceaseless play of situationally effective schemes, tactics, and strategies."[44] Here the question of effectiveness could easily return us to an Austinian performative analysis. At this level it is relatively easy to speak of baptism as a strategic practice for the initiation of persons into the Christian community: it is in the context of the Christian community that baptism effects initiation.

But Bell also argues, third, that ritual practice is *embedded in a misrecognition* of what it is in fact doing, that is, a "practice does not see itself do what it actually does"; it "sees what it intends to accomplish, but it does not see the strategies it uses to produce what it actually does accomplish."[45] Often, she writes, we are "apt to misrecognize the relationship between [a practice's] means and its ends in ways that promote its efficacy."[46]

[42] *Celebration of Demons,* 248.
[43] *Ritual Theory,* 81.
[44] Ibid., 82.
[45] Ibid., 87.
[46] *Ritual: Perspectives,* 81.

A parent may tell a child to "go play," and the child in response to the parent's query "What have you been doing?" may answer "Playing!" In this case both parent and child understand what "playing" and "go play" mean, but the child cannot speak about what playing involves while actually involved in the act of play. Misrecognition at this level may seem inconsequential. It becomes consequential when we attend to the ways by which misrecognition results in our blindness to what Bell calls the "schemes of privileged opposition, hierarchization, and circular deferment"[47] that produce or reproduce structures of power or disempowerment among those who participate in such practices.

Finally, given these characteristics, especially that of misrecognition, Bell argues that ritual practice is "able to *reproduce or reconfigure a vision of the order of power in the world.*"[48] It is at this point that Bell appears most in conflict with Kapferer. Where Kapferer's concern is with ritual performance as a disclosive and communicative event, Bell insists that ritualization as practice "is a particularly 'mute' form of activity . . . designed to do what it does without bringing what it is doing across the threshold of discourse or systematic thinking."[49] Ritualization, as practice, seems to communicate "without saying." (Perhaps this point echoes the commonplace claim that "actions speak louder than words.") These last two features of ritual practice raise the question of baptism's critical and transformative potential. They ask us to consider what we are doing beyond or in addition to initiation when we baptize. They ask us to consider the nature of the social, linguistic, ideological, and theological community into which we baptize.

Given these definitions and critiques, and perhaps more a blurring than clarification of the distinctions between performance and practice, I want to return to the model of ritual practice I anticipated in my discussion of Kapferer. Bell's further definition of ritual practice will help develop and clarify an understanding of ritual practice as disclosive of meaning, although we often misrecognize that meaning, experienced in the present, and providing the possibility for the transformation and the (re)construction of mean-

[47] *Ritual Theory*, 110.
[48] Ibid., 81. My emphasis.
[49] Ibid., 93.

ings and relationships. It is important to note that ritual practice often does each of these three things simultaneously. Our tendency in interpreting ritual practice has been to reduce meaning to one form exclusive of the other. I am arguing that the fullness of interpretation, the question of meaning, requires that we attend to all three forms. Nevertheless, I suggest in what follows that each form of ritual practice provides a particular type of strategic action and carries within it a primary correlative orientation to either past, present, or future. I name these forms manifestation, presentation, and emergence.

RITUAL PRACTICE AS MANIFESTATION
In this first form of ritual practice, the primary focus of the practice and of its interpretation is on the relationship of the ritual's participants to some paradigmatic event of the past of which the ritual event is now its re-presentation. Recalling Briggs's comment that in performance one assumes responsibility for "invoking the tradition,"[50] we see at least one line of continuity between this understanding of practice and the above descriptions of ritual as performance. At the same time, this very continuity opens this form to the critique expressed by Bell's concern that performance only enacts "prior conceptual entities."[51] Ritual practice conceived as manifestation is primarily, although not solely, concerned to sustain a relationship with the past. David Tracy's understanding of the "classic," explored in Chapter 2, provides the clearest theological parallel to this model. While Tracy argues for the classic's continuing ability to generate meaning, thus offering a definition that parallels our initial definition of practice, the classic's primary orientation is toward the past. It is to ask, "How do we make this past event, an event that continues to exercise some claim on us, meaningful today?" Within this form of ritual practice the primary concern is that the ritual performance function as a strategic practice for the disclosure of self, other, or ideology in continuity with a particular past.

Kevin Irwin's liturgical theological work *Context as Text* provides a second theological example of this form. Irwin attempts to shift

[50] *Competence in Performance*, 8.
[51] *Ritual Theory*, 38.

the focus of liturgical theology "from a philological-theological study of liturgical texts . . . to discussing these sources in light of their celebration, both past (to the extent possible) and present."[52] He turns to the liturgical context, which he understands as comprising "the three aspects of historical evolution, reformed rites and contemporary critical function,"[53] as a text that manifests meaning and is to be interpreted by the liturgical theologian. Irwin therefore understands liturgy to be "a privileged, though provisional encounter with saving events of the past experienced anew through the liturgy."[54] "By the very 'doing' of liturgy, the Church actualizes itself as the privileged locus where Christ's paschal mystery is operative for humanity here and now. Through liturgy, the Church enacts a paradigm against which other forms of devotion ought to be evaluated."[55]

Within this form of ritual practice, the liturgy becomes the means by which to mediate and manifest the "classic" event of Jesus Christ to the Christian community. This is not to say, as some have recently said, that it is time to shed our dependence on the tradition or on the past. It reminds us that, much as some might desire it, we cannot exist in a present that stands autonomously from the past. Our existence depends on some form of relationship to the past; the question is the nature or form of that relationship. Both Tracy and Irwin remind us that "we are not created *ex nihilo* each time we celebrate the liturgy. Rather our lives are once again set in proper order; we are always being refashioned as the baptized who are becoming more fully the holy ones of God."[56] As Bell also suggests, if "the exact repetition of an age-old ritual precedent is a strategic act with which to define the present, then no ritual style is autonomous."[57]

Victor Turner provides one other way to read this form of practice, especially in light of its continuities with the discussion of ritual performance. Turner writes:

---

[52] *Context and Text: Method in Liturgical Theology* (Collegeville, Minn.: The Liturgical Press, 1994) 55.

[53] Ibid.

[54] Ibid., 99.

[55] Ibid., 321.

[56] Ibid., 112.

[57] *Ritual Theory*, 101.

"In the sense that man [sic] is a self-performing animal—his performances are, in a way, reflexive, in performing he reveals himself to himself. This can be in two ways: the actor may come to know himself better through acting or enactment; or one set of human beings may come to know themselves better through observing and/or participating in performances generated and presented by another set of human beings."[58]

While Turner seems primarily to be speaking about the presentation of the self "outside" everyday life, he seems to assume that the self that comes to be known through ritual performance somehow pre-exists that performance, awaiting its manifestation or discovery through that performance. He seems to ignore the situatedness of those selves and the possibility that the self is not only manifested but constructed in the course of the ritual event. We are "self-performing" as Turner suggests, but, as we will see below when we consider a second form of ritual practice, that self-performance is not a reflexive act.

As a form of ritual practice, a focus on manifestation reminds us of our vital connection to personal, social, and cultural histories. Our presents and our futures are not possible without an accounting for such pasts. But, as a model of ritual practice, it is finally not enough. The fullness of our interpretation of the ritual event must account for its ability to manifest those saving events of the past in the present. Also, a strict orientation to the past and the reading of that paradigmatic past as the only critical principle by which to read the event ultimately fails to offer the possibility of a conditioned yet undetermined transformation suggested by the promise that all things will be made new. As Christians, we are baptized into the death and resurrection of Christ Jesus. While that death remains paradigmatic for our lives, we also await a resurrection like the resurrection of Christ but which is not Christ's. Through baptism, as a practice of manifestation, we enact continuity with the past. The temptation is to leave it at that—an event accomplished rather than a life begun. Is there a way to speak of baptism as a practice of the present?

---

[58] *Anthropology of Performance*, 81.

RITUAL PRACTICE AS PRESENTATION[59]

A statement by Catherine Vincie suggests a second form of ritual practice. Vincie writes, "Liturgy is not to be reduced to instrumental action whose sole aim is the production of justice in Christian life. Christian liturgy has a value in and of itself, it is praxis."[60] She is suggesting that liturgy is characterized as having some internal good that, in some way, stands on its own and can be internally defined. Although I have limited our discussion to the particular event of baptism, the statement still applies. Baptism has, in some way, a value in and of itself. Thus the primary focus of this model is on what ritual event *does* in the present.

Hans-Georg Gadamer, in his discussion of play within his broader discussion of hermeneutics, and Alisdair MacIntyre, with his notion of practice as defined by "internal goods," are of particular help in interpreting the present or presentational activity of a ritual event. While we may argue that Gadamer continues the notion of performance as manifestation, it is not a manifestation of the past but of the present: ". . . every performance is an event, but not one in any way separate from the work—the work itself is what 'takes place' in the event of performance."[61] The hermeneutical tasks of understanding, interpretation, and application are all interwoven; meaning is possible only in the context of the event itself. As Gadamer writes, ". . . understanding must be conceived as a part of the event in which meaning occurs"[62] and ". . . application co-determines [understanding] as a whole from the beginning."[63]

This understanding of practice is most fully realized in Gadamer's discussion of play, an event that fulfills its end only

---

[59] There is some similarity between my use of "presentation" and the "presentational" discourse identified by Susanne Langer. She differentiates between the "discursive" as represented in the linear conception of a text and which is therefore diachronic in its presentation, and the "presentational" as represented in symbol or image and capable of the synchronous presentation of multiple meanings. See Langer's *Philosophy in a New Key* (New York: Mentor Books, 1942) 78–79.

[60] "The Cry for Justice and the Eucharist," *Worship* 68:3 (May 1994) 197.

[61] *Truth and Method*, 2nd ed., trans. Joel Weinsheimer and Donald G. Marshall (New York: Continuum, 1993) 147.

[62] Ibid., 164.

[63] Ibid., 324.

while it is being done. As I indicated earlier, play requires a "self-forgetfulness"; it "fulfills its purpose only if the player loses [oneself] in play."[64] Play reaches presentation through the players; it has no goal but renews itself in constant repetition;[65] "all playing is being-played."[66]

In this sense ritual practice, while still realized in or as performance or, more appropriately, as a "doing," is not about the past but about the present. Ritual practice is the "being-played" as the past is encountered in the context of the present. It is not the manifestation of the past as past, but of the past as that which conditions a present that is now being "played." As Kapferer indicated, it is only the "immediately felt individual subjective encountering of a context of meaning and action" that permits us to find meaning in a ritual event as practice.[67] Practice defined as "presentation" as well as a point of encounter or engagement between past and present not only determines meaning but could be said to "be" meaning. This may account for why those responsible for the leadership of liturgy find it so difficult to fully participate as worshipers rather than as observers.

MacIntyre builds on this notion of practice as play by way of a set of definitions of practice, each revolving around his notion of practice as defined by "internal goods." He defines practice as

"any coherent and complex form of socially established cooperative human activity through which goods internal to that form of activity are realized in the course of trying to achieve those standards of excellence which are appropriate to, and partially definitive of, that form of activity, with the result that human powers to achieve human excellence and human conceptions of the ends and goods involved, are systematically extended." [68]

This definition has generated much fruitful discussion about the good of practice. For the purposes of this discussion, let me only highlight that the "goods" internal to a game are realized only by

[64] Ibid., 102.

[65] Ibid., 103.

[66] Ibid., 106.

[67] *Celebration of Demons*, 248.

[68] Alisdair MacIntyre, *After Virtue* (Notre Dame: University of Notre Dame Press, 1984) 187.

playing. When asked what an event "means," we could only repeat the event; when asked what a particular piece of music means, we can only play the music. When asked what baptism means, while we may have many words of explanation, in the end we can only baptize. (Of course, the warrants against rebaptism require new subjects of baptism, unlike needing a new piano to perform a piece of music.)

There is a tension here between the fixed and open nature of meaning in such presentations. The assumption tends to be that meaning somehow remains constant through each performance for both performer and audience. Yet MacIntyre reminds us that "practices never have a goal or goals fixed for all time . . . the goals themselves are transmuted by the history of the activity."[69] Even Turner can assent to such a statement: "Every social drama alters, in however minuscule a fashion, the structure (by which term I do not mean a permanent ordering of social relations but merely a temporary mutual accommodation of interests) of the relevant social field."[70] The meaning of what we play, even as it maintains some continuity with its "history of meaning," changes each time it is played. Christian liturgy as practiced by a particular community has a sense of sameness; week in and week out particular patterns are repeated, stories told, hymns sung. But the fact that it is another week, that it is yet another gathering of this community, that the Scriptures or hymns are different, that we have lived yet another week changes the meaning in the midst of the very sameness. We see here the continuity with Bell's definition of practice as situational, strategic, and especially as embedded in a misrecognition of what it is doing. That is, to say that we are playing requires that we stop playing and think about playing. The move from the "doing" to reflection on the "doing" changes its meaning. The move from the primary theology enacted in the liturgy to critical or systematic reflection on the liturgy changes its meaning.

Several cautions are in order in regard to this form of ritual practice. By turning to a consideration of the "internal goods" of a practice, it is very easy to approach a practice as if it could stand apart from its social, political, and cosmological contexts. Arguing

[69] Ibid., 193.
[70] *Anthropology of Performance*, 92.

that a practice such as baptism is valuable in and of itself tempts us toward both the objectification and the decontextualization of the practice. These are two temptations that we must avoid.[71] A third is the temptation to believe that everything that can be said is or will be said within the ritual event. On one level, this would lead to the (im)possibility of the signified being reduced to the sign. On another level, this leads to a denial or rejection of that which is either unknown and therefore remains unsaid or that which is unknowable and therefore unsayable, that is, the divine mystery.

To return to the example of meaning in Christian baptism, we could say, on the one hand, that baptism means what it accomplishes—initiation, membership, regeneration. But this, as Vincie reminds us, is to reduce it to matter of instrumental cause and effect. On the other hand, by attending to its nature as a practice of presentation we find that its meaning is not only in what it accomplishes in the present nor only in its relationship to the past, but also in the repeated "doings" that are part of the event itself—renouncing, affirming, confessing, sprinkling/pouring/immersing, welcoming, and so on. If, by our focus on the "doing" of meaning, we begin to understand the meaning of ritual practice as changing within each "doing," then we also begin to see a way to understand the transforming nature of a ritual practice and its potential influence on the future of persons and communities. This orientation toward the future I turn to next under the concept of "emergence."

RITUAL PRACTICE AS EMERGENCE
Within his discussion of meaning and understanding, Gadamer further identifies a relationship between what he called a "situated"

---

[71] Having said this, however, I note Bruce Marshall's argument that it is only in consideration of the distinctive internal goods of the eucharistic practice of the church that post-Constantinian Christians find any compelling reason to bother with the church:

The church's eucharistic worship . . . suggests that internal to Christian communal practice is not just any good but the chief good of human life: becoming a sharer in the divine nature. The suggestion that we should bother with the church because the Eucharist happens there is an utterly noninstrumental answer to the pressing post-Constantinian question—and for that reason one effectively suited to our times.

[Bruce D. Marshall, "Why Bother with the Church?" *The Christian Century* 113 (January 24, 1996) 76.]

knowledge and "open indeterminacy" that results in what he calls a "historically effected consciousness."[72] These terms offer some of the conceptual language by which we can speak in this third form about the future orientation of ritual practice. Here our concern can turn from the "mere" reproduction of power relationships, ideologies, or gender constructs to a focus on the means by which ritual practices may reconfigure or transform those relationships. Liturgy, in the end, cannot be "reduced to" instrumental action. Seeing liturgy as an emergent ritual practice enables us to more fully see liturgy as a constitutive and constructive act by which a community both produces its future and reconstructs its past. The liturgy may appear to stand on its own as an event of the present, but it is an act that stands in an active, constructive relationship to its past and our past; to the present, which is rewriting that past; and to the emerging future being "written" or performed in the liturgy itself.

We have already seen in Kapferer some indication of the concept of emergence, primarily in reference to the structure of a practice emergent in a context that is itself ordered through the process of a performance.[73] Briggs speaks of a concept of emergence along similar lines, as "the way that the structure and content of performances are shaped by the specifics of the social interaction in which they occur."[74] Both Kapferer and Briggs attend to the possibilities for ritual structures to emerge from the performance of the ritual event. I am arguing here that meaning as well as structure emerges within the ritual practice.

The work of the philosophical psychologist George Herbert Mead provides some of the clearest statements about emergence and its relationship to past, present, and future. Where Gadamer speaks of the relationship of the past and present in terms of the "historically effected consciousness," Mead speaks to the relationship of present and future under the category of "passage," where

[72] *Truth and Method*, 340. The relationship between "situated knowledge" and "open indeterminacy" as a framework for "emergence" seems to echo Erikson's conclusion that "any true ritualization is ontologically grounded and yet pervaded with the spontaneity of surprise," an "unexpected renewal of a recognizable order in potential chaos." Erikson, "Ontogeny," 621.

[73] *Celebration of Demons*, 248.

[74] *Competence in Performance*, 11.

"what is taking place conditions that which is arising."[75] While Mead at times interchanges the words "conditioning" and "determinative," he is usually careful to preserve a distinction between the two, the former offering the possibility of an open future, the latter offering only closure. He is therefore able to say that while the conditioning past or present is necessary (and in fact, the conditioning past is always "there"), it does not determine the full reality of that which is emerging.[76]

As if to caution against a closed determinism, Mead writes, "The past is there conditioning the present and its passage into the future, but in the organization of tendencies embodied in one individual there may be an emergent which gives to these tendencies a structure which belongs only to the situation of that individual."[77] That is, while we may read a particular ritual practice in light of what it reveals about past and present, its "true" meaning emerges from the practice itself. This emergence is dependent upon history and tradition, yet it is relative to the social status, condition, and context of those who now engage in the practice. Not only does the future open in an undetermined way, but even the past takes on a "hypothetical" character. Our readings of the past become valid only "in so far as they present a history of becoming in nature leading up to that which is becoming today, in so far as they bring out what fits into the pattern that is emerging from the roaring loom of time."[78] There are at least two implications of such a reading. First, in part from our attempts to account narratively for our presents, the emergent character of the present and future results in the rewriting or reconstruction of our pasts. Second, the character of emergence as related to the future invites an open reading of the present (as a future past). That is, the future may reveal that which could not be said or which was unsayable in a particular present. Is this not the hope that Christians live by?

A reading of Christian baptism as an emergent practice calls our attention to the pragmatic concern for the character of life that

[75] *Philosophy of the Present*, ed. Arthur E. Murphy (Chicago: University of Chicago Press, 1932) 21.

[76] Ibid.

[77] Ibid., 17–18.

[78] Ibid., 21.

arises out of the practice. Mead encourages our attention to this concern and invites us to move from instrumental action, which speaks of a determinative relationship of cause and effect, toward a more open teleology in which the past conditions but does not determine future action. Within this final form of ritual practice, we might also begin to speak eschatologically—as an anticipated but undefined end toward which our practice, baptism, is oriented. Here our orientation in baptism shifts from a primary focus on reproducing one paradigmatic life or on the enactment of individual new birth or spiritual regeneration to a primary focus on the life that is yet to be, even as that life offers the possibility for reconstructing our histories.[79]

I have attempted to trace the theoretical development from ritual process to a concern for performance and practice. I have also attempted to develop an argument for an understanding of practice that, while inclusive of manifestation and presentation, leads toward emergence and requires the interaction of all three forms of interpretation. Missing, however, is the concern Bell claims in her work for issues of ideology and power and, more generally, for ethical practice. In my discussion of baptism, I have left these issues largely implicit and need now to more explicitly name them.

The emergent reading of sacramental practice I have proposed here enables a move from the assumed relationship *lex orandi, lex credendi* to a constitutive relationship with what Don Saliers calls the *lex agendi* (the law of action) and Kevin Irwin calls the *lex vivendi* (the law of living). While we may distinguish the laws of practice/action from the laws of living/ethics, I believe that in a reading of sacrament as "emergent practice" there can finally be no distinction. Sacramental action, while not reducible to ethics, is itself an ethical practice, a situated, strategic event "embedded in a misrecognition of what it is doing" and both/either reproducing or reconfiguring the order of power in the world. Our images, practices, and understandings of Christian baptism remain conditioned by tradition, exercising claims to power and truth through mani-

[79] Both the Wesleyan understanding of sanctification and the transformative processes and practices of the (Roman Catholic) Rite of Christian Initiation of Adults (RCIA) suggest such an emergent character. I return to Wesley and sanctification in Chapter 7.

festation and presentation. But as a particular emergent ritual practice, baptism is oriented toward a future that remains open before us. For Christians it is an expression not only of "having been saved" but also of "being saved." As such, it offers the potential for the transformation of its claims to power and truth. It does so even as the nature of the resurrection, the shape of the resurrection body, and the coming of the eschaton remains imaged, imagined and narrated, but finally undetermined before us.

To this point, I have spoken about baptism as a particular practice of manifestation, presentation, and emergence. What, then, does it mean to speak more broadly about liturgical catechesis as a strategic liturgical and sacramental ecclesial practice? In terms of Bell's definition of ritual practice, liturgical catechesis is, first, situational. It is a catechesis, a process of formation that shapes faith, character, and consciousness, that puts faith into our bodies and bone marrow, occurring in the context of the liturgical practices of a particular community of faith and with particular persons. It is, second, strategic in the sense that it has particular ends it seeks: a way of being in the world, of knowing who and whose we are.[80] A practice/event is a unit of meaning combining persons and circumstances, a social uniting of past and present, and a non-neutral form of learning.

This may remind us of Rebecca Chopp's definition of practice: practices are "socially shared forms of behavior that mediate between what are often called subjective and objective dimensions. A practice is a pattern of meaning and action that is both culturally constructed and individually instantiated."[81] Bell puts it this way: What ritualization does is actually quite simple: it temporally structures a space-time environment through a series of physical movements . . . thereby producing an arena which, by its molding of the actors, both validates and extends the schemes they are

---

[80] Bell's definition of ritual practice suggests that my inclusion of "strategic" in my definition of liturgical catechesis as (strategic ecclesial) practice is redundant. I include it at this point as my own strategic emphasis.

[81] *Saving Work*, 15. See note 3 above. And, as Bell writes in her description of practice theory in the study of ritual, "rather than ritual as the vehicle for the *expression* of authority, practice theorists tend to explore how ritual is a vehicle for the *construction* of relationships of authority and submission. Bell, *Ritual Theory*, 82.

internalizing.[82] Combining these definitions, I argue that, as ritual practice, liturgical catechesis is a social uniting of past, present, and future and a "pattern of meaning and action" that is culturally constructed and *communally* instantiated. It is on these terms that we speak of liturgical catechesis as an *ecclesial* practice.

Regardless of how we define "worship" and its purposes, its ongoing practice reproduces various social orders and transforms others. In some cases it continues to reproduce a pattern of patriarchy, hierarchical power structures, and disempowerment. However this is true, it is also reconfiguring the worldview of those engaged in its practice: it gathers in one place rich and poor, male and female, the powerful and the disenfranchised. For good or ill, for the sake of the world or the sake of churchly institutions, it puts into play a way of being in the world and a form of knowledge about institution, self, and world. Unless sustained by force, the worldview reproduced in practice is conditioned rather than determined. The seeds of transformation wait to blossom.

At the same time as it is situational and strategic, liturgical catechesis is a practice of misrecognition. In one sense, we might argue that in the liturgy we misrecognize who the actors of the liturgy are and what the liturgy does. As difficult as it is for many liturgical communities to understand that it is the community as a whole that is the actor, rather than the preacher or presider, choir, music director, and other "professionals," this represents only one level of misunderstanding. If the liturgy intends the "glorification of God and the sanctification of humanity," then we must acknowledge that this liturgical "transaction" involves God as subject and actor.

It is this latter misrecognition that sets up the final characteristic of ritual practice, the reproduction or reconfiguring of a vision of the order of power in the world. Where we assume that the liturgy is only a human practice, we obscure the transforming work of God in and for the world, the *"praxis* of God." It then becomes a practice of what we have seen and known (reproduction) rather than a practice of what we do not yet see and what we cannot yet imagine on our own (reconfiguring). I explore how liturgical catechesis is a practice of God and the gathered community in the next two chapters.

[82] Ibid., 109–110.

What does it mean to speak about liturgical catechesis in terms of my threefold model of ritual practice? It is, first, following Gadamer, a "work" that takes place only in the doing, in its performance.[83] Once we move to critical reflection on that action, the meaning changes. Liturgical catechesis is a practice of knowing (and unknowing) possible only in the context of liturgical sacramental action. In this sense, what it manifests and reveals is in a constant state of reconfiguration and reinterpretation. But as a knowing/unknowing dependent on performance, liturgical catechesis is presentational rather than discursive. As Connerton observed, this presentational practice constructs an argument for a way of being and of knowing ourselves in the world that is written in and on our bodies as well as our minds.

Second, liturgical catechesis not only enables but also "practices" an ongoing connection between the past, present, and future. As such, it claims the conditioning but non-determinative power of personal, social, and cultural histories for our present and future. It proclaims the story and vision of the Christian community, of our history with God and God with us. This story conditions our reading of our histories and our expectations for the future. Even so, as an act of presentation, liturgical catechesis is an act of the present in which meaning is not "understood" but "performed." What we come to know liturgically remains largely unknown outside our performance of the liturgy. A response at the presentational level to the question of what we have come to know or understand in the liturgy requires that we do the liturgy, knowing full well that in this doing our knowing will not be the same.

That our knowing will not be the same enables us to say that liturgical catechesis is, third, an emergent practice. Liturgical catechesis is a practice of persons and communities actively producing a future and reconstructing or rewriting the past. As an emergent knowing, liturgical catechesis produces a "reading" of self and community in the present that is undetermined, looking to and from the future to the present. Even as our presentational knowing depends upon liturgical performance, that performance continuously orders and reorders our emergent knowing. Here liturgical

[83] I note here that in following this definition we find a way to recover the root sense of liturgy as "public work."

catechesis claims what writers about liturgy and catechesis do not see: its inherently self-critical and self-transformative potential. The repeated standing before God in vulnerability and humility, the repeated naming of oneself as God's beloved, summons person and community to ongoing conversion. Liturgical catechesis asks, "If we have prayed this way and if we believe this way, should we not act this way?"

The tensions between manifestation, presentation, and emergence, and the conditions of liturgical catechesis as strategic ecclesial practice, return us to our starting point with the tensions between the expressive, constitutive, and normative characteristics of liturgical practice. As we saw in Kapferer's work, ritual performance does result in the expression of the beliefs and structures of a community. Yet we also saw that this performance was simultaneously a means by which a community constitutes and reconstitutes itself, an active participation that constructs tradition and its interpretation, a participation that itself orders the structures of practice. Is not this ordering a way of defining person and community, of setting the boundaries of meaning and understanding? Is not this "writing" and "rewriting," this "incorporating" and "inscribing," in body, mind, and spirit—all that I have claimed is involved in liturgical catechesis—a "practicing" of ourselves?

To this point in the book, I have attempted to address the meaning of "practicing," leaving relatively unexplored the concept of "ourselves." In the next two chapters we will explore who are we and who we practice ourselves to be and how this is practiced in the liturgy. The chapter that follows these asks and attempts to answer the question "To what end are we practicing ourselves?"

Chapter Five

Trinitarian Grammar and the Christian Self

From Thee our being we receive[1]

To this point, I have proposed a way to speak about and understand liturgical catechesis as a particular practice of the church through which the church forms its people in a particular way of being. I have also argued that as a consequence of our liturgical practice, worship teaches us. Central to this understanding are several claims explored in the previous chapters: (1) Christian liturgy is simultaneously constitutive and normative for the shape of Christian life as well as expressive of that life, even when those norms are contested. (2) As a practice of the church, liturgical catechesis unites past, present, and future in a pattern of meaningful action. (3) As meaningful and strategic action, liturgical catechesis is a practice of Christian persons in Christian communities.

In addition to these claims, I have attempted to develop a foundation that supports a fourth claim that serves as a corrective to the ways in which *liturgical catechesis* as a practice of the church is understood. With this fourth claim, I have proposed that, as a "strategic ecclesial practice," the liturgical catechesis enacted *in Christian worship* is neither instruction *for* liturgical participation

[1] Hymn 248, "Hail, Father, Son, and Spirit, great," stanza 3, in *The Works of John Wesley*, vol. 7: *A Collection of Hymns for the use of the People called Methodists,* ed. Franz Hildebrandt and Oliver Beckerlegge (Oxford: Clarendon Press; New York: Oxford University Press, 1983) 389.

113

nor critical reflection *on* that participation, but a formative practice in its own right. Although United Methodists continue to neglect both instruction for participation in worship and critical reflection on that participation, especially with adults who are new to the Christian faith and the United Methodist traditions, we have also neglected the formational and catechetical power of liturgical practice itself.

In light of these claims and this understanding of liturgical catechesis, I concluded the previous chapter with the question, "Who are we and who do we practice ourselves to be?" Put another way, where the previous chapters led us toward an understanding of liturgical catechesis as "strategic ecclesial practice," this and the following chapters attempt to address the questions "Practice of *what*?" and "To what end?"

In answer to *what,* in this and the next chapter I want to develop an understanding of the Christian person as a person in relation to other persons-in-relation and to a relational God. This self-in-relation I call, following Catherine LaCugna's use of the term, the *theonomous self,*[2] a self that is neither self-determined (autonomous) nor completely other-determined (heteronomous), but defined by the character of one's relationship with God. The claims listed above suggest that, beyond the primary doxological character of the liturgy, liturgical practice shares a pastoral function common to both catechists and liturgists. This pastoral function emphasizes the constitutive or constructive role of liturgical practices. This constitutive work is, in part, about the formation, molding, shaping and constructing of persons within our particular faith traditions and practices. Consequently, the particular liturgical traditions and practices of our churches determine, at least in part, the understanding or nature of the Christian "self" to be constructed.

Although our North American religious culture seems to suggest otherwise, we cannot speak of generically religious or "faithed" selves any more than we can speak of some generic "spirituality." There are always the questions "What faith?" "What spirits?" "What spirituality?" We can speak only of religious selves located

[2] *God for Us: The Trinity and Christian Life* (New York: HarperCollins, 1991) 316, n. 136, for her brief but suggestive use of this term. I provide a thorough discussion when I return to this term below, p. 144.

within and shaped by particular traditions and practices, differentiated as well by the particular traditions of each church within the
larger Christian community. While we might speak broadly about
the shared identity of Christian selves as that identity is named by
the Christian story, even here we must acknowledge that a Christian self formed in a United Methodist liturgical context differs
from a Christian person formed in a Greek Orthodox liturgical context. We share the confession that "Jesus is Lord," but the way in
which this confession is written on our bodies and in our minds
and spirits looks and feels as different as the spaces in which these
communities worship. The identity proposed by Warner Sallman's
picture of Jesus that hangs in so many Protestant Sunday School
rooms—romanticized, comfortable, Northern European, male—is
different from that proposed by the Orthodox icon of Christ
Pantokrator—mysterious, transcendent, and other.

The character of Christian life and the question of Christian selfhood in the interstices between modernism and post-modernism,
Christendom and post-Christendom, as we have seen in the competing claims described in Chapter 2, are not without their own
difficulties and competing claims. Where the substance of this
book depends upon an argument for the construction of faithed
selves, post-modern theories assert or deny the possibilities of a
self in any form. Where some communities question what lies in
the heart of a person, at the core of one's being, post-modern theorists question the existence of an essential or core self. In the midst
of these competing claims and challenges, how shall we speak of
and define the Christian self in a manner that frames a horizon for
the self within a community of faith situated in the stream of
Christian tradition and practice?

As questions about Christian formation, these questions may be
asked more frequently by catechists than by liturgists. Even so,
where religious educators have emphasized instruction for and in
worship and liturgists have emphasized theological reflection on
the texts and practice of worship, it has been uncommon for either
to attend to the explicitly formative character of liturgical practices
and their role in the social construction of the self. Yet again it may
not be at all clear why in a discussion of liturgical practice we need
to explore the concepts of the socially constructed and relational
self. Let me name three reasons to pursue this discussion. First, an

understanding of the self as socially constructed provides a corrective to our cultural assumptions about the self as an autonomous and fixed essence existing independently within the matrix or web we call "world." Second, an understanding of the constructed relational self provides a needed antidote to what some see as the radical or perhaps toxic individualism of North American culture. Third, the implicit faith "grammar" practiced in Christian liturgy is a grammar of human "becoming" in relationship to God and one another that is grounded in the communion of persons we call Trinity.

In spite of these reasons, the idea of the constructed relational self is not without its problems. Again, let me address just three. First, a definition of the self as a social relational construction is open to the criticism that this definition results in a form of determinism that removes the possibilities for power, freedom, and self-determination from the individual. Rather than remove such possibilities, however, our acknowledgment of the self as a social relational construction reveals the hidden ways in which we are not free. In light of the discussion of *misrecognition* as a component of ritual practice in the previous chapter, this should give liturgists cause for attending to this question.

Second, a social-relational understanding of the self may be seen as detracting from or obscuring the distinctive interrelatedness of body, mind, and spirit within each person. Although this seems to diminish our individuality, the discovery that we must attend to the bodies, minds, and spirits of those around us reveals the isolation and narcissism with which we live.

Third, one could argue that the nature of the constructed self, because it is a unique construction of experiences, traditions, and relationships, serves to reinforce rather than challenge individualism. What I experience and come to know through that experience is uniquely my experience, my knowledge, unshared and unshareable at some level with any other person. And yet, our inclination to describe and share these experiences invites us back into conversation and relationship with those around us as we seek affirmation or at least recognition of these experiences and our interpretations of them.

Given these possibilities and problems, how might we best describe the liturgically or sacramentally constructed (practiced) self? I want to begin with the question of liturgical practice as a faith grammar, with the intent of moving toward an exploration of Trinitarian relationality as a model for Christian personhood and community. In particular, I want to explore the "cultural-linguistic" framework for doctrine proposed by George Lindbeck in order to examine the Trinitarian grammar of Christian liturgy as a framework for and mode of social relatedness.

A second step addresses the question of a Trinitarian-relational God. Here I will develop a conversation with the relational Trinitarian theologies of Catherine LaCugna, Jürgen Moltmann, and Leonardo Boff, each of whom explores the social-historical character of our knowledge of God and of God's revelation of Godself to humanity. Also significant in the work of these three theologians is their attempt to recover a theology of the Trinity as a practical theology of the relatedness of human existence. These two steps result in my situating the liturgically formed self in the "relatedness" of God. A third step takes up the particular question of the relational self, guided by a conversation with the social psychology of George Herbert Mead, the philosophical psychology of John Macmurray, and the neo-Piagetian psychology of Robert Kegan.

This conversation brings us full circle, as it were, bringing us back to the question of a liturgical grammar of relationality by way of an exploration of the self as a construction which occurs in particular cultures of relatedness and which results in the formation of the *theonomous* self. In the chapter that follows, I will look explicitly at several liturgical practices in which we put this Trinitarian-relational grammar into play.

LITURGY AS A GRAMMAR OF AND FOR FAITH

In this tensive time between Christendom and post-Christendom, when the very idea of "self" is contested, how might we speak about the liturgical construction and practice of the religious self? George Lindbeck's cultural-linguistic model for doctrine and theology has proved to be a generative proposal for the work of theological reflection.[3] This model is not only congruent with the

---

[3] Reinhard Hütter provides a recent critical but appreciative reading of Lindbeck's contribution to this conversation between doctrine, theology, and practice in *Suffering Divine Things: Theology as Church Practice*, trans. Doug Stott (Grand Rapids, Mich.: Wm. Eerdmans Publishing Co., 2000) 40–69.

discussion in the preceding chapter on ritual as performance and practice but also provides a framework for a discussion of liturgy and the self. Of particular help is his attempt to move contemporary theological discourse out of a location in modern individualism and into the socio-cultural linguistic framework provided by the specific practices of the Christian faith.

Lindbeck has been primarily concerned with the ways in which Christian doctrine may function in a "postliberal age." To this end, he has distinguished among three primary approaches to doctrine. The first, the "cognitive" approach to doctrine, "stresses the ways in which doctrines function as informative propositions or truth claims about objective realities."[4] Catechism, "traditional" Sunday School models of religious education, and liturgies dominated by word and instructional preaching, such as the Protestant "preaching service," offer parallels to this approach.

The second, "experiential-expressive" approach "interprets doctrines as noninformative and nondiscursive symbols of inner feelings, attitudes, or existential orientations," and highlights the "resemblance of religions to aesthetic enterprises."[5] On the educational side, the modern religious education movement, particularly as influenced by Dewey, most clearly illustrates this approach. On the liturgical side, the growing concern for the quality of music in worship during the 1950s, the attempts at "creative liturgy" during the 1970s, and the more recent versions of "contemporary worship" fall into this category.

The cognitive approach reflects, to some extent, the self as defined by the Enlightenment, emphasizing rationality, tradition, and harmony. The experiential-expressive approach reflects a self that is consistent with the Romantic emphasis on the rights of the individual, the play of free imagination, and the power of individual feeling or sentiment to define a way of life. Lindbeck sees the experiential-expressive as the primary mode of religious discourse in modernity and as reflecting the individualism of much contemporary Protestant piety, certainly within the mainstream of United Methodism.

But what mode of discourse is appropriate in post-modernity? Here Lindbeck offers a third way, which he calls the "cultural-

---

[4] *The Nature of Doctrine* (Philadelphia: Westminster Press, 1984) 16.
[5] Ibid., 16.

linguistic." This approach utilizes insights from the cognitive and experiential-expressive approaches but provides a means for the critique of individualism, as well as a balance between reason and sentiment, tradition and imaginative creativity, the social and the individual. This critical and constructive third approach emphasizes "those respects in which religions resemble languages together with their correlative forms of life and are thus similar to cultures (insofar as these are understood semiotically as reality and value systems— that is, as idioms for the construction of reality and the living of life)." In this model doctrines function as "communally authoritative rules of discourse, attitude, and action."[6] For example, within a Trinitarian Christian framework, the ecumenical church requires that the Three-in-One be held in tension with the One-in-Three as we attempt to describe the fullness of the Trinitarian God.

Lindbeck's cultural-linguistic proposal offers a model of a socially constituted universe of religious discourse within which the individual is situated and with which the individual is engaged in conversation toward the construction of the self. This universe of discourse reaches beyond language to include ritual and symbolic practices as well—sacramental actions, prayer, and hymn singing. As socially constructed universes of discourse, particular religions function as "comprehensive interpretive schemes, usually embodied in myths or narratives and heavily ritualized, which structure human experience and understanding of self and world."[7] In this

---

[6] Ibid., 18.

[7] Ibid., 32. Although he does not develop this understanding of ritual practice as a universe of discourse, Lindbeck does hint at the performative aspect of doctrine as a grammar of faith. Lindbeck reflects on Austin's understanding of "performativity," which I discussed in the previous chapter, and the implications of this for understandings of religious "truth." He concludes, "a religious utterance . . . acquires the propositional truth of ontological correspondence only insofar as it is a performance, an act or deed, which helps create that correspondence" (65). He argues, further, that "meaning is constituted by the uses of a specific language. . . . The proper way to determine what 'God' signifies . . . is by examining how the word operates within a religion and thereby shapes reality and experience" (114). While his discussion of the cultural-linguistic approach can lead to an analytical-cognitive focus on the grammatical structures of doctrines and practices, Lindbeck points, I think, toward an understanding of cultural grammar in which the grammar is "realized" only as it is put into practice.

approach to doctrine, a particular religion functions as "a kind of cultural and/or linguistic framework or medium that shapes the entirety of life and thought," "similar to an idiom that makes possible the description of realities, the formulation of beliefs, and the experiencing of inner attitudes, feelings, and sentiments," and "a communal phenomenon that shapes the subjectivities of individuals rather than being primarily a manifestation of those subjectivities."[8] In light of this approach, I would argue that a particular religion is therefore a particular "culture of embeddedness," or perhaps even a web of cultures, in which both an individual and a social group find definition and develop. Each particular religious culture, as a community of strategic ecclesial practices, embeds its members in particular narratives, acts of piety and mercy, and ways of viewing the world. The Christian religious, liturgical, and spiritual life is, therefore, always particular rather than generic.

This cultural-grammatical framework also suggests a sequence of development in the religious individual. The individual initially develops embedded in the culture of a religion (and its field of discourse) whereby the religion "has" the individual, that is, where the religion provides the structure for the definition of the self, toward a culture whereby the individual religiously has the content of a religion.[9] Initially, a religious culture surrounds and holds us. As we

[8] Ibid., 33. Although few religious educators have given Lindbeck's work much attention, these two points have been taken up indirectly by those working with the question of religious education in a pluralistic context. The value of education into and by a particular "culture of embeddedness" is described by Bert Roebben in "Do We Still Have Faith in Young People? A West-European Answer to the Evangelization of Young People in a Post-Modern World," *Religious Education* 90:4 (Fall 1995) 327–345. Roebben writes:

"Teaching the reasons which underlie the rule of social life, of language, of customs, and so on is fundamentally a dynamic process. The educator initiates the child not only in the rules but at the same time in the reasons for the rules; immerses the child not only in the customs of a certain community, but also in the purposes for these customs; teaches the child not only 'values,' but at the same time the process of 'valuing,' that is, the giving of reasons why someone considers something valuable; imparts to the child not only the 'articles of faith' but also the reasons why he or she considers faith to be such a precious good" (338).

[9] I am indebted to Gabriel Moran's discussion of the distinction between the development of a "religion" which one has and the "religious" as a par-

practice this culture (and other cultures in which we are embedded), we internalize it in body, mind, and spirit. As we do so, the religion is no longer "other" but part of our very life and breath.

In positing a cultural-linguistic model for doctrine, Lindbeck describes a dialectical process between "knowing about" a religion and "being" religious. The difficulty that Lindbeck identifies for the development of a Christian person in a particular doctrinal culture is a difficulty that old-line/mainline churches seem to acknowledge with a wink and then to ignore. "Fewer and fewer contemporary people are deeply embedded in particular religious traditions or thoroughly involved in particular religious communities."[10] Although liberal mainline churches like the United Methodist Church are quick to acknowledge the adverse effects suffered by children orphaned or abandoned, many have been slow to acknowledge the adverse effects of separation from the particularity of a religious community under the assumption that human persons are in some way generically religious or "faithed" and will find their way on their own.

In the pre-Constantinian context in which Christianity was a minority among other religious traditions, the church required processes of Christian formation and initiation—liturgical and catechetical practices—that drew individuals into the particularity of the Christian community's way of life as much as, if not more than, its way of belief. From the particularity of this way of life, Christian people interacted with the diverse beliefs of their social-political world. It was only in a context that assumed a "Christian world" that these communal practices diminished in importance. The challenges of our own pluralistic context present us with the

---

ticular way of being in the world. See Gabriel Moran, *Religious Education Development* (Minneapolis: Winston Press, 1983) 148–156.

[10] *Nature of Doctrine*, 21. While some have criticized Lindbeck for positing a new "confessionalism" or "fideism" susceptible to the problems of the "cognitive" approach to doctrine, this criticism only holds if we accept that a particular cultural-linguistic universe univocally defines the self. If we accept that this particular (religious) universe of discourse is in dialectical relationship to the self and with other religious fields of discourse, and that there is a developmental process that moves from "knowing about" religion to a way of "religious being," the charge of confessionalism does not hold, at least for the development of the religious self.

need to once again claim those practices that provide a way of life and belief from which to interact with our world. To claim the liturgy as a normative and constitutive practice for the Christian life is to claim the liturgy as inherently catechetical.

This developmental process is more than a process of tradition-ing, formation, or education. We may still make a case for claiming "faith" as a verb—faith is something we do—rather than as a noun—faith as something or some content independent of our ac-tion.[11] I think of this dialectical process between the individual and a religious culture of embeddedness as a process of "faithing." The process moves between the structure of a religious grammar, a reli-gious grammar which "has" the individual or which the individ-ual has as content (I think, I believe, I know) and a religious grammar as a mode of being related in and to self, other, the world, and God (I am, we are). It is a process that moves between epistemology and ontology, between knowing and being (or being known). Although the church generally unites profession of faith and baptism in one rite, it is one thing to make a profession of faith (I believe in . . .) and another to be baptized in response to that profession (a distinction heightened by the Orthodox formula "You are baptised . . ."), both in terms of the action itself and the use of it as a reminder of our status within the faith community. The dis-tinction between the two is seen in the difference between the Apostles' Creed and the Nicene-Constantinople Creed in their cur-rent ecumenical forms: the former begins "I" believe and is appro-priate as an individual confession of faith to its baptismal context; the latter begins "We" believe and is appropriate to its context in the weekly assembly of the Christian community.[12] What *I* believe is what I have as the content of my faith. What *we* believe is not substantially different in content, but as a communal form of belief

[11] Moran, *Religious Education Development*, 124. In particular, see James W. Fowler and Sam Keen, *Life Maps*, ed. Jerome W. Berryman (Waco, Tex.: Word, 1985) 18. It may be linguistically awkward to enact this claim (as arguments against the use of inclusive language for humanity or for God have also con-tended), but I do not believe that such awkwardness necessarily prevents our linguistic reconstruction.

[12] A helpful discussion of this difference between the two creeds is provided in *Confessing the One Faith* (Geneva: WCC Publications, 1991) 15.

what we believe provides a framework, a grammar in which *I believe*. We saw a similar interaction between the *I* and *we* in the discussion (Chapter 3) of the Affirmation of Faith of the United Church of Canada and its use by TUMC (pp. 69ff.).

Lindbeck's cultural-linguistic model emphasizes that what "I" believe is always and already situated within the context of what "we" believe and that there is no sense of an "I" believing without the believing "we." "Faithing" the self is therefore a social-relational process that yields people who cannot be generically religious, as they cannot be generically "selved." We must be "faithed" in particularity by particular practices and stories. As Lindbeck observes, "different religions seem in many cases to produce fundamentally divergent depth experiences of what it is to be human."[13] Different grammars yield different selves, just as particular cultures of embeddedness yield particular senses of the self.

The "essential" religious self is a self defined as embedded in and arising from the changing relationships to and with those who symbolize particular socio-linguistic religious cultures. It is a self "faithed" in and toward particular forms of social relatedness. As S. Mark Heim has argued, "the actual ends that various religious traditions offer as alternative human fulfillments diverge because they realize different relations with God." If as Christian people we claim a Trinitarian faith, this shapes the character of our relationships with God, one another, and the world. As Heim also argues, "'Knowing' God as Trinity is a way of life, a nurturing and growth into closer communion with God across a range of relations that fully encompasses our lives."[14] What, then, does it mean for us to speak about a "social-relational self"? And if this self is not generically religious, where does a Trinitarian grammar lead us in understanding this self as a Christian self?

THE SOCIAL-RELATIONAL SELF

By turning first to an explicit psychological social-relational grammar, I hope to provide a foundation for the Trinitarian theological perspectives that follow and to develop a correlation between the

[13] *Nature of Doctrine*, 42.
[14] "The Depth of the Riches: Trinity and Religious Ends," *Modern Theology* 17:1 (January 2001) 30.

psychological grammar of the social self and the theological grammar of the Trinity. Here I draw on the philosophical psychological work of John Macmurray, the social psychological work of George Herbert Mead, and the recent, neo-Piagetian developmental psychology of Robert Kegan.

Mead, Macmurray, and Kegan share common concerns for the development of person in community, for the *a priori* role of the community in that development, and for the person's ability to act in and with that community. They all assume that to some extent the social—whether we speak of a society, a collective, or some other description of a human "whole"—precedes the individual and provides a matrix, web, or culture in which the human self arises and develops. Mead describes his concern as an attempt to explain "the conduct of the individual in terms of the organized conduct of the social group, rather than to account for the organized conduct of the separate individuals belonging to it."[15]

Macmurray's concern is similar. Over against a description of the person as the isolated or autonomous "I," he describes a self that exists only as an agent in active relationship to an Other. Thus for Macmurray, the self is constituted by mutuality and relationship.

Kegan, while concerned with the conduct of individuals, also understands the developmental process of the individual as a process of changing social relationships.

Where Mead is helpful in speaking of the socially constructed self, Macmurray is helpful in speaking of the self as an agent in relation, and Kegan in speaking of the socially related self and the developmental issues of those relationships.

Within the social psychological framework Mead explicates in the lectures collected as *Mind, Self and Society,* he is particularly helpful in pointing to the relationship between language or symbolic gesture, self-consciousness (what Mead calls "mind"), and the social. He argues that the development of "mind" requires communication or a "conversation of gestures." Such a conversation of gestures requires a relational/social context.[16]

[15] *Mind, Self and Society,* ed. Charles W. Morris (Chicago: University of Chicago Press, 1934) 7.
[16] Ibid., 49–50.

Three points in Mead's work are important to this discussion. First, it is through the sharing of gestures, in conversation with another person, that the self, or sense of self, develops. Second, meaning, as well as the self, is constructed in the course of the interaction between the self and another, that is, in relationship. Third, meaning has its existence "entirely within [the social or relational] field itself" and thus pre-exists the individual.[17] For Mead, the self and the sense of self as meaningful do not and cannot develop in isolation; they develop only in relationship where the "conversation of gestures" may occur. As Mead writes, the self "arises in the process of social experience and activity, that is, develops in the given individual as a result of his relations to that process as a whole and to other individuals within that process."[18] The social construction of the self is a dialectic construction, a co-determinate relationship between self and other made possible only by a series of relationships between two persons, and between the subjective "world" of the individual and a larger social world.

In terms of a sense of unity or coherence of the self, Mead offers two conclusions. First, the "unity of the self is constituted by the unity of the entire relational pattern of social behavior and experience in which the individual is implicated, and which is reflected in the structure of the self."[19] Second, because he describes this unity in terms of relational patterns rather than essences, the self "is not so much a substance as a process in which the conversation of gestures has been internalized within an organic form."[20] Here Mead reminds us of the important relationship between our given

[17] Ibid., 78.

[18] Ibid., 135.

[19] Ibid., 144, n. 4. In this statement Mead both anticipates the direction of the Trinitarian theologies reviewed in the following section and provides a link between the theology of the Trinity and psychology of self. Reading Mead in light of that discussion, we could easily replace "self" with "God." This is to say that the Christian God is constituted by the relational pattern of the three Persons of the Trinity and the historical behavior and experience in which they are implicated. This relational pattern, as we will see in the discussion of the Trinitarian theologies of Jürgen Moltmann, Leonardo Boff, and Catherine LaCugna that follows, is reflected in the nature of Godself.

[20] Ibid., 178. It may be helpful here to recall the discussion in Chapter 3 of the inscription and incorporation of meaning in the body through ritual practice as represented in the work of Paul Connerton. See pp. 75ff.

biological construction and the social environment in which that body/mind is nurtured or not nurtured. The self as relational process continues the internalization of this conversation of gestures throughout the life span. In more poetic form, Mead writes:

"The self is not something that exists first and then enters into relationship with others, but it is, so to speak, an eddy in the social current and so still a part of the current. It is a process in which the individual is continually adjusting himself [sic] in advance to the situation to which he belongs, and reacting back on it."[21]

Yet as I think about the relationship of eddy and current, I am reminded that while the eddy depends on the current for its life force, the eddy also spins in upon itself. To be caught in an eddy is, at one and the same time, to be caught in the current and separated from the flow of the current. The psychological eddy may become a narcissistic whirlpool.

This brief review of Mead introduces the major themes of the self as socially constructed, as related, and as processual. John Macmurray provides a description of the self that draws upon the conversational relationship described by Mead. He expands Mead's concern for the social self in his development of the relational patterns of behavior that shape the development of the self. Where Mead defined these relational patterns as a "conversation of meaningful gestures," primarily linguistic in form, Macmurray extends these shared patterns to focus on the shared agency of self with other. To this end, Macmurray provides two interrelated arguments united under the heading of his Gifford lectures as "The Form of the Personal." In the first part of his argument, he develops an understanding of the self as agent. In the second part, his attention is on the nature of the self as person-in-relation. As both of these arguments are relevant to our discussion here, I will briefly summarize each.

Foundational to Macmurray's argument for the "form of the personal" is a shift from understanding the self as "subject" to self as "agent." With this shift Macmurray challenges the priority of autonomous individualism as constitutive of or normative for human selfhood as he finds it represented in modern (Kantian) philosophy. For him, to speak of the person as subject is to represent the person

---

[21] Ibid., 182.

as an "isolated, purely individual self" disconnected from God, world, and community. The existence of this isolated self denies the agency, the capacity to act upon the world and be acted upon by it, that is characteristic for the human person. The denial of human agency required to create the isolated self results in what Macmurray can only call a fiction.[22]

Having identified the self as agent, Macmurray further argues that not only is the isolated self a fiction but also the "idea of an isolated agent is self-contradictory. Any agent is necessarily in relation to the Other. Apart from this essential relation he [sic] does not exist."[23] In the turn from fiction to self-contradiction, Macmurray finally concludes that the isolated self is self-negating. "The solitary self can only mean the self in reflection, self-isolated from the world, withdrawn into itself."[24] This withdrawal from the world, from relationship, is a withdrawal of agency and, therefore, a withdrawal of the self as agent from the world. While reflection is a form of internal action, it is not a form of agency or engagement with the world; it is an action of "standing back" from the world, from experience, from engagement with other agents, and from the world itself.[25]

In terms of *who* we are and *whose* we are, there are at least two consequences of the self as agent that are of particular importance to this discussion. The first has to do with our knowledge of self

[22] *The Self as Agent* (London: Faber and Faber, 1957) 38.
[23] *Persons in Relation* (London: Faber and Faber, 1961) 24.
[24] *Self as Agent*, 141.
[25] Here it is important to note, I think, what Macmurray means and does not mean by "experience." Experience is a pattern of action in the world and, therefore, in relationship. "'Experience' is a practical concept, referring to whatever is apprehended in action, in distinction from what is thought in reflection." Experience is a consequence of agency (Macmurray, *Self as Agent,* 115.) In this regard, Macmurray echoes Mead's distinctions between experience, intelligence, and knowledge. For Mead, experience refers to that portion of life in which the person acts in reference to the environment. Intelligence is the ability to use past experience in the modification of a response or selection of a stimulus in "meeting the difficulties that arise in the life process." [George Herbert Mead, "The Process of Mind in Nature," in *Philosophy of the Act*, ed. Charles W. Morris (Chicago: University of Chicago Press, 1938) 404–405.] Knowledge is a hypothesis tested and found true as it allows a person to proceed with action and which can serve as a basis for action in the future (Mead, "History and the Experimental Method," in *Philosophy of the Act,* 95).

and other. Because the self is identified by its agency in or engagement with the world, our ability to know another is determined by our engagement or relationship with the other. "I can know another person as a person only by entering into personal relation with him."[26] Our knowledge of the other, as with our knowledge of ourselves, is determined by our action with the other and the other's action with us. "Since the agent is part of the Other, he [sic] cannot modify the Other without modifying himself, or know the Other without knowing himself."[27] Here Macmurray speaks of self and other as co-determining agents or "primary correlates": "Any determination of [self or other] must formally characterize the other also. The form of the Self and the form of the Other must be identical: the categories through which both are thought must be the same. If I am the agent, then the Other is the other agent."[28] In Macmurray's schema this is as true for the relation between persons as between persons and God.

Second, like Mead, Macmurray sees this co-determinative agency in relation to the history and future of persons. By action in the world persons in relation determine the past, as action completed, and condition the future, as action yet to be completed and therefore open or incompletely realized.[29] Macmurray suggests that this co-determinacy by agents affects both public and personal life. At the public level, the co-determination of the past through the completion of shared action results in the development of a public memory, a story identifying that this is who we are or have been in this relationship. For Macmurray, common action requires such common or shared public memory.[30] At the personal level, the co-determination of the past and conditioning of the future result in a modification of action and thought. The mutual action of agents, as a modification of individual action, brings about a change in worldview and expectations for our world.[31]

[26] Macmurray, *Persons in Relation*, 28.
[27] Ibid., 166.
[28] Ibid., 79.
[29] *Self as Agent*, 134.
[30] Ibid., 214.
[31] Ibid., 185.

Throughout his discussion of the self as agent, Macmurray anticipates a conclusion that does not come until the second volume of his lectures: a person's "proper existence [is] as a community of persons in [personal and mutual] relation."[32] With language that clearly anticipates what we will find in Robert Kegan's work, Macmurray writes, "If the *terminus a quo* of the personal life is a helpless total dependence on the Other, the *terminus ad quem* is not independence, but a mutual interdependence of equals."[33] He concludes, "[T]he primary and distinctive character of personal behavior" is "the mutuality of the personal." With relationship or mutuality as the distinctive marker of the personal, with the co-determinative agency of self and other as constitutive for selfhood, we discover the necessity of the other for our sense of self. "The reference to the personal Other is constitutive for all personal existence."[34]

One difficulty with Macmurray's proposal is the argument that this relational self is or becomes heterocentric. The heterocentric self locates one's "center of interest and attention in the other" in such a way that the *ideal of the personal* is "a universal community of persons in which each cares for all the others and *not one for himself* [my emphasis]." Nevertheless, Macmurray also argues that this ideal of the personal as a community of mutual interdependence provides "the condition of freedom—that is, of a full realization of [one's] capacity to act—for every person."[35] He finds this ideal represented in his image of God as "the idea of a personal Other who stands in the same mutual relation to every member of the community."[36]

---

[32] *Persons in Relation*, 12, 61.

[33] Ibid., 66. The development of persons in relation we find represented here is not what we find represented in the moral psychologies of Piaget or Kohlberg, which assume a developmental sequence from heteronomy (total dependence on the other) to autonomy (as independence of the self from which the autonomous persons stands in relation to others). Here Macmurray clearly anticipates not only Kegan but also the feminist critiques that build upon an ethic of care and mutuality.

[34] Ibid., 69.

[35] Ibid., 158, 159.

[36] Ibid., 164. As we find in the pragmatism of Mead, Macmurray argues that "all meaningful knowledge is for the sake of action, [although here Mead would argue that action is for the sake of knowledge] and all meaningful action for the sake of friendship" (*Self as Agent*, 15).

Where Mead situates the development of the individual within a social/relational matrix, and Macmurray within the co-determinative and mutual agency of self and other, Robert Kegan provides the means by which to describe the changing character of that matrix through a developmental stage sequence. Where Mead speaks of the "social current" in which the individual is implicated, Kegan speaks of cultures of embeddedness. For Mead, the individual may be "caught" for a time in a particular eddy of the stream and is at risk of being dissolved by the stream (a risk Mead apparently wants to avoid). For Kegan, in contrast, the individual rises in and through particular cultures, growing as a self in continuously expanding matrices of relation and taking as content for the self what in the previous stage had provided structure to the self. Where Mead points primarily toward a linear conception of developmental relationships, Kegan speaks of a spiral of development and a plurality of "cultures," pointing toward the possibility for our synchronous participation in multiple cultures or universes of discourse. (In this way, perhaps, he points toward a sense of the self as "perichoretic," which we will explore in the next section.) But like Mead, Kegan argues that meaning is located in the gesture (if we take the grasping of an infant as a symbolic gesture) and in the social. Meaning is,

"in its origins, a physical activity (grasping, seeing), a social activity (it requires another), a survival activity (in doing it, we live). . . . It cannot be divorced from the body, from social experience, or from the very survival of the organism. Meaning depends on someone who recognizes you. Not meaning, by definition, is utterly lonely."[37]

Meaning, with the self, requires relationships, conversations, and languages; in such lies the possibility for being recognized and being known, for re-cognizing, re-knowing, and re-creating the sense of self. Relationship makes both meaning and the transformation of self-meaning possible.

In speaking about cultures of embeddedness and social meaning-making, Kegan points toward particular changing modes of relatedness in which we construct the self. These modes range from the "incorporative self" of the infant in dependent relationship to

[37] *The Evolving Self* (Cambridge, Mass.: Harvard University Press, 1982) 18–19.

parents, taking in sustenance as well as the world around it, to the "interindividual self" of the mature adult in relationship with other (mature) adults. Kegan argues that an individual both grows "out of" a culture and transforms or recovers that culture as content for the next. Like Mead, Kegan describes this growth process as "an evolution that is imagined to go on not within the body alone but within the life-surround, an evolution which continually reconstructs the relationship of the organism to this bigger environment, an evolution more of the mind than of the brain."[38] The development of the self takes on the character of a lifelong evolution of subject-object relations, the development of "a succession of qualitative differentiations of the self from the world, with a qualitatively more extensive object with which to be in relation created each time," and thus "successive triumphs of 'relationship to' rather than 'embeddedness in.'"[39]

At some point, then, the flow of self/meaning must break free from the eddy and rejoin the main current of the stream. This is not, however, so that the self can be swept along at the mercy of the stream. The structure or definition of the self and other/social is for Kegan, as for Mead, co-determined: "a person's evolution intrinsically creates anew 'the other' with which the person can be in relation, that as a person evolves those of us around him [her] become something fundamentally different to him [her]."[40] Unlike Mead, Kegan offers a model that preserves a balance between several developmental poles: between differentiation and integration, separation and attachment, and autonomy and inclusion.[41] His model suggests that a continuous dance between "emergence" and relationship, each occurring so that the other might also occur, more accurately describes the development of the self than eddies in a stream of life. The "other" (or our conception of the other) who is created anew includes parents, communities of care, and God.

What Kegan, Macmurray, Mead, and Lindbeck all call our attention to is the fact that "the human coherence of our lives is

[38] Ibid., 71.
[39] Ibid., 77.
[40] Ibid., 140.
[41] Ibid., 108. Like Mead, this balancing act suggests another connection with a concern we will see in Moltmann and Boff to articulate a way to preserve unity in the midst of diversity and diversity in the struggle for unity.

enhanced by life in a community of considerable duration, a community which gathers and subtends its era-specific expressions of support."[42] As Mead states, "A person learns a new language and, as we say, gets a new soul. He [sic] puts himself into the attitude of those that make use of that language."[43] What, then, does it mean for our understanding of this social-relational self if it is "faithed" in a Trinitarian grammar?

FAITH IN A TRINITARIAN RELATIONAL GOD

It is not uncommon for church people as well as their pastors to ask why we should bother with a doctrine as confusing and debated as the Trinity. For many, the Trinity is a metaphysical question irrelevant to our daily lives and better left to philosophical theologians. Clearly, I believe otherwise. A Trinitarian grammar has practical implications for the way we think about the shape of Christian life and for the ways in which we practice being Christian selves in the liturgy.

As one among those attempting to move discussions of the Trinity out of the level of metaphysics and into a level that addresses the practical shape of Christian life and practice, Douglas Ottati characterizes his response to the question, "Does the Trinity make any sense?" in the following way:

"Trinitarian theology makes sense as a continuation of a biblically initiated exploration into experiences of redemption and into an apprehension of God that is part of saving faith. It describes the Christian community's distinct experience of faithfulness and new life, and it points to the God who is beyond our comprehension."[44]

Of importance in this statement is the way in which Ottati affirms the distinctive narrative character of a Trinitarian faith in and for the Christian community. By claiming that the Trinity points "to the God beyond comprehension," Ottati also reminds us of the symbolic character of Trinitarian language. It is analogical language about God by which we approach the mystery of God. Yet, because it is analogical and symbolic, it never completely reveals

[42] Ibid., 261.

[43] *Mind, Self, and Society*, 283.

[44] "Being Trinitarian: The Shape of Saving Faith," *Christian Century* 112: 32 (Nov. 8, 1995) 1044.

God. At the same time, it provides a grammar or structure by which we continue the narrative and revelation of God's ongoing practice in the world.

This re-examination of the Trinitarian grammar of the Christian faith is prompted, in part, by challenges to the particular relational language of "Father, Son, and Holy Spirit" that have arisen within feminist theological communities. It is also prompted, as Ottati indicates, by an attempt to retrieve, perhaps preserve, the Trinitarian language about God as language that is relevant to the faith of Christians today. But I would argue that this re-examination is prompted also by the shifting understanding of "personhood"— whether in reference to the human or divine person—from that rooted in autonomous individuality to an understanding rooted in relationality and community.

Among those who address these questions in the development of a theology of the Trinity are Jürgen Moltmann, Leonardo Boff, and Catherine LaCugna.[45] The three share a starting point in Karl Rahner's maxim that the immanent Trinity (God in Godself) is the economic Trinity (God for or in relationship to us, God's action in history), and the economic Trinity is the immanent Trinity.[46] This maxim points them toward a common conclusion: humanity can and does know God through God's action in our history and our history of relationship with God. (That being said, they also conclude that there is something of God that remains unknown or unknowable as well, even as our constructions or experiences of history remain partial or incomplete. As Frances Young reminds us, "There are good reasons for being wary of using the doctrine of Trinity in speaking about community as if the internal relationships within God were known to us.")[47] Each uses Rahner's maxim to argue that God's history with us

[45] These three represent the beginning of new and creative thinking about the Trinity, particularly in attempting to work toward a "practical theology" of the Trinity. Their work has been critiqued and developed by Elizabeth Johnson, *She Who Is* (New York: Crossroad, 1993); David Cunningham, *These Three are One* (Malden, Mass.: Blackwell Publishers, 1998); Paul Fiddes, *Participating in God* (Louisville: Westminster John Knox, 2001); and Bruce Marshall, *Trinity and Truth* (New York: Cambridge University Press, 1999), among others.

[46] *The Trinity* (New York: Herder and Herder, 1970) 22.

[47] "Essence and Energies: Classical Trinitarianism and 'Enthusiasm,'" in *Trinity, Community, and Power: Mapping Trajectories in Wesleyan Theology*, ed.

reveals a pattern of relationship that corresponds to the internal relationship of the three-personed God—Father, Son, and Spirit—and that this pattern of relationship is normative for the pattern of human relationship and being. Each also attempts, as much as possible, to avoid talking about the mystery of God in Godself except as Godself is made known in God's practice in history.

In their constructive work on the Trinity, Moltmann, Boff, and LaCugna have three additional components in common. First, they share an understanding that language about the Trinity is inherently and primarily doxological, a point more developed in LaCugna and Moltmann than in Boff. Second, they attempt to develop a social-relational doctrine of the Trinity from their reading of the history of God with us. Third, each retrieves the theological concept of perichoresis as a schema for naming a particular form of relatedness that affirms unity-in-diversity and diversity-in-unity. As Moltmann writes, this results in a "social doctrine of the Trinity, according to which God is a community of Father, Son, and Spirit, whose unity is constituted by mutual indwelling and reciprocal interpenetration."[48] From the shared starting point and these three common components, they point toward a common goal: a correlation between the divine society of the Trinity and human society.[49] These three points warrant further exploration.

M. Douglas Meeks (Nashville: Abingdon Press, Kingswood Books, 2000) 130. Some would also argue, as a corollary to the first conclusion, that God in Godself *must* be as God reveals Godself to be in historical relationship with us. In this regard, see Ted Peters's discussion of Eberhard Jüngel. Peters writes: "Jüngel assumes that God could not be nonrelational within God's own being and then become relational through mutual interaction with the creation. . . . There must exist a correspondence between God's life with the world and what goes on within the divine life apart from the world." Ted Peters, *God as Trinity: Relationality and Temporality in Divine Life* (Louisville: Westminster/John Knox, 1993) 92.

[48] *The Trinity and the Kingdom*, trans. Margaret Kohl (Minneapolis: Fortress Press, 1993) viii. Boff similarly writes, "The Trinity . . . is the revelation of God as God is, Father, Son, and Holy Spirit in eternal correlation, interpenetration, love, and communion, which make them one sole God." He adds his own emphasis, however, as he adds, "The fact that God is triune means unity in diversity." Leonardo Boff, *Trinity and Society*, trans. Paul Burns (Maryknoll, N.Y.: Orbis Books, 1988) 3.

[49] Peters, however, attempts to argue that Boff is unable to go as far as Moltmann in establishing this correlation. Peters writes, "Although Boff wants

THE TRINITY IS REVEALED IN DOXOLOGY
Glory be to the Father, and to the Son, and to the Holy Spirit. For
Moltmann, the praise and worship of the church is the situation in
Christian life for the assertion of the Trinity. More than this, he ar-
gues that praise and worship—doxology—are required to release
"the experience of salvation for a full experience of that salvation."[50]
Through the doxological rule of prayer the church gives expression
to its "experience of God in the apprehension of Christ and in the
fellowship of the Spirit." In other words, "[t]heological talk about
God stems from doxological talk to God, and remains talk before
God."[51] Or, as we noted in the opening chapter, the law of prayer
establishes the law of belief. There is a willingness in Moltmann to
say that doxology is theology, even if not all theology is doxology.
These two statements also indicate that even as doxology expresses
theology, it gives rise to or generates theology. As we have seen in
earlier parts of this discussion, especially in Chapter 1, this is crucial
to the understanding of liturgical catechesis being developed here.
To say that doxology is theology is to say that the performance of
the liturgy is an inherently theological practice and, in that, a practice of theological (and grammatical) formation.

Boff agrees with Moltmann's statement that "theological talk
about God stems from doxological talk to God," that doxology
precedes theology, but has some reservations about equating the
two: "First we profess faith in Father, Son and Holy Spirit in prayer
and praise (doxology). Then we reflect on how the divine Three are
one single God in perichoretic communion between themselves

---

to work with a correlation between a divine society and a human society on a
nonhierarchical basis, the divine society of which he speaks is in fact a monarchy; and because this monarchy is shrouded in eternal mystery apart from the
time in which we live, no genuine correlation with human society can be
made. (Peters, *God as Trinity*, 114). Peters bases this argument on a reading of
Boff that assumes that God as Father stands independent of creation, a point
that Boff takes pains to argue against. See Boff, *Trinity and Society*, 14–16 and
169 to the contrary.

[50] *Trinity and the Kingdom*, 152.

[51] Jürgen Moltmann, *The Spirit of Life: A Universal Affirmation*, trans. Margaret
Kohl (Minneapolis: Fortress Press, 1992) 73. And, Moltmann would add, "Doxological terms remain inescapably bound to the experience of salvation and do
not go speculatively beyond it. They remain related to the experience of salvation

(theology)."[52] Boff seems to argue that the language of prayer, liturgy, and human experience is an unreflective, perhaps even naive, form that requires theological comment and elaboration.[53] He reserves the theological catechetical work of the liturgy to "post-performative" reflection. Nevertheless, his affirmation that doxology, as prayer and praise to the Trinity, precedes theological reflection at least situates doxology as the source of that reflection.

LaCugna, like Moltmann, argues more specifically for "theology in the mode of doxology" as the most appropriate form of language with which to speak about the doctrine of the Trinity.[54] Doxology is itself a mode of response to the Christian experience of encounter with the self-giving love of God in Christ through the Holy Spirit.[55] As a mode of response to or in saving faith, LaCugna's maxim becomes "soteriology culminates in doxology," a maxim Charles Wesley captured when he concluded the hymn "Love divine, all loves excelling" with the words "lost in wonder, love, and praise." We see, hear, and recount God's works of salvation, "pray the name of God given to us" in God's history with us, and "enter into relationship" with this "God who names Godself."[56] LaCugna reminds us that "[d]oxological affirmations are . . . not primarily definitions or descriptions. They are performative and ascriptive, lines of thought, speech and action which, as they are offered, open up into the living reality of God himself."[57] This

---

precisely because they are directed towards the God himself whose salvation and love has been experienced" (*Trinity and the Kingdom*, 153). Boff is not satisfied with the doxological binding of the doctrine of the Trinity, arguing that this refusal to go beyond Scripture and liturgical tradition "is hardly theology; it has more to do with exegesis and spirituality" (Boff, *Trinity and Society*, 114). This comment betrays an assumption on his part that theology is somehow other than prayer, exegesis, and spirituality.

[52] *Trinity and Society*, 232.

[53] Ibid., 155–156.

[54] *God for Us*, 320.

[55] Ibid., 324.

[56] Ibid., 335.

[57] Ibid., 336. She is citing "The Filioque Clause in Ecumenical Perspective" in *Spirit of God, Spirit of Christ: Ecumenical Reflections on the Filioque Controversy*, Faith and Order Paper 102, ed. L. Vischer (Geneva: WCC Publications, 1981) 10.

John Calvin seemed to know well. His shorter catechism begins with the familiar reminder that the chief end of humanity is to worship God and to enjoy God forever.

As we will see in the discussion of the eucharistic prayer in the next chapter, the Trinitarian prayer of thanksgiving puts into play not only a theology of the triune God but a way of being in relationship to that God in prayer and praise. "Union with God and communion with each other are actualized through doxology."[58] That is, the practice of doxology puts into play a Trinitarian grammar that is as much about us as it is about God, even as it generates that grammar.

THE HISTORY OF GOD WITH US
REVEALS A SOCIAL-RELATIONAL GOD

Given their shared assent to the maxim that "the economic Trinity is the immanent Trinity," Moltmann, Boff, and LaCugna all assert that the history of God with us as a history of the persons of God[59] provides or reveals a social-relational doctrine of the Trinity. All three also "accept the modern understanding of personhood as a subject that is the center of action" but "add to it the idea that personality and mutuality belong together."[60] In Moltmann's most recent work, however, he recognizes the experiential need for "a many-dimensioned concept of experience" posed by postmodern plurality. To this end, he argues that we abandon "the narrow reference to the modern concept of 'self-consciousness,' so that we can discover transcendence in every experience, not merely in experience of the self."[61] As we will see, LaCugna provides a slightly different emphasis to this understanding.

Rather than focusing on the question of personhood, Moltmann moves quickly from the assumption that persons are subjects to a discussion of the particular character of the relationships between the persons of the Trinity. His beginning point for this discussion is

[58] LaCugna, *God for Us*, 345.

[59] I do not believe it important here to trace the whole of the discussion about the understanding of *person* and its relationship to *hypostasis*, *prosopon*, and *persona* at this point. Both Boff (*Trinity and Society*, 58–64) and LaCugna (*God for Us*, 243–250) trace this history.

[60] Peters, *God as Trinity*, 106.

[61] *Spirit of Life*, 34.

a second assumption, that the historical event of Jesus Christ, the incarnate person, is constitutive for the divine life of the Trinity as a whole. The narrative of this person Jesus is the narrative by the New Testament "of the relationships of the Father, Son, and the Spirit, which are relationships of fellowship and open to the world."[62] A theology of the Trinity, then, is less about the distinctive work of the individual persons of the Trinity than about the character of the relationship between those persons.[63] As he writes,

"The Father, the Son, and the Spirit are by no means merely distinguished from one another by their character as Persons; they are just as much united with one another and in one another, since personal character and social character are only two aspects of the same thing. The concept of person must therefore in itself contain the concept of unitedness or at-oneness, just as, conversely, the concept of God's atoneness must in itself contain the concept of the three Persons. This means that the concept of God's unity cannot in the Trinitarian sense be fitted into the homogeneity of the one divine substance, or into the identity of the absolute subject either; and least of all into one of the three Persons of the Trinity. It must be perceived in the perichoresis of the divine Persons."[64]

Although modern eyes and ears may be drawn to the concern for the "unitedness" or "at-oneness" within the person, here the person of God, Moltmann pushes us away from just such focus. Rather, he calls our attention, on the one hand, to the social-relational history of each particular person of the Trinity as definitive for the "personal" history of each person. On the other hand, by focusing on the intertwining of personal and social, Moltmann calls our attention to the image of diversity present in the unity of the triune God. It is this intertwining of personal as social-relational that points to the perichoretic nature of the persons of the Trinity. That is, we cannot talk about the character or person of God in Godself without talking about the interrelationship of the three persons of God and the char-

[62] *Trinity and the Kingdom*, 64.

[63] This is made clear, I think, in the shape of Moltmann's most recent systematic project, which begins with a discussion of Trinitarian relationship and then moves to a discussion, in separate volumes, of each of the persons of the Trinity.

[64] *Trinity and the Kingdom*, 150. On perichoresis, see below, pp. 142ff.

acter of their relationship to one another. For Moltmann, relatedness is constitutive of the persons of God.

Boff, perhaps more strongly than Moltmann, begins from the distinct subjectivity of each of the persons of God in order to describe what can and cannot be revealed about God. To this end, he describes three meanings of "person": The person is, first, "an existing subject . . . distinct from others." The distinctiveness of the person is necessary for relationship; without it there is only a blurring of identities, symbiosis, or dissolution of person as subject. This distinctiveness "emphasizes what cannot enter into relationship, being the condition that makes relationship possible."[65]

Second, from the position of distinctiveness, the subject participates in a "relational ordering of one [subject] to another."[66] As Boff writes, "each divine Person is a center of interiority and freedom, whose . . . (nature) consists in being always in relation to the Other persons."[67]

Finally, in this relational ordering, the person can further be described as a being-for, a knot of relationships: "All three Persons affirm themselves as an 'I,' not in order to close in on themselves, but in order to be able to give themselves to the other two."[68] Here Boff's social agenda becomes clear. The relationship of the persons—in this case, the persons of God—is not only a relationship *with* the other but a relationship *for* the other person. This relationship *with* and *for* the other creates both dialogue and communion, the unity of person and other.[69] Distinctively in Boff, this relational ordering also provides a critical theological principle for the relationship between Christianity and politics, between the law of prayer and the law of living:

"A Christianity too much focused on the Father without communion with the Son or interiorization of the Spirit can give rise to an

[65] *Trinity and Society*, 88.

[66] Ibid., 87.

[67] Ibid., 89. In this and the following, Boff most clearly articulates the language of the modern autonomous subject while, at the same time, articulating a corrective to that view. Even as he argues for the preservation of the self as a "center of interiority and freedom," this center has an otherward focus, the being-for, the giving of the self to and for others.

[68] Ibid., 116.

[69] Ibid., 116, 5.

oppressive image of God as terrifying mystery, whose designs seem unforeseeable and absolutely hidden. A Christianity fixated on the Son without reference to the Father and union with the Spirit can lead to self-sufficiency and authoritarianism in its leaders and pastors. Finally, a Christianity excessively based on the Spirit without links to the Son and his ultimate reference to the Father can favor anarchism and lack of concern."[70]

Perhaps this is one way of arguing that the church requires the Trinity and a theology of the Trinity in its fullness as the critical principle in its life as church.

Like Moltmann and Boff, LaCugna recounts the history of Trinitarian theologies, particularly those of the Cappadocians and the thirteenth-century Orthodox theologian Gregory Palamas, as a prelude to her own reconstruction of the Trinity as a model for Christian life. At the heart of her discussion lies an understanding of Trinitarian theology as a theology of relationship, a theology that affirms the "essence" of God as "relational, other-ward, that God exists as diverse persons united in a communion of freedom, love and knowledge."[71] Unlike Moltmann and Boff, who begin with the individual person in order to move toward an understanding of relationship, LaCugna begins her discussion of the Trinity with the question of relationship. She writes, "The heart of the doctrine of the Trinity lies here. The definition of divine person as a relation of origin means that to be a person is to be defined by where a person comes from; what a person is in itself or by itself cannot be determined."[72]

Also unlike Moltmann and Boff, who primarily use theological resources in the development of their arguments, LaCugna builds especially on the work of John Zizioulas and John Macmurray.[73]

---

[70] Ibid., 15. S. Mark Heim argues in a similar fashion: "The Christian theological tradition suggests that mistakes about the Trinity affect Christian life. But without a living sense of the Trinity, we contract the range in which God can share that nature with us, and the scope of our relation to God diminishes. This is so in connection with our prayer life, for instance, which is partial if limited to the approach to a generic 'God' or to Jesus alone." Heim, "The Depth of Riches," 30.

[71] *God for Us*, 243.

[72] Ibid., 69.

[73] See John D. Zizioulas, *Being as Communion: Studies in Personhood and the Church* (Crestwood, N.Y.: St. Vladimir's Seminary Press, 1993); John Macmurray, op. cit.

This enables a "more equal" correlation between theology and psychology, Trinity and society, than we find in either Moltmann or Boff.

LaCugna argues that Macmurray's understanding of persons as agents in relationship situates persons in community as a constitutive context for their identity as persons. This emphasizes "community as the context in which true personhood emerges and apart from which persons do not exist at all." LaCugna therefore rejects any understanding of person as introspective, self-reflective, autonomous, or self-sufficient and extrapolates a definition of person as a "heterocentric, inclusive, free, relational agent."[74] She suggests that we can understand God as person (or as three persons) only by situating God as an agent in community or in a communion of persons.

In conjunction with her reading of the Cappadocians, LaCugna draws from Zizioulas an understanding of personhood as "being as relation." This enables her to claim that "God's To-be is To-be-in-relationship, and God's being-in-relationship-to-us *is* what God is."[75] Less tortuously, she is arguing that what God is in Godself, an identity that remains mysterious and unknowable, is constituted by relationship: the internal relationships between Father, Son, and Spirit, and the external relationships between these persons of God and creation. From this LaCugna can conclude that because humanity is created in the image of God, human "to-be" is "to-be-in-relationship" and human "being-in-relationship-to-God" is what we are. Even as our own identities are mysterious and not fully knowable, we know ourselves and are known, as God is known, by and in relationship.

LaCugna's reading of Zizioulas and Macmurray (more so than her reading of the Cappadocians) permits her to move toward a definition of human and divine being as "person-in-communion." Her goal throughout her discussion is to challenge us to think

[74] *God for Us*, 259. See Macmurray's understanding of "heterocentric" and "freedom" above, p. 129. Elizabeth Johnson similarly argues that "the Trinity provides a symbolic picture of totally shared life at the heart of the universe. It subverts duality into multiplicity. Mutual relationship of different equals appears as the ultimate paradigm of personal and social life. The Trinity as pure relationality, moreover, epitomizes the connectedness of all that exists in the universe." *She Who Is*, 222.

[75] *God for Us*, 250.

about the persons of the triune God as not "in" God but in God's relationship with and for the "others" of Godself, the world, and all humanity, and to discover in these relationships the character of our own lives as well as that of God. Like Moltmann and Boff, she concludes that God's identity as a personal agent in communion with Godself and creation as revealed in the history of God-with-us requires a Trinitarian theology that is social-relational.

THE PERICHORETIC GOD

Also common to Moltmann, Boff, and LaCugna is their retrieval of perichoresis as a theological and, I think, psychological framework for speaking about the interrelationship of the persons of the Trinity. The history of this term is not always clear. However, its earliest use was in reference to the intertwining of the human and divine natures in the person of Jesus Christ. Only later, in the work of John Damascene in the eighth century, is it used to refer to the (internal) inter-relationship of the persons of the Trinity.[76] Boff offers two definitions or descriptions of perichoresis: the first suggests a static state in which one being is contained within another, such as the indwelling of God/Father and Spirit in Christ. The second suggests a more dynamic state of interpenetration or interweaving of one person in and with others, indicating an active reciprocity between persons. An example of this active reciprocity: On the one hand, God/Father[77] acts in (or through) the Spirit and Mary in the incarnation of Jesus. On the other hand, God acts in and through Christ in the giving of the Spirit upon the church after the resurrection (in John) or at Pentecost (in Luke-Acts).[78]

For Boff, this perichoretic relationship is constitutive of the eternal and infinite communion of the persons of the Trinity. It is only

[76] While Moltmann, Boff, and LaCugna all summarize the discussions about perichoresis, a more thorough review is provided in Verna Harrison, "Perichoresis in the Greek Fathers," *St. Vladimir's Theological Quarterly* 35:1 (1991) 53–65. She traces its roots in the Christological work of Gregory Nazianzen to its adoption by Maximus Confessor and, finally, to its standardization in Trinitarian discussion in the work of John Damascene.

[77] As Trinitarian theologians make clear, while the name "Father" is problematic for many, substituting "God" in place of "Father" obscures the fact that Christ is God and that Spirit is God.

[78] *Trinity and Society*, 135.

in this interpenetration of the persons that we can speak about the unity of the one God.[79] As was said of their relationality, so we can say of the Trinitarian perichoresis: it is of the essence of God as it is revealed in the history of God with us. Even as God is related, intertwined, and interpenetrating within Godself, so this "union-communion-perichoresis opens outward: it invites human beings and the whole universe to insert themselves in the divine life," offering "a response to the great quest for participation, equality and communion that fires the understanding of the oppressed."[80] In this way the Trinity provides a grammar for the reciprocal participation of persons in community without requiring that diversity be sacrificed for such participation.

Moltmann expands on this image of openness within the divine perichoresis in a way that suggests the interrelated agency of the persons of the Trinity: "The trinitarian Persons do not merely exist and love in one another; they also bring one another mutually to manifestation in the divine glory."[81] Within the Trinity, this suggests an understanding of the agency of each person of the Trinity as an agency directed toward the other rather than the self. As Boff indicates, this suggests an openness toward and action on behalf of the Other as that Other is represented within God by the three persons and by the created Other presented in the human person. This openness suggests to Moltmann a correspondence of surrender and giving, care and relatedness between each of the divine persons of the Trinity.

Like Boff's suggestion that the perichoretic relationship within the Trinity responds to the quest for "participation, equality and communion," Moltmann argues that this perichoretic unity "corresponds to a human fellowship of people without privilege and without subordinances" and "to the experience of the community of Christ, the community which the Spirit unites through respect, affection, and love."[82] As in Boff, this perichoretic unity provides for Moltmann not only a means by which to preserve unity in the midst of diversity but to preserve diversity in the struggle for

[79] Ibid., 49.
[80] Ibid., 6, 11.
[81] *Trinity and the Kingdom*, 176.
[82] Ibid., 157–158.

unity. This perichoretic unity offers, then, a social-theological shape to the life of the church. "The true unity of the Church is an image of the perichoretic unity of the Trinity, so it can neither be a collective consciousness which represses the individuality of the persons, nor an individual consciousness which neglects what is in common."[83]

Finally, as if to summarize what Moltmann and Boff say about the perichoretic character of the Trinity as it points to the character of human being and community, LaCugna points to the way in which perichoresis expresses the idea that "the three divine persons mutually inhere in one another, draw life from one another, 'are' what they are by relation to one another." Within this, she highlights the importance of understanding perichoresis as a "being-in-one-another" that results in "permeation without confusion" rather than a blurring of self and other or dissolution of self in the other.[84] Perichoresis points to a way of life in and with others that preserves distinctiveness without it becoming individualistic, autonomous, or isolated. The Trinitarian grammar is a grammar about God and person by which we name God and ourselves in and by our history of relationship, or agency, with one another.

THE THEONOMOUS SELF:
THE SELF IN RELATION TO A RELATIONAL GOD

Through the preceding conversation between the cultural-linguistic faith grammar proposed by Lindbeck, the social-relational psychologies of Mead, Macmurray, and Kegan, and the Trinitarian faith grammar present in the theological explorations of Boff, LaCugna, and Moltmann, I am arguing that it is as difficult and as inappropriate to speak of expressive-experiential individualism as the norm of human religious "being" as it is to speak psychologically of the fully autonomous, separative individual as a norm of human "being." In terms of the constitutive and normative claims of liturgical practices in the formation of the Christian self, this argument summons us beyond the concern for personal happiness and holiness as practices related to the private or solitary person. It also summons us to a concern for the ways in which these goals

---

[83] Moltmann, *Spirit of Life*, 224.
[84] *God for Us*, 270–271.

are situated within and defined by the particular liturgical practices of particular communities of faith. I have argued also that the construction of a "faithed" self embedded in the particular sociolinguistic culture of Christianity embeds the self in a culture of relatedness structured by a Trinitarian grammar enacted in Christian narrative and practice. Given the plurality of cultures in which the human self lives and the various narratives that have arisen from and within a Christian grammar, we need now to describe a coherent and unitive sense of our many selves in relatedness to God as practiced in Christian liturgy.

The discussions of the preceding sections suggest a web of criteria and images with which to describe this Christian self. A summary of these images and criteria may be helpful. The prevailing images in the discussion of the relational theologies of the Trinity build upon an understanding of the revelation of the Trinitarian God in the practice of God's agential relatedness to humanity through creation, liberation, consolation, incarnation, passion, resurrection, and inspiration. The practice of God reveals Godself as mutually indwelling persons moving within one another in a reciprocal interrelatedness that Christian tradition calls "perichoresis." This the church celebrates and names in its doxological practice, whether in a form speaking of the co-equal glory of the three persons, "to the Father and the Son and the Spirit," or in the processual form, "to the Father through Christ in the Spirit."

While this practice of interrelatedness is oriented with and for the other, it is a practice that moves from the distinctiveness of the persons of God as relational agents to the distinctiveness of the other persons as relational agents. That is, the pattern of relatedness we find in the images, practices, and experiences of the Trinity is a pattern that moves from one person of the Trinity to another, creating a community that flows outward from the person into creation, humanity, and the future.

In the patterns described by the social psychologies above, the shape of human life and personhood reflects these theological patterns of relatedness, community, and outward-directedness. The human person, and the human sense of self, arises in a social context. Patterns of relatedness and mutuality, from the unequal mutuality of the mother and child to the equal "intermutuality" of adults in mature relationship, shape the emerging sense of self. For

Mead, these changing patterns of relatedness develop primarily through language; for Macmurray and Kegan, through agency and other forms of relatedness and care. All three suggest the development of the human self through relationships of "co-determination" between persons. The interaction of persons determines both self and other, establishes and interprets a pattern of action (focused on the past), and conditions the shape of the future. As Kegan identified, this co-determination of persons yields a balance between differentiation and integration, separation and attachment, autonomy and inclusion. In doing so, it makes possible the participation of the person in increasing matrices of relationship.[85]

Two statements by Kegan and Moltmann provide the clearest correlation between the perichoretic relationships of the Trinity and what Kegan calls the intersubjective self. Kegan argues that any particular culture of embeddedness must do three things to adequately serve the development of the human person as a person in relation. It must, first, hold securely, so as to provide confirmation as well as recognition of who the person has become. Second, "it must let go in a timely fashion" so as to assist in differentiation and contradiction. Third, "it must remain for recovery" during those transitional periods when the developing person "is leaving behind what seems still like itself and which the [person] must recover as part of its new organization."[86]

Moltmann's exploration of the perichoretic nature of the Trinity uses similar language. "In order to know one another, the lovers need not only union but detachment; not merely desire but also the setting-free; not solely the going out of the self but the withdrawal of the self too; not community alone, but also personhood."[87] The history of God in Christ, perhaps surprisingly, offers a concrete example of these patterns of relatedness. Does not God's pronounce-

---

[85] So, too, in Erik Erikson's work, as I noted in his treatment of ritual and ritualization in Chapter 3. In Erikson the progressive unfolding of psychosocial ritual forms from the numinous to the judicious, dramatic, and formal enable this balance Kegan describes. Erikson unwittingly (so it seems) describes this self balance in terms of the appropriate balance or median of virtue as we find named in Aristotle's discussion of the relative mean of virtue as established by the exercise of practical wisdom.

[86] *Evolving Self,* 158.

[87] *Spirit of Life,* 262.

ment that Jesus is God's beloved Son in the accounts of Jesus' baptism and transfiguration speak of confirmation, recognition, and personhood? Do not the accounts of the passion, death, and resurrection of Christ, from the prayers in the garden to the lamentation from the cross, speak of differentiation, contradiction, union, and detachment? Do not the resurrection and the outpouring of the Holy Spirit provide the framework for the recovery of the new self, the setting free of the person, and the gift of community?

These images and criteria suggest a number of ways we might describe the culture of embeddedness and the sense of self offered by liturgical practice for the construction of the Christian person as a person in relation to a relational God. To the extent that our postmodern context permits any language about "self," it requires us, at the least, to address the multiplicity of the self as well as the unitive sense of self. The temptation in this age of fragmentation may be to run toward and hang on to anything that provides integration and unity. Doing so, however, risks sacrificing the diversity of human being and community, committing Christians to liturgical, theological, and practical fundamentalisms. In this framework we may succeed in establishing a sense of self that, in its quest for unity, succeeds in so differentiating itself from others that it moves toward sectarianism, otherness, and autonomous communities. But there is another temptation expressed by those who turn from an emphasis on unity to multiplicity: to succumb to the relativity of self, belief, and practice. Our current North American context seems intent on pitting these two options against each other. The Trinitarian theologies and social-relational psychologies explored in this chapter address these concerns, offering ways to name the self that are neither reductive (the One) nor fragmentary (the many).[88] They also offer a way to name the self and to identify a culture of embeddedness that serves the perichoretic self.

[88] Among those theologians who emphasize the unitive sense of self or the unity (and difference) of the self in relationship to God, I think of Teilhard de Chardin's "divine milieu" and H. Richard Niebuhr's "responsible self." Both suggest models of relationality between persons and between persons and God but are so concerned to preserve the unity of the self and of God as to prevent any discussion of the multiplicity of the self or the tri-unity of God. Among those who seem to overemphasize multiplicity at cost to unity, I think of Catherine Keller's "web of interconnectedness." Keller guards against the

It is in the language and imagery of the perichoretic Trinity, particularly as developed in Catherine LaCugna's work, that I believe
we find a model of the relational self that meets the bipolar re-
quirements we find in Kegan and Moltmann. Perhaps surprisingly,
the language of perichoresis is both echoed in and returns us to the
interrelational language of Mead:

"our own selves exist and enter into our experience only in so far
as the selves of others exist and enter as such into our experience
also. The individual possesses a self only in relation to the selves of
other members of [one's] social group; and the structure of [one's]
self expresses or reflects the general behavior pattern of this social
group to which [one] belongs."[89]

It is in the divine perichoresis, the dance of the Trinity, the communion of persons, that we find an adequate way of describing the multiplicity of a self faithed in relation to God. It is here that we discover
the impossibility of either a pure heteronomy, as a "naming oneself
with reference to another," or a pure autonomy, as a "naming oneself with reference to oneself." Both of these options are destructive
of persons through the domination and oppression of the first and
the narcissism of the second. In the dance of the Trinity we find
"persons in relation" named only as they can be, in reference to another who is also oneself in relation. It is here in the dance that we
find the source and reference for the truly "theonomous" self, a self
"named with reference to its origin and destiny in God," an origin
and destiny of relatedness to and with God.[90]

---

implicit (and often explicit) hierarchy and patriarchy found in the "radical
monotheisms" as represented by Niebuhr. Nevertheless, her description of the
self as defined by only its web of relationships results, at least in appearance,
in the eddies described by Mead disappearing and the stream emptying into a
broad and deep lake. Where Teilhard de Chardin and Niebuhr end with the
One, Keller only sees the many. See Pierre Teilhard de Chardin, *The Divine
Milieu* (New York: Harper and Row, 1968) 114–116; H. Richard Niebuhr, *The
Responsible Self* (New York: Harper and Row, 1963) 122–125; and Catherine
Keller, *From a Broken Web: Separation, Sexism and Self* (Boston: Beacon Press,
1986) 180–181, 225–227.

[89] *Mind, Self, and Society*, 164.

[90] LaCugna, *God for Us*, 290. It is worth noting that even with her brief reference to the "theonomous self," LaCugna never once cites Tillich's use of the
term, despite the imaginal parallels between their use of it. Tillich's discussion

It is the theonomous self as "a relational self in relationship to a relational God" that best describes not only the socially constructed self but the self related in and emerging from the particular culture of embeddedness of Christian liturgical practice. In the divine perichoresis of the Trinity it becomes possible to take the attitude of a related/relational God to oneself, to see oneself as an object of God's relatedness, and to see God as an "object" of our own relatedness. This perichoretic relatedness, or theonomy, also

---

of "theonomy" is not extensive, but he repeats it several times in his work and gives it careful definitional attention. Tillich distinguishes theonomy from autonomy and heteronomy, less in terms of negation or contrast than in terms of a Hegelian sublation *(Aufhebung)*. Autonomy refers to a form of reason and action of the individual person by which the person obeys the law of reason found within the self, affirming and actualizing the structure of reason "without regarding its depth" or its rootedness in the ground of being itself. [*Systematic Theology* 1 (Chicago: University of Chicago Press, 1951) 83.] The autonomous self seems to be the paradigm of the modern rational subject.

In contrast to the autonomous self is the heteronomous self, with which theonomy is most often confused. Heteronomy "issues commands from 'outside' on how reason should grasp and shape reality," imposing itself on the functions of reason (Tillich, 83.) Heteronomous reason claims the authority of God and speaks in an unconditional and ultimate way, as do tyrants and dictators. It is a form in which impersonal structure rather than personal presence is the priority. [David Novak, "Theonomous Ethics: A Defense and a Critique of Tillich," *Soundings* 69 (Winter 1986) 437.] Tillich sees such authority expressed in myth and cult as the means to dominate "autonomous cultural creativity from the outside." [*The Protestant Era*, trans. James Luther Adams (Chicago: University of Chicago Press, 1948) xvi.] Heteronomy is hierarchical and authoritarian, autonomy individualistic and "self-complacent." Heteronomy dominates culture, autonomy exhausts and empties culture.

Theonomy, in contrast, "does not mean the acceptance of a divine law imposed on reason by a highest authority" but the uniting of the structure and ground of reason in God and manifest in the "theonomous situation." (Tillich, *Systematic Theology* 1:85.) Tillich describes such situations as periods that

> "do not feel split, but whole and centered. Their center is neither their heteronomous authority but the depth of reason ecstatically experienced and symbolically expressed. Myth and cult give them a unity in which all spiritual functions are centered. Culture is not controlled from outside by the church, nor is it left alone so that the community of the New Being stand beside it. Culture receives its substance and integrating power from the community of the New Being, from its symbols and its life" (*Systematic Theology* 1:148–149).

meets Kegan's three criteria for a "culture of embeddedness." It offers (1) the confirmation and recognition that I am a self in relationship to God and God is in relationship to me; (2) differentiation and contradiction, that in relationship I am not God but self, and God is not me but God, and while we are many, we are also one; and (3) a place of stability where the self can "find" or recover that which had been "lost" in development, where I and those with whom I am in relationship are transformed.

How, then, do we liturgically practice this Trinitarian pattern as a "grammar" not only for Christian doctrine and belief but also for the shape of Christian living? This is the question of the next chapter.

J. Mark Thomas describes the theonomous period this way: "In theonomy, the churches are transformed into a holy community with universal inclusiveness, and 'more embracing unities' are created, including those excluded from particular communities (family, friendship, class)." ["Theonomous Social Ethics: Paul Tillich's Neoclassical Interpretation of Justice," in *Being and Doing: Paul Tillich as Ethicist*, ed. John J. Casey (Macon, Ga.: Mercer University Press, 1987) 121.]

Tillich's description of the theonomous situation as "ecstatically experienced and symbolically expressed" provides a significant link to LaCugna's construction of the theonomous self, particularly her discussion, through Zizioulas, of *ecstasis* and of the role of liturgical doxology as a framework for and mode of that expression.

Chapter Six

Trinitarian Grammar and Liturgical Practice

O let us on thy fullness feed[1]

Throughout this book I have been exploring an assertion that sacramental liturgical practices are means of meaningful, constitutive, and normative action by which the church and Christian people give expression to who it and they are and by which church and persons "practice" themselves as Christian in a Trinitarian mode. In this chapter I want to explore this assertion in the context of particular liturgical practices. My exploration falls into three parts. In the first, I examine several Trinitarian prayer forms that John Wesley had in hand or edited. In the second, I explore two contemporary Methodist eucharistic prayers as forms of meaningful action in which we "practice ourselves" in a Trinitarian mode. In the third, I briefly explore how the practices of baptism, or baptismal reaffirmation, and confession also serve the practice of the theonomous self.

THE WESLEYS AND THE TRINITY
Lindbeck's cultural-linguistic proposal, explored in the previous chapter, attempts to address the problem of Christian discourse in a post-Constantinian, postliberal age. In John and Charles Wesley's

[1] Hymn 493, "Saviour of all, to thee we bow," stanza 5, in *The Works of John Wesley*, vol. 7: *A Collection of Hymns for the use of the People called Methodists*, ed. Franz Hildebrandt and Oliver Beckerlegge (Oxford: Clarendon Press; New York: Oxford University Press, 1983) 682.

day, Christian discourse was in the process of moving into the still Constantinian but "enlightened" liberal modern age. In some ways the Wesleys struggled to hold on to the cultural-linguistic structures of Scripture and prayerbook as Enlightenment philosophy moved to set aside the sense of Scripture as a "realistic narrative" of the world.[2] Yet in a context that increasingly privileged human experience, both John and Charles attempted to provide a means of accounting for Christian experience within the scriptural narrative of the world. Perhaps one of the marks of the early Methodist movement was its ability to hold the experiential and cultural-linguistic structures together. This seems to be particularly true in the ways in which both John and Charles appropriated the language of Scripture and prayerbook in their sermons and hymns. This is also true in John Wesley's understanding of the particular and instituted means of grace as forms of meaningful action that are constitutive of and normative for the Christian life, as we explored in the first chapter.

The Wesleys' *Hymns on the Trinity* and *Hymns on the Lord's Supper* have received significant attention as primary expressions of their Trinitarian and eucharistic theology.[3] The various writers remind us that the Wesleys expected their hymns to be read in private devotion as well as sung in corporate worship. In this way the hymns instructed and formed the Methodist societies in particular understandings of Christian faith and doctrine. These writers also re-

[2] In Gary Dorrien's recent brief summary of postliberalism, he describes this loss of Scripture as realistic narrative in the Enlightenment. See "The Origins of Postliberalism: A Third Way in Theology," *Christian Century* 118:20 (July 4–11, 2001) 16–21.

[3] See J. Ernest Rattenbury, *The Eucharistic Hymns of John and Charles Wesley* (London: Epworth Press, 1948; rpt. and rev. Cleveland: OSL Publications, 1995); Kathryn Nichols, "Charles Wesley's Eucharistic Hymns: Their Relationship to the Book of Common Prayer," *The Hymn* 39:2 (April 1988) 13–21; Teresa Berger, *Doxology in Hymns?* (Nashville: Abingdon Press, Kingswood Books, 1994); Barry E. Bryant, "Trinity and Hymnody: The Doctrine of the Trinity in the Hymns of Charles Wesley," *Wesleyan Theological Journal* 25:2 (Fall 1990) 64–73; David Tripp, "Methodism's Trinitarian Hymnody: A Sampling, 1780 and 1989, and Some Questions," *Quarterly Review* 14:4 (1994) 359–385; Geoffrey Wainwright, "Why Wesley Was a Trinitarian," *Drew Gateway* 59:2 (1990) 26–43; and Wilma J. Quantrille, *The Triune God in the Hymns of Charles Wesley*, Ph.D. dissertation, Drew University, 1989 (Ann Arbor: UMI, 1993).

mind us that the hymns and hymnals provide the most systematic working out of the Wesleys' theology. I do not intend to repeat their work here. My concern is with the tradition of prayer the Wesleys inherited and shaped. Are there seeds of their Trinitarian theology in the liturgical texts which shaped them and which they used throughout their lives as Anglican priests?

In asking these questions, I am suggesting that John and Charles brought and offered to Methodist doxological practice and theology what they themselves practiced doxologically. Two examples will suffice. The first, a eucharistic preface for the Feast of Trinity, comes from John's edition of the 1662 *Book of Common Prayer* for the North American Methodists:

> It is very meet, right, and our bounden duty,
> that we should at all times, and in all places give thanks unto thee,
> O Lord, Holy Father, Almighty, Everlasting God.
> Who art one God, one Lord;
> not one only person, but three persons, in one substance.
> For that which we believe of the glory of the Father,
> the same we believe of the Son, and of the Holy Ghost,
> without difference or inequality.[4]

This eucharistic preface represents something of an *inclusio* for the Wesleys' Trinitarian theology; they first received this liturgy in their own Anglican formation and then commended it to the new church as it took shape in North America. As with the creed and articles of religion, this preface summarizes the doxological and doctrinal language for the Trinity that was read and heard in John's letters and sermons and sung in Charles' hymns over the preceding fifty years. It also summarizes the Trinitarian faith contained in the (abridged) *Articles of Religion* John included in *The Sunday Service.* It states in doxological form the "fact" of the Trinity

---

[4] *John Wesley's Prayer Book: The Sunday Service of the Methodists in North America*, introduction, notes, and commentary by James F. White (Cleveland: OSL Publications, 1991) 135. In light of recent eucharistic reforms, it is interesting to note that with the exception of the doxology in the post-communion prayer, the Holy Spirit is not otherwise mentioned in the eucharistic prayer of the *Sunday Service.* Aside from this preface, the only other place the Trinity is explicitly named is in the *Glory to God in the highest*, recited by the congregation following the post-communion prayer.

that John believed and beyond which he would not speculate.[5] We might argue that his repeated experience with the language of *person* and *substance* as found in this prayer permitted nothing "to constrain him" from using it in preaching, conversation, and reflection.[6] Unsurprisingly, it does not deviate from the Trinitarian faith articulated in the Nicene-Constantinopolitan Creed: three persons, one substance, without difference or inequality.

The second example is an excerpt from the prayer for Sunday morning as found in "A Collection of Forms of Prayer," first printed in 1733 and continuing in print into the early nineteenth century. Here Wesley provides a (non-eucharistic) prayer that finds its most worthy parallel in the eucharistic prefaces of the Eastern churches.[7] Again, it is an explicit practice of Trinitarian doxology. I quote only part:

> Glory be to thee, O most adorable Father,
> who, after thou hadst finished the work of creation,
> enteredst into thy eternal rest.
> Glory be to thee, O holy Jesus,
>   who having through the eternal Spirit,
> offered thyself a full, perfect, and sufficient sacrifice[8]

[5] See "Letter to a member of the society," August 3, 1771, in John Wesley, *The Works of John Wesley*, XII, ed. Thomas Jackson (London: Wesleyan Methodist Book Room, 1871) 293; and "On the Trinity," Sermon 55, in John Wesley, *The Works of John Wesley*, vol. 2: *Sermons*, ed. Albert Outler (Nashville: Abingdon Press, 1984) 376–377.

[6] "On the Trinity," 378.

[7] It is unfortunate that, as Wesley's first publication, a critical edition of these prayers is not yet available. John makes one reference to these prayers outside of the 1775 preface printed in *Works*, XIV, ed. Jackson, 270–271. This comes in the context of a letter of May 14, 1765, tracing the development of his understanding of perfection. There he indicates that the prayers were printed for the use of his pupils (ibid., 213.) The preface of 1775 provides a helpful summary of the spirituality formed in and by these prayers: "to comprise in the course of petitions for the week the whole scheme of our Christian duty" (ibid., 270). This scheme is further described under five headings: (1) renouncing ourselves, (2) devoting ourselves to God, (3) self-denial, (4) mortification—dying to the world and the things of the world, and (5) Christ living in me. As this last stage is representative of fulfilling the law, Wesley suggests a sixth stage, the step into glory (ibid., 271–272).

[8] Here Wesley seems to echo the "offertory prayer" as found in the *Book of Common Prayer*.

for the sins of the whole world,

didst rise again the third day from the dead,

and hadst all power given to thee both in heaven and on earth.

Glory be to thee, O blessed Spirit,

who proceeding from the Father and the Son,

didst come down in fiery tongues on the Apostles on the first
    day of the week,

and didst enable them to preach the glad tidings of salvation to a
    sinful world,

and hast ever since been moving on the faces of men's souls,

as thou didst once on the face of the great deep,

bringing them out of that dark chaos in which they were involved.

Glory be to thee, O holy, undivided Trinity,

for jointly concurring in the great work of our redemption,

and restoring us again to the glorious liberty of the sons of God.

Glory be to thee, who, in compassion to human weakness,

hast appointed a solemn day for the remembrance of thy
    inestimable benefits.[9]

As text and practice commended to the Methodists throughout John's life, this, too, seems to provide a Trinitarian *inclusio* around his theological work. On the theological level, as Geoffrey Wainwright reminds us more broadly of Wesley's Trinitarian theology, this prayer is an example of Trinitarian doxology grounded in the soteriological work of the Trinity.[10] A "Father-Creator, Jesus-Redeemer, Spirit-Sanctifier" division of labor was unthinkable and unprayable for Wesley. As represented here, the work of creation is the work of Father and Spirit; the work of redemption, the work of the three-personed but undivided Trinity.

The doxological character of these examples point us to John's argument in his sermon "On the Trinity" that the doctrine of the Trinity is something that is more to be practiced than to be understood. As Thomas Oden summarizes, "The manner in which God is three in one can be left to honest, humble adoration and celebration as a mystery of faith."[11] The Wesleys' resistance to "speculative theology" is also reflected in Charles Wesley's eucharistic hymn "O

---

[9] *Works*, XI, ed. Jackson, 203.

[10] Wainwright, "Why Wesley Was a Trinitarian," 26, 33, 35.

[11] *John Wesley's Scriptural Christianity*, (Grand Rapids: Zondervan, 1994) 47.

the depth of love divine." Wesley wrote: "Ask the Father's wisdom how: Christ who did the means ordain; angels round our altars bow to search it out in vain."[12] In this way, as liturgical theologian Aidan Kavanagh has suggested, the liturgy serves as a means through which the church transacts or works out its "faith in God under the condition of God's real presence in both church and world."[13] Such practices of humble adoration and celebration lead us precisely where speculation will not, to the lived understanding of the triune faith. These two examples, while expressions of Wesley's Trinitarian faith, are offered to the Methodist societies and church as a means by which they may be formed in this faith and by which they may "practice" themselves as "Christian" in a Trinitarian mode. As Ted Campbell observes in his discussion of the Wesleyan doctrine of God, "the goal of salvation is to restore the lost image of God, which is a Trinitarian image."[14]

THE TRINITARIAN-RELATIONAL GRAMMAR OF EUCHARISTIC PRACTICE

As Geoffrey Wainwright has argued, "The sacraments, in the plural, are signs to sharpen our vision of the divine presence in the world" and enable us "to shape our will and our action conformable with God's in configuration with Christ."[15] As such, it is possible to understand liturgical practice, and in particular eucharistic prayer and action, as a practice of a Trinitarian-relational grammar that shapes person and community.

Let us look, then, at two recent Methodist eucharistic texts as doxological modes for the practice and expression of this grammar.[16] These two texts reflect new self-understandings that

[12] *The United Methodist Hymnal* (Nashville: The United Methodist Publishing House, 1989) 627.

[13] *On Liturgical Theology* (New York: Pueblo Publishing Co., 1984) 8.

[14] "'Pure, Unbounded Love' Doctrine about God in Historic Wesleyan Communities," in M. Douglas Meeks, ed., *Trinity, Community, and Power: Mapping Trajectories in Wesleyan Theology* (Nashville: Abingdon Press, Kingswood Books, 2000) 91.

[15] Geoffrey Wainwright, *Doxology: The Praise of God in Worship, Doctrine and Life* (New York: Oxford University Press, 1980) 408.

[16] I am using the "normal" texts of the United Methodist and British Methodist churches as presented in "Word and Table I" in *The United Methodist Hymnal* 9–10, *The United Methodist Book of Worship* (Nashville: The United Methodist Publishing House, 1992) 36–38, and "Holy Communion for

might not have been possible prior to the ecumenical work that preceded them. Both texts reflect the ecumenical consensus regarding the overall content and shape of the eucharistic prayer.[17] They reflect, also, the recovery of a more explicit Trinitarian pattern. Both texts include, in some order and fashion, thanksgiving, anamnesis, invocation of the Spirit, communion of the faithful, and the meal of the kingdom. When outlined, we find that the two prayers are identical in their structure and orientation toward a Trinitarian pattern, with eight common elements: (1) *sursum corda*, (2) thanksgiving to God, (3) Sanctus/ Benedictus, (4) anamnesis/commemoration of Christ,[18] (5) institution narrative, (6) memorial and acclamation, (7) epiclesis/invocation of the Holy Spirit, and (8) Trinitarian doxology.

UNITED METHODIST

It is right, and a good and joyful thing,
always and every where to give thanks to you,

Ordinary Seasons (First Service)" of *The Methodist Worship Book* (Peterborough, England: Methodist Publishing House, 1999) 192–194. That these patterns are normative for the church seems a disputed point, especially in North America. On this, it is worth noting that the services of the church, as part of the *Hymnal* and *Book of Worship*, require authorization by the General Conference. Also, the ordinal of the North American church asks elders to receive the liturgies of the church. The preface to *The Methodist Service Book* (Peterborough, Eng.: Methodist Publishing House, 1975), in a discussion of the relationship between free and fixed prayer in Methodist liturgical life, argues that the forms presented in the book "are not intended, any more than those in earlier books, to curb creative freedom, but rather to provide *norms* [my emphasis] for its guidance" (vii). The preface to *The Methodist Worship Book* states that these words still apply (viii). A concise review of these issues, of the development and reform of these services, and of liturgical life throughout world Methodism is provided in Karen B. Westerfield Tucker, ed., *The Sunday Service of the Methodists: Twentieth-Century Worship in Worldwide Methodism* (Nashville: Abingdon Press, Kingswood Books, 1996).

[17] On this consensus, see *Baptism, Eucharist and Ministry* (Geneva: World Council of Churches, 1982) 10–17, as well as Thomas Best and Dagmar Heller, eds., *Eucharistic Worship in Ecumenical Contexts* (Geneva: World Council of Churches, 1998).

[18] I am aware that some would reserve the designation *anamnesis* to that portion of the prayer following the institution narrative that is concluded by the memorial acclamation. I am convinced, however, that items 4-6 constitute the fullness of the re-membering and re-presenting of Christ.

157

Father almighty, creator of heaven and earth.
You formed us in your image and breathed into us the breath
    of life.
When we turned away, and our love failed, your love remained
    steadfast.
You delivered us from captivity,
made covenant to be our sovereign God,
and spoke to us through your prophets.
And so, with your people on earth and all the company of heaven
we praise your name and join their unending hymn:
Holy, holy, holy Lord . . .
Holy are you, and blessed is your Son Jesus Christ.
Your Spirit anointed him to preach good news to the poor,
to proclaim release to the captives and recovering of sight to
    the blind,
to set at liberty those who are oppressed,
and to announce that the time had come when you would save
    your people.
He healed the sick, fed the hungry, and ate with sinners.
By the baptism of his suffering, death, and resurrection
you gave birth to your church,
delivered us from slavery to sin and death,
and made with us a new covenant by water and the Spirit.
When the Lord Jesus ascended, he promised to be with us always,
in the power of your Word and Holy Spirit.
On the night in which he gave himself up for us. . .
And so, in remembrance of these your mighty acts in Jesus Christ,
we offer ourselves in praise and thanksgiving
as a holy and living sacrifice,
in union with Christ's offering for us,
as we proclaim the mystery of faith:
Christ has died . . .
Pour out your Holy Spirit on us gathered here,
and on these gifts of bread and wine.
Make them be for us the body and blood of Christ,
redeemed by his blood.
By your Spirit make us one with Christ,
one with each other, and one in ministry to all the world,

until Christ comes in final victory and we feast at his heavenly
banquet.
Through your Son Jesus Christ,
with the Holy Spirit in your Holy Church,
all honor and glory is yours, almighty Father, now and forever.
Amen.

BRITISH METHODIST

We praise you, gracious Father, our Maker and Sustainer.
You created the heavens and the earth and formed us in your
own image.
Though we sinned against you, your love for us was constant,
and you sent your Son Jesus Christ to be the Saviour of the world.
Sharing our human nature, he was born of Mary, and baptized in
the Jordan.
He proclaimed your kingdom, by word and deed,
and was put to death upon the cross.
You raised him from the dead; you exalted him in glory;
and through him you have sent your Holy Spirit,
calling us to be your people, a community of faith.
And so, with angels and archangels and all the choirs of heaven,
we join in the triumphant hymn:
Holy, holy, holy Lord . . .
Holy God, we praise you that on the night in which he was
betrayed. . .
Remembering, therefore, his death and resurrection,
and proclaiming his eternal sacrifice,
we offer ourselves to you in praise and thanksgiving,
as we declare the mystery of faith:
Christ has died . . .
Send down your Holy Spirit that these gifts of bread and wine
may be for us the body and blood of Christ.
Unite us with him forever
and bring with the whole creation to your eternal kingdom.
Through Christ, with Christ, in Christ,
in the power of the Holy Spirit,
we worship you in songs of everlasting praise.
Blessing and honour and glory and power
be yours forever and ever. Amen.

While similar in shape and theology, these texts also reveal subtle theological distinctions. The United Methodist prayer tends toward compartmentalizing the persons of the Trinity. For example, the preface focuses on God as Father and "creator of heaven and earth" and of humanity without naming the other persons of the Trinity. In doing so, it recounts God's covenant faithfulness and redeeming work prior to the incarnation of the Son. In contrast, the preface in the British Methodist text names the whole Trinity, offering thanksgiving explicitly to the Father through Jesus Christ the Son, through whom the Holy Spirit is sent.[19] Both prayers also tend to speak of God's creating relationship to humanity to the neglect of the rest of creation, in contrast to other recent eucharistic prayers.[20]

As anamnesis and commemoration of Christ's life, death and resurrection, the United Methodist prayer gives more attention to the emancipatory praxis of Christ, uniting it to the work of the Spirit that anoints Christ for this work and will be poured out upon us. It includes in this praxis the inauguration of the eschatological time. This attention to emancipatory praxis is distinctive among the recent generation of eucharistic prayers; it provides a doxological expression of the Wesleyan commitment to personal and social holiness. As anamnesis, it operates here to "reappropriate Christ in the present so that we are caught up into his very being and are continuing the redemptive history of God-with-us. Thus, in our corporate memory, recited and proclaimed, we are given identity in Christ and a foretaste of the ultimate messianic banquet."[21] The intent is to enable the Christian community to re-

[19] The second prayer for Ordinary Seasons in the *Methodist Worship Book*, 203–207, is shaped more like the United Methodist prayer in its compartmentalization of the persons of the Trinity. This second prayer is distinctive in that it begins "God our Father and Mother."

[20] For example, the preface to eucharistic prayer A in the Presbyterian *Book of Common Worship* (Louisville: Westminster/John Knox Press, 1990) names God as Lord, creator and ruler of the universe, who has made all things and sustains them by God's power (69). The first preface for Ordinary Time recounts God's creation of light and darkness, the sea and land, the universe, all of which God calls good. These acts of creation are recounted before the narrative of God's creation of humanity (133).

[21] *Companion to the Book of Services* (Nashville: Abingdon Press, 1988) 39.

ceive "a history more powerful than mere 'remembered events' and a future far greater than natural expectation" in order "to love, to serve, and to worship God 'between the times' of God's redemptive acts in Christ and the coming in final victory of God in Christ at the end of history."[22]

The anamnetic character of the British text is more concise. With the exception of the institution narrative, it is limited in place to the preface. In creedal fashion the text remembers Christ sharing our human nature, born of Mary, baptized in the Jordan, dying, raised from the dead, and exalted in glory. This narration provides a balance of the incarnate (sharing, born, baptized) and glorified (dying, raised, exalted) Christ. Narration of Christ's relational praxis is limited to naming Christ's proclamation of the kingdom "by word and deed" and recounting the gifting of the Holy Spirit through him.

As anamnesis gives way to oblation, both prayers describe the offering as an offering of ourselves in praise and thanksgiving. In the United Methodist prayer, the community offers itself in praise and thanksgiving and is joined with Christ's offering for us. Its self-offering is a means by which it remembers Christ's offering. In the British prayer the community's offering of praise and thanksgiving comes in response to its remembrance of Christ's offering. In both prayers it is the human community, the church, rather than the bread and cup, that is offered as "a holy and living sacrifice."[23] The language at this point in each prayer also reflects different attitudes about the character of the community. United Methodists seem more assertive with their offering: "and so, in remembrance . . . we offer ourselves . . . as a holy and living sacrifice." The British are more reticent: "Remembering . . . and proclaiming . . . we offer ourselves to you."

[22] Ibid., 39–40.

[23] This raises a question about the nature of the gifts of bread and wine. Both liturgies provide for the bread and wine to be brought to the table with "the other gifts" of the community or for the bread and wine to be uncovered if already in place. With the former action, bread and wine are given dual meaning as the gifts of the people *and* the gifts of God. Such meaning is less clear in the latter action, where the already present gifts are uncovered or unveiled. The former suggests a divine-human cooperation in the gifts, perhaps a Wesleyan synergism. The latter suggests a Wesleyan prevenient presence of God's gifts and grace.

Finally, as thanksgiving and anamnesis turn to epiclesis and petition, we find several subtle contrasts. In the British prayer the Holy Spirit is invoked so that the gifts of bread and wine may be the body and blood of Christ, but the Spirit is not directed upon the gifts. The petition that we may be united with Christ and brought into the kingdom is directed, as the whole of the prayer is, to the Father, without direct action from the Spirit. In contrast, the United Methodist prayer invokes the power of the Spirit upon the gifts and the people with explicit missional intent. The prayer intends our transformation through the Spirit "that we may be for the world the body of Christ" and that by the power of the Spirit we may be made one with Christ and with one another for the sake of ministry to the world. Overall, both prayers are addressed to the Father, who acts through Christ and the Spirit. Yet, the British prayer emphasizes the christological narrative, "remembering . . . his death and resurrection, and proclaiming his eternal sacrifice," and the United Methodist prayer gives more balanced attention to the work of each person of the Trinity.

The practical intent in both prayers is clearly to offer God thanks and praise, to commemorate the event of Jesus Christ, and to invoke the Holy Spirit in relationship to the primary symbols of bread and cup, all as a means of effecting the communion and community of the faithful. In spite of identical structures and much common language, I have emphasized the modest differences between these two prayers as a way to keep our attention on the Trinitarian grammar they practice in doxology.

I have three concluding points concerning these two texts as they relate to my question of the Trinitarian grammar of the liturgy as the doxological practice of the Christian self. First, these prayers are marked by an eschatological expectation that names a horizon of meaning for particular Christian communities.[24] This horizon is

---

[24] My intent here is a brief note, not exhaustive study. Geoffrey Wainwright's *Eucharist and Eschatology* (New York: Oxford University Press, 1981) continues to provide the most comprehensive historical and theological review of this theme. One of the Wesleyan hymns on the Trinity provides an example of the linking of Trinity, eschatology, and person. In Hymn 19 in the Wesleys' *Gloria Patri, etc., or Hymns to the Trinity* (London, 1746), especially stanzas 3-4 (stanza 1 is addressed to the Father, stanza 2 to the Son), we find the following:

defined by the pairings of memory and hope, history and future, creation and eschaton. These juxtapositions are most clearly imaged with language that speaks of the "already but not yet" character of the eucharist in which we thank the Triune God for what has been accomplished and, proleptically, for what will yet be accomplished. We are present *now* at the Lord's table; at the same time, we anticipate our presence at the table of the messianic banquet. We offer our thanksgiving this Lord's Day in anticipation of our participation in the Day of the Lord.

The United Methodist prayer, in particular, ties our memory and history to events of failed love and unfaithfulness on the part of humanity. Hope and future are dependent on God's steadfast love in spite of such failing, on God's liberation of humanity from its captivity, and on the covenant God initiates. The events of creation (although limited in these prayers to creation of the human creature) and Christ's final victory enclose the actions of liberation and covenant.

Second, these prayers provide an intersection of existential, transcendental, and political horizons and meanings. In eucharistic practice the community of faith models and engages in emancipatory practice, re-memorative creativity, and prescriptive achievement. As it does so, however, it doxologically names these activities as God's activity, in which the community now participates. More simply, it is the place where individual lives in all their brokenness meet with the reality of the community, city, and nation yearning for their own perfection and where all these encounter the limitations of their createdness and creatureliness in a holy transaction with God. As David Power helps us see, in the symbolic nature of the liturgy the "symbols dare to express a totality of meaning [which we may not grasp], to present to the human mind

---

O Spirit of Might, of Joy, and of Love,
Who guidest us right To mansions above,
Whose hallowing Graces for Heaven prepare:
We pay Thee our Praises 'Till Glorified there.

There, there we shall see The Substance Divine,
And fashion'd like Thee Transcendently shine,
Thy Personal Essence So bold to explain,
And wrapt in thy Presence Eternally reign.

the ultimate and the transcendent. The imagination dares to speak beyond knowing. It presents the ultimate not as acquired but as desirable, not as attained but as attainable."[25] At the level of relationships between persons as well as those between persons and God, we are confronted with the historical character—the successes and failures—of those relationships. At the same time, we see or hope for relationships that are yet to be or are becoming.

The petitions to share in and be made one with the body of Christ for the world make this clear in both prayers. The United Methodist prayer expands the meaning of this transformation in its explicit work of anamnesis and proclamation. The time has come and now is when the poor hear the good news, captives are released, the blind are healed, and the oppressed set at liberty. Although the British prayer speaks more clearly of Christ's exaltation in glory, both prayers look toward Christ's final coming in glory, which remains on the distant horizon, around the bend, as it were. But in our doxological transaction the existential and political horizons are seen to intersect now, in the fact of the resurrection, in Christ's ability to "overcome every power that can hurt or divide us."

As a critical grammar of the self, these prayers are distinctive in the absence of the language of individualism and autonomy. Both prayers speak in the plural: Christ's historic activity is now occurring with *us*. *We* have turned away and our love failed, *we* are delivered from captivity, slavery and death, *we* are promised Christ's presence in Word and Spirit, *we* are made one body in Christ for the world, *we* are brought with the whole creation into the kingdom. In this, both prayers reveal a grammar of relatedness to persons and world that has political ethical consequences, a relatedness of persons that exemplifies a relationship we might name as *lex orandi statuat lex vivendi*, "the law of prayer establishes the law of living." Speaking in the plural also simultaneously subverts clerical attempts to usurp the eucharistic prayer as private prayer and challenges the dominant individualistic piety found in many of our churches. These actions are emphasized in the British prayer as the congregation speaks the whole of the concluding doxology rather than only offering the concluding "Amen."

[25] *Unsearchable Riches: The Symbolic Nature of the Liturgy* (New York: Pueblo Publishing Co., 1984) 173.

Finally, this horizon of meaning provides a vision of both the moral ideal and the ontological reality of human existence grounded in the as yet unfinished Trinitarian revelation of Godself. Each prayer, Trinitarian in shape and address, speaks of God's presence, agency, and relationship in history and creation, as well as of the expectation for relationship with God beyond history. The doxological work of the Christian community speaks of the pattern of God's self-communication, God's "practice," as displaying a "trinitarian logic; . . . a relational onto-logic that shows the very form and content of the divine life as triune."[26] Each prayer provides a grammar of thanksgiving to God, through Christ, in the Holy Spirit that names "who we are, whose we are, and where God is leading us." This refers to the inaugurated yet unfinished inbreaking of God's dominion into the world and our liminal status on the threshold of that inbreaking. It is the juxtaposition of the "not yet" with the "already" of Christ's presence at the banquet table and in the world. It is also the juxtaposition of our presence and anticipated presence at the Lord's table.

The reality of eucharistic practice is that all of this happens now as we are gathered about the Lord's table Sunday after Sunday. The ideal, the moral vision, is that while all creation is invited to the feast, we are in ministry to the world until that is made to happen. Eucharistic practice, then, "sharpens our vision," "shapes our will and action," and forms us in the life of Christ. More than this, it provides the practice of seeing, hearing, tasting, touching, and smelling the divine presence. As such a tangible practice, it shapes our will and action, molds us into the image and likeness of Christ, and prepares us for the life of glory. These eucharistic prayers, as prayer texts, enable us to proclaim our faith.

And yet, several disclaimers are in order. These eucharistic texts in themselves cannot tell us how often any particular church celebrates eucharist (a problem for many of our churches), whether people stand or sit for the prayer, or whether the bread and wine are to be received sitting in the pew, kneeling at the altar rail, or standing in procession. They do not tell us about the character of the bread and wine (or grape juice) or of the gestures that may or

[26] Don Saliers, *Worship as Theology: Foretaste of Glory Divine* (Nashville: Abingdon Press, 1994) 71.

may not accompany the word actions of the text. They do not reveal the nature of the preaching and praying that form the context for the great thanksgiving, nor do they tell us about the people who are engaged in this performance. They do not describe the configuration of the building and the placement of the table, or the sights and smells present to the community. A fuller practical theology would require that we attend to such questions. As we saw in the congregations described in the Introduction, the presence or absence of these texts, or texts like them, also has implications for the grammar of prayer and faith in each congregation. Even so, while these prayer forms do not tell us many things, as prayer forms they do represent a grammar of prayer and faith. As texts, they represent normative theological statements by the church. As texts that Christians pray, sing, and perform, they represent normative doxological practices of the church.

Another proviso: while the eucharistic prayer shapes the "source and summit" of the liturgy—the celebration of the eucharist—it is incomplete in itself. It requires the balance of Word read, proclaimed, and engaged, of prayers that gather up the joys and sorrows of the community, of song, gesture, and dance, of silence and stillness interweaving with one another or starkly juxtaposed against the other.[27] This is itself a critical point for the grammar of the liturgy as a whole. Each portion of the liturgy makes a distinctive contribution to the performance of the whole. In some cases these practices support, complement, and fill out what is more concisely expressed in doxological form in the eucharistic prayer. In other cases these practices stand in strong, critical tension with the grammar of the eucharistic prayer.

For now, we will have to be content with the intended faith grammar as it is presented rather than the grammar performed or practiced. Nevertheless, if these texts are received as the normal

[27] For a discussion of the character of juxtaposition exemplified by the liturgy, see Gordon Lathrop, *Holy Things: A Liturgical Theology* (Minneapolis: Fortress Press, 1993). Among the liturgical juxtapositions Lathrop describes are those of "our actions and symbols with biblical words, word and table, Sunday meeting and seven-day week, texts-with-preaching and thanksgiving-before-eating, holy people with "the one holy Lord," praise and beseeching (see pages 11, 21, 52, 53). For Lathrop, it is in these chains of juxtaposition that meaning is created (65).

and, I would argue, normative way in which the church gives thanks, remembers, and enacts God's saving Word, they articulate in the content of the prayer who and whose we are even as they point to our future in and with God.

OTHER LITURGICAL PRACTICES

While the eucharist is central to the liturgical, sacramental, spiritual, and missional life of the church, it does not, nor can it, bear the entire weight of the formation of the theonomous self. In light of the criteria presented above, I want to name, primarily by way of questions rather than propositions, several sets of ecclesial sacramental practices that correspond to and nurture the theonomous self as described in the previous chapter.

First, in baptism, confirmation, and the reaffirmation of baptismal vows we find practices, a liturgical catechesis, of Trinitarian relatedness that provide most clearly for the nurture of confirmation and recognition, not of something done to us in our personal past, but of who we have become and are becoming. As a practice of Trinitarian faith, baptism provides what is perhaps the most explicit articulation of this faith. The church universally baptizes "in the name of the Father, Son, and Holy Spirit." Among the ecumenical creeds of the church, the baptismal creed we know as the Apostles' Creed gives further expression and definition to this faith. But, as I noted earlier in this chapter, this creed is also about personal (though not "private") faith. It is an articulation in the midst of community of what "I" believe as a self in relation to God.

The questions that baptismal practice, as a practice of the theonomous self, raises are these: We must ask of ourselves and our communities how these practices support or negate the construction of persons-in-relation. Does our understanding and use of these practices focus only on individual faith? Or are we drawn into a faith that is both "ours" and that of the Christian community? Our answers to these questions will vary, of course, according to the particular baptismal practices and theologies of particular communities.

Second, in the practices of both private and public confession and penance we find the practices and liturgical catechesis that most clearly nurture differentiation and contradiction. Here we speak of what we have done and left undone and hear most clearly the promise of God's relatedness despite our tendencies toward unrelatedness. The ongoing practice of reconciliation with the community and with God draws us into a depth of relationship and relatedness. Here we are reminded that we are not the whole of the body and that the body, to be whole, has need of us. Here we must ask how Christian communities receive the many and various gifts presented to the community by its diverse members. At the same time, we must identify and transform those practices that polarize rather than differentiate the members of the community.

A final eucharistic note: Baptism, creed, penance, and reconciliation remind us of the grammar in which we are embedded. Yet it is in the practice, the liturgical catechesis, of faithfully gathering at the eucharistic table where we are both sustained for and joined in solidarity to the world, where we can return again and again to receive what had been "lost" and to continue the transformation of the world. Here we must question the adequacy of Christian reflection on the sacramental life (mystagogy) and of our need for ongoing eucharistic formation. Does our gathering at the table lead us back into the world? Does our gathering model a way of being in and knowing the world? Does our sharing in the eucharistic bread deepen our critical solidarity with the world? Is this practice truly a practice of theonomous selves, reflecting the Trinitarian pattern of God's salvific relationship to and with the world? Is this a reflection of God's self-giving that so overflows with love that all creation is brought into relatedness with God and one another? Or is the grammar of conversion and transformation so hidden that it never finds its way into our experience?

As enacted and embodied prayer, these practices are also the means by which we do our faith and the faith is done to us. In them, our praise of God is a practice of the Christian self. Augustine was correct when he wrote that when you receive the eucharist, "it is your own mystery which you receive."[28] To paraphrase Augustine,

[28] Sermon 272 in Migne, *Patrologia Latina* 38 (1861), col. 1247: "Would you understand the body of Christ? Hear the apostle say to the faithful: 'You are the body and the members of Christ.' If, then, you are Christ's body and his members, it is your own mystery which you receive. It is to what you are that you reply Amen, and by replying subscribe. For you are told: 'The body of Christ.' and you reply, 'Amen.' Be a member of the body of Christ, and let your 'Amen' be true." [Trans. Mary Collins, *Worship: Renewal to Practice* (Washington: Pastoral Press, 1987) 291.]

it is in these practices that "we receive who we are" or, in a less passive voice, where we "practice who we are becoming." But this raises a final set of questions that require our attention: Who are we becoming? To what end do we practice ourselves?

Chapter Seven

A Vision of Christian Life

Changed from glory into glory[1]

In the previous chapter I argued that liturgical practices provide the means by which Christian persons are formed in a pattern of relationship to a relational God. These practices are the means by which we receive who we are, as we heard Augustine reminding us, and practice who we are becoming. Who we are becoming, I have argued, is a theonomous self. But what is the end of this becoming?

Two hymn texts provide partial though imaginal answers. In her "Hymn of Promise," a text increasingly sung at funerals, Natalie Sleeth offers one answer.[2] Although she intends her hymn to speak of the resurrected life that follows death, her verse "in the end is our beginning" offers a larger vision of the life we live today. It suggests a vision of the Christian life that is lived in light of an eschatological horizon. It suggests not "when" or "if" but "because." We live in glory today because of the hope of glory that is yet to be. We view our beginning as Christian persons from the perspective of a goal that, as not yet fully disclosed, offers a vision of hope and the

---

[1] Hymn 374, "Love divine, all loves excelling," stanza 3, in *The Works of John Wesley*, vol. 7: *A Collection of Hymns for the use of the People called Methodists*, ed. Franz Hildebrandt and Oliver Beckerlegge (Oxford: Clarendon Press; New York: Oxford University Press, 1983) 547; *The United Methodist Hymnal* (Nashville: The United Methodist Publishing House, 1989) 384.

[2] *The United Methodist Hymnal*, 707.

requirement that we live toward that goal in faith rather than certainty. Charles Wesley offers a similar vision in his familiar stanza:

Finish, then, thy new creation; pure and spotless let us be.
Let us see thy great salvation perfectly restored in thee;
changed from glory into glory, till in heaven we take our place,
till we cast our crowns before thee, lost in wonder, love, and
    praise.[3]

Unlike Sleeth's concern for life after death, however, there is in Wesley a concern for the life of glory in the midst of life, an expectation that the life of glory is progressively revealed and practiced in the shape of the Christian person's present life. This expectation shares a long and rich theological heritage. As hymn texts that are read and sung repeatedly in many congregations, these hymns provide a means by which the eschatological vision of Christian life is rehearsed and "put into play" in the patterns of Christian living.

Like these hymn texts, the eucharistic texts discussed in the previous chapter also put into play the pattern of a life that is "already but not yet" realized. (See p. 163 in Chapter 6.) In the offering of these prayers, the church intercedes on behalf of the whole Body of Christ in expectation of the life of glory. In the British Methodist prayer this intercession is gathered in one petition: "Unite us with him for ever and bring us with the whole creation to your eternal kingdom." So, too, the United Methodist prayer: "By your Spirit make us one with Christ, one with each other, and one in ministry to all the world, *until* Christ comes in victory and we feast at his heavenly banquet." Although the British Methodist prayer looks toward the eschatological day, the United Methodist prayer invites a more active expectation; the community prays *until.* The community gathers at the table to break bread and share the cup *until* Christ comes in glory, *until* we are changed fully into glory. The community prays in expectation that its prayer will change or shape it in ways that both anticipate its future life and look at the present in terms of that anticipated future in such a manner that the future shapes it now.[4] As Don Saliers notes, "All petition to God that is

---

[3] Ibid., 384.

[4] See Don Saliers, *Worship as Theology: Foretaste of Glory Divine* (Nashville: Abingdon Press, 1994) 228. Similarly, but perhaps more cautiously, Jürgen Moltmann writes, "The regenerate person is not as such already existent and

faithfully grounded in praying with Christ is eschatological in the sense of manifesting our openness to God's future for us, while revealing the reality of God's intention to act toward us in accordance with God's unfailing promise."[5] More than this, this faithfully grounded petition is a means by which we practice our intention to act in and with God.

Geoffrey Wainwright captures some of this co-intentionality (synergy) in his comprehensive review of the eschatological themes of the eucharist. Three of his statements are of particular relevance to this discussion. In the first he writes of the "already but not yet" character of the eucharist:

"It would seem possible to consider the eucharist as a provisional instance of that glorification of men [sic] and nature by God which will make the new heavens and the new earth, and as the anticipation of that glorification of God by men and all creation which will be the final and complete acknowledgment of His universal kingdom."[6]

What is "already" is provisional; it is *until*. There is more to come. In this sense what is "already" is "not yet." But *what* is provisional, *what* is anticipated? It is God's work of glorifying humanity and all creation in anticipation of humanity's and creation's work of glorifying God. God and humanity work in a pattern of co-intentionality from the future through the present to the future.

Second, Wainwright argues, as I have argued in earlier chapters, that this eschatological work of God and humanity does more than *express* the unity or disunity and love or lack of love within the church and among God's people. He writes, "The eucharist both expresses an already existing unity among the Lord's people and it

---

that regeneration belongs to the reality present to us only as something to be expected. The regenerate person is ahead of himself [sic], as it were; he lives from what is coming to meet him, not from what already exists in him." *The Spirit of Life: A Universal Affirmation*, trans. Margaret Kohl (Minneapolis: Fortress Press, 1992) 151.

[5] *Worship as Theology*, 78.

[6] *Eucharist and Eschatology* (New York: Oxford University Press, 1981) 104. With similar intent, Alexander Schmemann writes, "It is the very essence of the Christian faith that we live in a kind of rhythm—leaving, abandoning, denying the world, and yet at the same time always returning to it, living in time by that which is beyond time, living by that which is not yet come, but which we already know and possess." "Liturgy and Eschatology," in *Liturgy and Tradition*, ed. Thomas Fisch (Crestwood, N.Y.: St. Vladimir's Seminary Press, 1990) 95.

also increases and deepens their love for one another until such time as it will have borne its full fruit in the perfect peace and unity of heaven."[7] Here is that word again: *until.* Although expressive, eucharistic practice is a means toward that deepened "perfect" love; it changes us as it constitutes us as Christian people. It is not (only) our expression of a human reality but also the expression of something beyond us, toward which we live and move, the expression of a perfection and unity that comes into our midst as God's continuing work among us. Alexander Schmemann states it this way: "The unique . . . function of worship in the life of the Church and in theology is to convey a sense of this eschatological reality; and what eschatology does is to hold together things which otherwise are broken up and treated as separate events occurring at different points in a time sequence."[8]

This brings us to Wainwright's third statement: "From the eschatological perspective . . . the eucharist is more important for what it makes of us than for what it expresses as being already true of us."[9] Even as we engage in the "making" of eucharist, we are ourselves being made eucharistically. As Augustine has reminded us, it is ourselves that we are receiving when we receive the bread and cup. Even as we pray "make us one with Christ and one with each other" as Christ's faithful people, we are being made in that unity and communion. We are being constituted by our liturgical practices as persons in relationship to a relational God, as theonomous selves. The liturgical catechesis of this theonomous self occurs in the intertwining of these expressive, constitutive, and normative liturgical practices.

With this understanding of liturgical practice as the means by which we practice ourselves in a theonomous relationship, how do we more fully describe the "end" of this practice? In describing this end, I want to explore two traditions that make similar claims about the function of the liturgy and of sacramental practices in relationship to their end. The first explores the Eastern Orthodox understanding of *theosis,* or "divinization," and the role of the

---

[7] *Eucharist and Eschatology,* 142–143. It is helpful to remember here that even as our eucharistic practice manifests the unity and love of the church, it offers an eschatological critique of the church's ongoing disunity and lack of love.

[8] "Liturgy and Eschatology," 95–96.

[9] *Eucharist and Eschatology,* 143.

sacramental life in this process. The second explores John Wesley's understanding of Christian perfection and the role of the "means of grace" in achieving this perfection. Although these appear to be widely disparate traditions, recent Wesleyan scholarship is demonstrating Wesley's reliance upon and compatibility with the Orthodox tradition.[10]

THE ORTHODOX CONCEPT OF THEOSIS

The Eastern Orthodox traditions name the process of being changed "from glory into glory" and the character of the Christian life that is "already but not yet" as theosis, or "divinization." Theosis is the gradual movement of persons toward the attainment of likeness to God in virtue, wisdom, and knowledge of God. This movement, in the words of an Eastern monk, "is aimed at union *(henósis)* with God and deification *(theosis)* . . . a sharing, through grace, in the divine life."[11]

This process of divinization is rooted in three theological claims: that human persons are created in the image and likeness of God (Genesis 1:28), that humanity retains in its nature the essential quality of life graced by God, and that, in its freedom, humanity has the potential for losing or attaining a likeness to God. This process of divinization is rooted in the past, ongoing, and future work of God in Jesus Christ through the Holy Spirit. It is a process that, in its fullness, is Trinitarian. But it is also a process that depends on the distinctive work of Jesus Christ. As Vladimir Lossky writes, "The descent of the divine person of Christ makes the human person capable of an ascent . . . in the Holy Spirit."[12]

[10] See especially A. M. Allchin, "Our Life in Christ: In John Wesley and the Eastern Fathers," in *We Belong to One Another*, ed. A. M. Allchin (London: Epworth Press, 1965); Ted A. Campbell, *John Wesley and Christian Antiquity* (Nashville: Abingdon Press, 1991); Brian Frost, *Living in Tension Between East and West* (London: New World Publications, 1984); Randy Maddox, *Responsible Grace* (Nashville: Abingdon Press, Kingswood Books, 1994) and "John Wesley and Eastern Orthodoxy: Influences, Convergences and Differences," *Asbury Journal* 45:2 (Fall 1990) 29–53; and Albert Outler, "John Wesley's Interest in the Early Fathers of the Church," in *The Wesleyan Theological Heritage*, ed. Thomas C. Oden and Leicester R. Longden (Grand Rapids, Mich.: Zondervan, 1991).

[11] A Monk of the Eastern Church (Lev Gillet), *Orthodox Spirituality* (London: SPCK, 1945) 22.

[12] *In the Image and Likeness of God* (Crestwood, N.Y.: St. Vladimir's Seminary Press, 1985) 97.

In the Orthodox tradition, our creation "in the image" of God provides the starting point of this journey; our re-creation "in the likeness" of God is our potential and goal. Our creation and re-creation in the image and likeness of God identify what is and what is yet to be in the shape and character of human life. The person created "'in the image' is the person capable of manifesting God in the extent to which his [sic] nature allows itself to be penetrated by deifying grace. Thus the image . . . can become similar or dissimilar."[13] The shape of human life progressing toward similarity to the likeness of God, the divinized or theonomous self I described in the previous chapters, is therefore neither autonomous nor closed in upon itself. The theonomous self is open to the gift and life of grace such that it can both receive this gift and represent it and God in the world. In contrast, the non-theonomous self is marked by a stance of dissimilarity, separation, and enclosure, as represented by the image of the "self-made man."

Humanity in the image and likeness of God is, and requires, a life of relationship and openness to others and to God. Because it is open and progressing toward the likeness of God, it demands that we speak about life that continues to be or is *being* saved, that participates in the "working out" of our salvation, that continues toward holiness, that moves toward a future with God. We therefore cannot define the shape of divinized human life as that which *has been* saved. It is a life that is not only manifest but also emergent; as such it parallels the way in which ritual practices function in our lives (see Chapter 4, pp. 105ff.). John Meyendorff writes, "[Our] relationship to God is both a givenness and a task, an immediate experience and an expectation of even greater vision to be accomplished in a free effort of love."[14] That our relationship to God is given reminds

[13] Ibid., 139. Stanley Harakas supplements this: "While 'image' emphasizes the ontological beginning of man, 'theosis' emphasizes the ontological *telos* of man. Both say that 'true man,' 'true humanity,' 'perfect and complete humanity' is realized only in relationship with the divine prototype." *Toward Transfigured Life* (Minneapolis: Light and Life, 1983) 28.

[14] *Byzantine Theology* (New York: Fordham University Press, 1974) 2. Meyendorff supplements this statement later in the book: "The 'natural' participation of man [sic] in God is not a static givenness; it is a challenge, and man is called to grow in divine life. Divine life is a gift, but also a task which is to be accomplished by a free human effort. This polarity between the 'gift' and

us that this transformation occurs first by the grace and glory of God. That our relationship to God remains a task reminds us that the completion of human "likeness" to God requires our attention and our "practice," our cooperation and our intention. Mantzaridis writes, "By submitting himself [sic] freely to God's will and being constantly guided by [God's] grace, man can cultivate and develop the gift of the 'image,' making it a possession individual, secure, and dynamic, and so coming to resemble God."[15]

How do we cultivate and develop this gift of the "image"? In one sense, we cannot. Only God accomplishes this work, and God's work and grace cannot be confined to any one mode or form of human action. As many Protestants argue (and sing), so, too, do the Orthodox: God works in strange and mysterious ways, God's wonders to perform. Nevertheless, this is not an invitation to disregard the ritual sacramental life of the church, only a reminder that "the Spirit blows where it will."[16] With this very Protestant caution in mind, the Orthodox argue that the ritual sacramental life of the church is the "normal" means by which God works—and in which humanity participates or cooperates—to "divinize" humanity through the power of the Holy Spirit. This cooperative work calls upon the Christian person to make use of "every mystery, every ordinance, every method available to the Christian life . . . toward the acquisition of the gifts of the Spirit and theosis—union with God."[17]

---

the 'task' is often expressed in terms of the distinction between the concepts of 'image' and 'likeness.' It is the final destiny and end for which [humanity] was created by God. It is the aim and purpose of the Christian life: union and free communion with God" (139). See also Georgios I. Mantzaridis, *The Deification of Man* (Crestwood, N.Y.: St. Vladimir's Seminary Press, 1984) 7: "The word 'likeness' . . . expresses something dynamic and not yet realized, whereas the word 'image' signifies a realized state, which in the present context constitutes the starting point for the attainment of the 'likeness.'"

[15] *Deification of Man*, 21.

[16] A Monk of the Eastern Church writes that this idea that "God is not bound to the sacraments" does not mean "that a man [sic] could disregard, or slight, or despise, the channels of grace offered by the church without endangering his soul. It means that no externals, however useful, are necessary to God, in the absolute sense of this word, and that there is no institution, however sacred, which God cannot dispense with." *Orthodox Spirituality*, 32.

[17] Robert G. Stephanopoulos, "The Orthodox Doctrine of Theosis," in *The New Man*, ed. John Meyendorff and Joseph McLelland (New Brunswick, N.J.: Agora Books, 1973) 157.

The liturgical sacramental life of the church offers to the Christian person and community the means and methods by which and with which to experience, practice, and develop God's gifts of reconciling and transforming, justifying and sanctifying grace. The liturgical sacramental life of the church points toward union with God even as it makes manifest the presence of God's dominion in the present. The church's sacramental life transmits and makes accessible through created means the uncreated grace of God to God's creation. It provides the means through which God's creation (humanity) approaches and receives that which is uncreated.[18] In the burning bush, manna in the desert, and water from a rock, God approaches humanity and we approach God. In the healing of the sick, the curing of the blind, the giving of a cup of water, the feeding of the hungry with bread and fish, and the gathering of a community for a festive meal, God continues to approach us and open the way for our approach to God. God's practice of being God is also our practice of being "in the image and likeness" of God. As John Meyendorff argues, this sacramental practice is, at least for the Orthodox, not an "imitation" of Jesus but the practice of coming to life in Christ. It is a cooperative participation in Christ's deified humanity enacted by means of water, oil, bread, wine, song and prayer.[19] We do not copy Jesus, but are clothed in the life of Christ. We are made Christ's, and we are made "christs."

This participation, as Meyendorff also reminds us, is an "already but not yet." It is a participation in the dominion of God that is present but still anticipated, a participation in divine life that is only now seen in the sacraments/mysteries of the church. For the Orthodox, the sacramental life of the church is the means by which we now participate in the divine life. What is yet to be is present in the divine liturgy. What we are yet to be, joined with the saints around the throne of God, we are in the liturgy as we sing the angelic song, "Holy, holy, holy Lord." Here in the liturgy the Christian community, not only living "in Christ" but as the Body of Christ, anticipates and enters into the kingdom of God. In doing so, it discovers that this sharing in divine life, while extra-ordinary, is the "natural" state of humanity.[20]

[18] Mantzaridis, *Deification of Man*, 41.
[19] *Byzantine Theology*, 164.
[20] Ibid., 191.

Although this participation is revealed as both a natural and a present reality in the sacraments, the "not yetness" of this life requires the continued cooperative growth of each individual through the liturgical sacramental life of the church. Again, Meyendorff: "The Kingdom to come is already realized in the sacraments, but each individual Christian is called to grow into it, by exercising his own efforts and by using his own God-given freedom with the cooperation of the Spirit."[21] In this sense, the liturgical sacramental life of the Church takes on a certain urgency for the individual and the community. While the liturgical sacramental life of the community provides the context, means, and theological shape of this cooperative work, it also represents the primary mode for the community's practice until the kingdom that has come is realized in its fullness. As I have argued throughout this book, liturgical practices not only constitute the self and the Christian community in the context of community but also are a means by which the kingdom of God is also constituted in the present. As a practice until the kingdom is realized, so, too, the Church realizes in its practice the inbreaking of that kingdom. While firmly rooted in the present, the sacramental liturgical life of the community presents to the community an eschatological interpretation of that present.

What is clear in this brief summary of the Orthodox perspective is the relationship between the eschatological fulfillment of humanity in its acquisition of the "likeness of God," the ongoing work of divinization, or theosis, and the sacramental liturgical life of the church. The eschatological fulfillment of humanity in the image and likeness of God is anticipated by the eschatological present manifest in the liturgy. Because this future is manifest in the present, the present liturgical work is the primary means by which (or in which) the Christian individual and community work out or realize their future as the future of humanity in and with God. As Paul reminds us in the letter to the Philippians, we work out our own salvation with fear and trembling even as God in Christ is at work in us (Philippians 2:12-13). Although this liturgical work is the cooperative work of humanity in the power of God's grace, this work is first the work of the Trinity, of God through Christ in the Spirit.

[21] Ibid., 176.

As I argued in the previous chapters, it is this Trinitarian framework that provides the primary grammar and narrative for our understanding of the Christian person in relation to God, for the theonomous self. As a liturgical work that remains a mystery, we are unable to explain *how* it works, only that, in faith, it does by the power of God. As a liturgical work of the kingdom, it is both the *end* and the beginning of our life with God, our work of being "saved," of being remade in the likeness of God.[22]

JOHN WESLEY, SANCTIFICATION, AND THE MEANS OF GRACE

Like the Orthodox, John Wesley understands the Christian experience of sanctification as a process that is supported and encouraged by sacramental practice. My intent in the following is to review John Wesley's understanding of the relationship between sanctification and the means of grace. In so doing, I want to not only suggest the similarities between his position and that of the Orthodox but also to note how an understanding of the Orthodox position enriches our understanding of Wesley.

Wesley's understanding of sanctification as a lifelong process and his concern for the "methodical" use of the means of grace in support of that process clearly drew from his reading of the early church fathers. Even so, Wesley resisted the language of theosis or divinization and rejected the ascetical life as the normative shape of the Christian life (even as his own life clearly embraced such asceticism). As Ted Campbell indicates in his review of Wesley's use of early church writings, Wesley was cautious in his edition of the Pseudo-Macarian homilies, from which he drew much of his understanding of sanctification, and excised the language of divinization and ascesis from his edition.[23]

In place of the language of theosis or divinization, Wesley uses "sanctification" and "Christian perfection." By these terms he

[22] On this point, United Methodist Don Saliers provides, in his own conclusions, an apt summary of the Orthodox position: "Faithful liturgy is the fundamental imaginal framework of encounter with God in Christ, which, in the power of the Holy Spirit, forms intentions in and through the affections oriented to God revealed in Christ as their goal and ground." *Worship as Theology*, 175.

[23] *John Wesley and Christian Antiquity*, x.

means, in the most concise form, "pure love reigning alone in our heart and life."[24] Wesley more fully defines Christian perfection as "loving God with all our heart, mind, soul, and strength. This implies that no wrong temper, none contrary to love, remains in the soul and that all the thoughts, words and actions are governed by pure love."[25]

A third description, found in the early essay, "A Farther Appeal to Men of Reason" (1745), in which Wesley provides a defense of the Methodist movement and argues for its continuity with the beliefs of the church, echoes the language of the early church. Here Wesley describes Christian perfection as "a present deliverance from sin, a restoration of the soul to its primitive health, its original purity; a recovery of the divine nature; the renewal of our souls after the image of God, in righteousness and true holiness, in justice, mercy, and truth."[26] It is clear in each of these statements that salvation and sanctification, for Wesley, are concerned with this life, with life in the midst of life, rather than life after death.[27] In the present the Christian person is freed from the power of sin and healed of the "sin-sick soul." This present experience of liberation and healing begins the process of the renewal of the image and likeness of God in the Christian person. This renewal, on the one hand, recovers the "natural" ontological status of the Christian person as a person of grace. On the other hand, this recovery of life in the image and likeness of God transforms the social-ethical relationships between the person and other persons and between the person and God such that these relationships are defined by God's justice, mercy and truth.

[24] "Thoughts on Christian Perfection," in *John Wesley*, ed. Albert Outler (New York: Oxford University Press, 1964) 293.

[25] Ibid., 284.

[26] Cited in Harald Lindström, *Wesley and Sanctification* (Stockholm: Almgvist and Wiksells Boktryckery A. B., 1946; reprint, with a foreword by Timothy L. Smith, Wilmore, Ky.: Francis Asbury Publishing Co., 1980) 100.

[27] Theodore Runyon underscores this point: "The axial theme of Wesley's soteriology is the renewal of the image of God. Therefore, salvation is more than being declared righteous and being admitted to heaven. It is, following the Eastern pattern, participation in the nature and reality of God through the Spirit." *Wesleyan Resources for Ecumenical Theology*, J. D. Northey Lectures, Candler School of Theology, Emory University, 1993, 10.

Wesley acknowledged the difficulties the Christian person faces in attaining such perfection and was ambivalent about its attainability in this life. At the same time, he was willing to admit to "degrees of perfection" or to a process of being made perfect:

"Christian perfection, therefore, does not imply (as some men seem to have imagined) an exemption either from ignorance, or mistake, or infirmities, or temptations. Indeed, it is only another term for 'holiness.' . . . Yet we may, lastly, observe that neither in this respect is there any absolute perfection on earth . . . . So that how much soever any man has attained, or in how high a degree soever he is perfect, he hath still need to "grow in grace" and daily to advance in the knowledge and love of God his Saviour."[28]

In making this claim, Wesley preserves the teleological emphasis of the early fathers and the tension between the "already and not yet" that he believed characterizes the Christian life of holiness and happiness.[29] For Wesley, the experience of salvation in the present life prepares the individual for the life of the kingdom and represents a present realization of that life. The present experience of sanctification, of happiness and holiness, provides an entrance into what remains future, the believer not only living and walking toward eternity but also living "the life of eternity, the life of love which characterizes the Kingdom of God."[30] The experience (to whatever degree possible) and practice of Christian perfection in this life prepare the person for the experience of perfect holiness in that life that is yet to come.

As a practical theologian, Wesley addressed his writings to particular audiences and arguments. In some cases and in response to the witness of some of those he believed demonstrated perfection in their lives, he seems to emphasize the "already" character of

[28] "Christian Perfection," in Outler, *John Wesley*, 258.

[29] Even here, Albert Outler argues, "The crucial term for Wesley was not *perfectus* but *teleios*—a dynamic understanding of 'perfecting' that had come to him from early and Eastern spirituality." "In this view, 'perfection' may be 'realized' in a given moment (always as a gift from God, received by trusting faith), yet never as a finished state." "John Wesley: Folk Theologian," in *The Wesleyan Theological Heritage*, ed. Thomas C. Oden and Leicester R. Longden (Grand Rapids, Mich.: Zondervan, 1991) 121–122.

[30] Henry H. Knight, III, *The Presence of God in the Christian Life: John Wesley and the Means of Grace* (Metuchen, N.J.: Scarecrow Press, 1992) 71.

Christian perfection. In other cases, particularly in reference to his own life, he emphasized the "not yet" of Christian perfection. Where he is consistent, we discover an experience of Christian perfection that is "already and not yet." As Wesley demonstrated in his preaching, his essays, and his own life, "Christ-likeness is not simply infused in believers instantaneously. It is developed progressively through a responsible appropriation of the grace, which God provides. Spiritual disciplines are essential to this process of growth."[31] On these points he is in agreement with the Orthodox.

How, then, does Wesley understand the role of these spiritual disciplines? Like the Orthodox, and in faithfulness to his Protestant context, Wesley was careful to argue that the sacraments of the church, along with other devotional practices, are means of grace rather than ends in themselves. As means, they are not intended to limit the place or manner in which God works in human lives. Nevertheless, Wesley understood these means, especially those he calls the "instituted means"—prayer, fasting, eucharist, searching the Scriptures, and "Christian conference"—as the normal means through which God works in human lives. Other means may arise appropriate to particular times and places (these Wesley calls the "prudential means"), but the instituted means remain constant for the Christian community.[32] Recalling the discussion of ritual practice in Chapter 4, these instituted and prudential means of grace are forms of ritual practice by which we are constituted bodily and socially, as embodied selves in relationship to other embodied selves. Thus, the person seeking sanctification waits

NB

"not in careless indifference or indolent inactivity, but in vigorous and universal obedience; in a zealous keeping of all the commandments; in watchfulness and painfulness; in denying ourselves and taking up our cross daily [these Wesley elsewhere names the

---

[31] Maddox, "John Wesley and Eastern Orthodoxy," 39.

[32] Wesley's own understanding of the importance of hymn singing to Christian formation argues for an understanding of such as a "prudential" means of grace (see below, p. 199). For Wesley, I think it was clear that, to the extent that the texts produced and sung in the Methodist movement echoed the language of Scripture and the prayerbook, hymn singing was a "prudential means of grace" that supported or complemented the "ordinary" means of searching the Scriptures and prayer.

"general" means of grace]; as well as in earnest prayer and fasting and a close attendance on all the ordinances of God [the "instituted" means of grace]."[33]

For Wesley, the Christian person awaits the fullness of perfection and sanctification in active cooperation with the work of God.

In his review of Wesley's understanding of the means of grace, Henry Knight summarizes this understanding as follows: "The means [of grace] form an interrelated context within which the Christian life is lived and through which relationships with God and one's neighbor are maintained."[34] Within this context and pattern of relationships, the "Christian life is correspondingly enabled to grow in love."[35] That is, the means of grace function as practices of the Christian self in relationship to God and neighbor. They "increase our sensitivity to God's presence through the experience and practice of love in the Christian community and in service to the world," "counteract despair or complacency in the Christian life by moving us outward from ourselves," and place us "in loving relationships with God, other Christians, and the world."[36] Important in this last statement is its distinctive contrast with what much popular understanding of salvation and sanctification would have us believe: that such is about *my* life with God, *my* life after death, and that such has little to do with my relationship to you and salvation/sanctification as social practices.

As these practices develop our relationship to God, they also develop our awareness of, and ability to be in relationship to, other persons and to the world. As practices by which we recover the image and grow into the likeness of God, the means of grace recover and transform the patterns of our relatedness in the world. The life of holiness and happiness is an ethical and ontological life of love for God and for the world.

When, in his adaptation of the Anglican articles of faith for the church in America, Wesley retained the article that defines the church as the place where the sacraments are duly administered, he was claiming for the church the power and the means by which

[33] "Thoughts on Christian Perfection," in Outler, *John Wesley*, 294.
[34] *The Presence of God*, 2.
[35] Ibid., 15.
[36] Ibid., 13.

it will continue to practice its own transformation. He was claiming, even as his followers began to separate themselves from the Church of England, the institutional church as the context in which these relational practices will be offered, practiced, and developed. Although the Spirit may blow where it will, the "instituted" means of grace provide the normal patterns by which God works in us and by which we are drawn to the practices of God. The means of grace are the "source" of our experience of sanctification, the place in which this sanctification is made manifest, and the context in which this experience of sanctification continues to develop. Knight writes, "They will work against our forgetting God or confusing God with self; they will help us truly know who God is and, as a consequence, who we are before God and who God calls us to be."[37] Wesley made this point in his discussion of prayer in one of his sermons:

"The end of your praying is not to inform God, as though He knew not your wants already; but rather to inform yourselves, to fix the sense of those wants more deeply in your hearts, and the sense of your continual dependence on him who only is able to supply all your wants. It is not so much to move God—who is always more ready to give than you to ask—as to move yourselves, that you may be willing and ready to receive the good things he has prepared for you."[38]

Some might resist the human focus on this statement, but it makes its point well. Sacramental liturgical prayer, as well as other forms of prayer, is a means by which we open ourselves to God and the gifts of God's grace. Through such prayer we open ourselves to the transformation wrought by the Holy Spirit and practice ourselves in light of the eschatological hope of what we shall yet become. We remember and anticipate the way of God in our lives, and we remember and anticipate our way in God's life. Yet Wesley would be quick to remind us, as would the Orthodox, that this is a cooperative work, done with and in response to God's grace.

[37] Ibid., 48.
[38] "On the Sermon on the Mount, VI," in *The Works of John Wesley*, vol. 1: *Sermons*, ed. Albert Outler (Nashville: Abingdon Press, 1984) 577.

As I indicated at the beginning of this chapter, Wesley and the Eastern Orthodox may seem unlikely companions. Where the Orthodox emphasize our likeness or similarity to God, Wesley had a sharper sense of the possibilities for dissimilarity. Where the Orthodox have a stronger doctrine of creation read christologically, Wesley, reflecting the dominant Western theological understandings of humanity's fallenness, lacked this. But we begin to see, even in this necessarily brief review, that they share a number of common concerns. Five interrelated points are particularly evident here.[39]

Both believe, first, that the goal or teleology of the human life is life with God. This goal, in itself, is not exceptional. What is distinctive, however, is the strong emphasis the Orthodox and Wesley place on the teleological character of the Christian life. In the human quest for meaning, the Christian raison d'être is our life with God. What we do and how we do it in both our liturgical sacramental life and our social-ethical life—which are inseparable from each other—are shaped and judged by this goal.

Second, this goal, which we commonly call salvation or sanctification, is further defined as the restoration of the image and likeness of God in humanity. Whether we speak of theosis or Christian perfection, whether we speak of a life characterized by "the true experimental knowledge of God" or by "happiness and holiness," we (or our lives) intend a particular shape or pattern in this life with God. In Chapter 5 I argued that this pattern is best described in terms of the Trinitarian perichoresis, a pattern of mutual interrelationship and relatedness known in its fullest only within the mystery of the Triune God revealed in the history of God's praxis. The image and likeness of God that Christians remember, enact, and anticipate in liturgical and social praxis are a reciprocal participation of persons in community that (mysteriously) permits unity without requiring the sacrifice of diversity.

[39] I am drawing here on Albert Outler, "John Wesley's Interests in the Early Fathers of the Church," in *The Wesleyan Theological Heritage*, 103. There Outler identifies four additional parallels between Wesley and the Orthodox/early church: (1) "a therapeutic view of the ordo salutis as contrasted with any forensic one"; (2) "the person and primal agency of the Holy Spirit in Christian existence"; (3) "prevenient grace"; and (4) "the inspiration of Scripture and its pneumatological interpretation."

Third, Wesley and the Orthodox concur that the Christian life is defined by a "concordance of grace and free will," by the synergy of human striving and God's grace. It is this synergy that makes Christian perfection possible: God is always at work in humanity in the grace and power of the Holy Spirit making possible our response, cooperation, and striving. Neither tradition permits arguments for the human work of sanctification without God's gift of grace. Nor do they suggest that we are compelled in this work by God. The gift of grace is accompanied by the freedom of human response.

Wesley and the Orthodox also agree, fourth, that this synergy of human striving and God's grace is represented, on the human side, by ascesis and discipline in Christian living. In spite of contemporary discussions about these two traditions that suggest the Orthodox are more inclined to the contemplative life (personal holiness) and the Methodists to the active or political life (social holiness), Wesley and the Orthodox draw from common traditions and expectations that call for a balance between the two. The character and patterns of human response to the experience of God's grace are shaped and expressed in both liturgical and socio-political praxes. Christian life in the image and likeness of God, if we accept that this image and likeness are a pattern of relatedness to a relational God, requires human response that is both liturgical/contemplative and social, both mystical and political.[40] Human striving in response to God's grace takes the form of prayer and

[40] See Johann Metz, *Faith in History and Society: Toward a Fundamental Practical Theology*, trans. David Smith (New York: The Seabury Press, 1980) 77 and 95: "The spirituality of liberated freedom cannot therefore be limited to a pure experience of cult that is isolated and free from all the conflicts, repressions, and challenges of everyday life." See also his *Followers of Christ: The Religious Life and the Church*, trans. Thomas Linton (New York: Paulist Press, 1978) 42–44. There Metz writes, "The mystical aspect of following Christ never takes place in a vacuum; that is not something that happens in isolation from society or apart from a particular political situation, so as to be spared the antagonisms and sufferings of the world and to be granted the ability to maintain its own innocence by not being a participant" (43). For an extended discussion of Metz's distinction between the political and mystical and its relationship to the liturgy, see Bruce T. Morrill, S.J., *Anamnesis as Dangerous Memory: Political and Liturgical Theology in Dialogue* (Collegeville, Minn.: Liturgical Press, Pueblo Books, 2000) 50–57.

politics, the ritual sacramental media of bread and wine as well as the cup of water "for the least of these." Having said this, however, the project at hand requires an emphasis on the disciplined life practiced in rite and sacrament. These, for both Wesley and the Orthodox, are the primary means by which Christian persons practice and receive, are born into and nurtured for, the life of grace.

Finally, given the teleology of life with God in perfect love and the cooperative work by which persons are made perfect in love, this perfection is open-ended rather than absolute. Wesley argued that even those whose lives evidence Christian perfection continue to grow in that perfection. Here the teleology of the Christian life merges with the eschatology of that life. We live and grow in grace *until* God's day, the last day. From the Orthodox perspective, the Christian life is characterized by present experience and by a greater vision of what will be accomplished in perfect love. For Wesley, that vision is finally of communion with the Trinity: "And to crown all, there will be a deep, and intimate, an uninterrupted union with God; a constant communion with the Father and his Son Jesus Christ, through the Spirit; a continual enjoyment of the Three-One God, and of all the creatures in him."[41]

In this sense, we return to where we began this chapter. In the practice of ourselves through the means of grace, we practice what is both already and not yet in our Christian lives. What is already is a pattern of relatedness in and with the Triune God; what is not yet is the completion of our "being made perfect in love." This also returns us to the themes of the fourth chapter. When we understand liturgy as a ritual practice, we discover that liturgy does more than manifest or re-present the past in the present. As emergent practice, liturgical practice and liturgical catechesis speak to the present from the future, enacting the shape of that future—our "perfection in love" or our completion in the likeness of God—in the present liturgical practice of the Christian community.

AN "ALREADY BUT NOT YET" CONCLUSION
In this and the previous two chapters I have attempted to explore the "grammar" of the liturgy, and hence of the Christian self, by

[41] Sermon 64, "The New Creation," in *The Works of John Wesley*, vol. 2: *Sermons*, ed. Albert Outler (Nashville: Abingdon Press, 1984) 510.

way of the criteria of Trinity, relationality, and eschatology. I have argued that as we practice this grammar in the unfolding of the Christian liturgy, we find not only the means by which we narrate our lives as Christian people but also a means by which we shape and re-shape, anticipate as well as remember, who and whose we are. In our practicing of the liturgy, we are practicing ourselves, our past, our present, and our future, as created and redeemed in the image and likeness of God. Put in a definitional form, I have argued that liturgical catechesis, as a means by which we practice ourselves as Christian people, is (1) an eschatological practice, (2) in which the church makes eucharist and is made by eucharist and its other liturgical sacramental practices, and (3) in which past and future intersect in the present as the past is re-membered and the future is created even as it is anticipated.

By claiming the Orthodox and Wesleyan language of the "means of grace," I have also argued that the sacramental life of the church, while so clearly articulating God's praxis in and with the world, is a context in which we, as God's people, cooperate in that praxis. Liturgical sacramental practice provides the meeting point between God's work of salvation and our work of "being saved," God's present and our future. As this meeting point, liturgical practice and liturgical catechesis—to continue in the definitional mode—(4) communicates and gives meaning to the Christian community, (5) positing a visional horizon of emancipation, liberation and reconciliation defined by memory and hope, (6) which the worshiping community possesses in the present and to which it bears witness in word and deed, that is, in emancipatory praxis.

Finally, by claiming the language of theosis or perfection, I can complete my definition of liturgical catechesis as a practice of the theonomous self in the claim that (7) the liturgy is that threshold place in which the Christian community stands and from which it moves in expectation of God's new creation, crying "Maranatha! Come, Lord Jesus!" As we live with the unfulfilled hope of Christ's coming in glory, as we live within the making of the kingdom, we ourselves are being made, constructed, practiced. Each step forward along the road toward the promised land, each venture in faith, brings us one step closer to that horizon while, at the same time, it presents us with a reconfiguration of that horizon. The horizon lies ever before us as a vision that we are making and by which we are being made. We remember and proclaim that we are formed in God's image and filled by God with the breath of life. We are given purpose in commandment and the cry of the prophet for justice. We are joined with all of earth and heaven, with apostles and prophets, with all who live for God "beyond all time and space" that we may become the cosmic choir singing "Holy, holy, holy Lord." We make and are made a holy and living sacrifice. And, as we make eucharist, we are made one in Christ, one with Christ, one with each other, and one for all the world. We are changed from glory into glory.

Chapter Eight

Conclusion

A heart to praise my God[1]

We are made in eucharist as we make eucharist; we make ourselves even as we are ourselves remade; we are changed even as our relationship to the world changes; we are changed from glory into glory. These are bold claims to make about liturgical sacramental practice, and perhaps even bolder claims to make about the Christian sacramental life, for those shaped in a Protestant ethos characterized by a distrust of ritual and sacrament. But if we who are Protestants are honest with ourselves, we discover that this ethos of distrust has itself shaped our worship practices. In resisting ritual and sacrament, our practices of resistance have taken on a ritual character of their own, a ritual strategy by which to name and shape the Protestant life that has resulted in liturgical practices consistent with our intellectual roots in the Enlightenment. Here the individual expression of autonomous and private experience displaces the corporate work of the Body of Christ.[2] These same

---

[1] Hymn 334, "O for a heart to praise my God," stanza 1, in *The Works of John Wesley*, vol. 7: *A Collection of Hymns for the use of the People called Methodists*, ed. Franz Hildebrandt and Oliver Beckerlegge (Oxford: Clarendon Press, New York: Oxford University Press, 1983) 490; *The United Methodist Hymnal* (Nashville: The United Methodist Publishing House, 1989) 517.

[2] As Karen Westerfield Tucker argues, for example, "Following in the footsteps of Wesley before them, twentieth-century Methodists are prone to judge

practices also disregard or deny the normative and constitutive claims liturgical practices make on the community of faith. However, as we have seen, our performance of liturgy and sacrament is a matter of practicing ourselves, whether as Protestant, Catholic, or Orthodox. But what kind of self shall we practice?

In the preceding chapters I have argued that by giving attention to the grammar and narratives enacted in the sacramental liturgical practices of the Church, particularly in baptism and eucharist, we discover a "catechesis of the self" that encourages the development of the theonomous self, a self formed in relationship to a relational God. This catechesis of the self suggests that, while we must continue to engage in preparation of persons for participation in liturgy and must also engage in critical reflection on our liturgical practices, we must also learn to attend to the ways in which our liturgical practice is itself formational. Such an understanding of liturgical practice challenges the dominant Western ethos of worship as a private act done in a corporate setting. It suggests that liturgical sacramental practice, while an expression of the faith of a community, is a practice that norms and constitutes that community as a particular community of faith. It exercises claims upon us as a religious people. While our practice is a means by which the community of faith *enacts* a theological grammar and narrative, it is also the means by which the community *appropriates* that grammar and narrative.

Perhaps all that I mean by "liturgical catechesis" is that in our enactment of the liturgy we are presenting ourselves and the world with a worldview which is already partially seen and understood and which we, as the Church, are intent upon actualizing in the present. At the same time, these liturgical practices offer for our appropriation a vision of the world that is not yet realized, thereby critiquing our present experience and life. Through our enactment of liturgy and sacrament, even in all its diversity of performance,

the service of worship by its results or fruits, though often this is seen more in terms of individual benefit than in regard to the corporate edification and strengthening of the whole Body of Christ or as it concerns the faithful and faith-filled worship of God." "Sunday Worship in the World Parish: Observations," in *The Sunday Service of the Methodists: Twentieth-Century Worship in World Methodism*, ed. Karen Westerfield Tucker (Nashville: Abingdon Press, Kingswood Books, 1996) 330.

we name ourselves as Christian people and are named by the world as doing what Christians in every time and place do. The particularity of these practices to the Christian community as practices of the self does not yield a generically religious people, but a people "faithed" in an embodied pattern of relatedness to the one we call God and to those we call, and are summoned to call, our neighbors.

As I have already suggested, this understanding of liturgical catechesis leads to a pattern suggested by but elaborating upon Prosper's axiom *lex orandi lex statuat credendi*—"the law of prayer establishes the law of belief." The elaborated pattern suggests that the law of prayer also establishes the *lex vivendi*, "the law of living." This is a connection the Apostle Paul seemed to make in the twelfth and thirteenth chapters of his letter to the Romans. Between "present your bodies as a living sacrifice, holy and acceptable to God, which is your spiritual worship" (Romans 12:1) and "put on the Lord Jesus Christ, and make no provisions for the flesh, to gratify its desires" (Romans 13:14), Paul links doctrine and ethics, worship and life. There is no clear distinction between them.[3] Liturgy, represented by baptismal and eucharistic practice, is directly related to belief and life in the world. The catechesis of the self practiced in liturgy and sacrament is a catechesis for Christian belief *and* action.

The move toward an understanding of liturgical practice as normative and constitutive as well as expressive provides a framework within which to evaluate the relationship between liturgy and catechesis. In particular, it challenges understandings of this relationship that are inclined to reserve to catechesis the educational and critical interpretive work of Christian formation and claims a priority of *lex orandi* over *lex credendi*. (Even so, as feminist and liberation liturgical theologians have shown us, a mutually critical relationship is also required between the two.) What and how we pray shape what and how we believe. The way in which we participate in the life of relationship to God and neighbor is formed, modeled, and defined (for good or for ill) by the way in which our liturgical practices permit us to practice those patterns of relationship.

[3] See Ernst Käsemann, *Commentary on Romans*, ed. and trans. Geoffrey W. Bromiley (Grand Rapids, Mich.: Wm. Eerdmanns, 1980) 323–329, 360–364.

These patterns and practices of relatedness have variously permitted the church to be co-opted by the dominant cultural powers, such as we find in the Constantinian church, or to stand in critical tension with those dominant powers, as we see in various movements within the Protestant reformation. Both forms exist in the life of the church today. The contemporary challenge of liturgical catechesis is to understand the liturgical life of Christian communities as patterns of formation into particular forms of a moral way of life. This challenge suggests, as a point of critique, that trivial liturgy breeds trivial belief and trivial action.

The liturgical sacramental life of the Church does not stand alone in its catechetical-formative life. It does, however, provide the central strategic location to and from which instruction and action flow. It is the primary place in which the community participates in its "work of salvation" as the work of the Christian life on behalf of the world. It is the location in which an ecclesial and world consciousness is generated, imagined, and put into play in the world. That is, "liturgical catechesis" understood as I am arguing here is a form—a practice—of knowing intrinsic to the liturgical practices themselves.

Throughout the previous chapters I have spoken of liturgy not only as practice and catechesis but also as a practice and catechesis in which Christian people participate. What is done in liturgy is not a discussion about the liturgy nor a running commentary on the liturgy being performed. Liturgical practice is a participation in a knowing about God, self, and other that is enacted and embodied. Liturgy, as the common interpretation of its etymology makes clear, is a public work of the worship of God. As critical theological practices, sacramental liturgical practices enact patterns of meaning and mean patterns of action that are constructed in the cultural grammar of Christianity and instantiated in the context of Christian community. At this level there needs to be a mutuality among the *lex orandi* (prayer), *lex credendi* (belief), and *lex vivendi* (life) of the community.

In turning to the question of liturgy as performance and practice, my concern has been to move liturgical theological practice beyond its focus on text—even as I have given my own attention to the interpretation of liturgical texts—and toward an understanding of liturgical practice as a form of participation in a social theological system that critiques or legitimates particular social orders, positions, and powers. Our attention to this form of participation encourages a discussion of liturgy as a complex of practices that structure our interpretation of church and world, self and other, and God. In speaking of liturgy as a practice in which we participate, we name liturgy as a "strategy of differentiation." The catechetical-formative actions in which we participate as Christian people differentiate us from the Rotary Club and the synagogue, from the bath house and ritual washing in the Ganges. While in each of these places we may participate in a meal or a bath, the Trinitarian grammar and narrative of the Christian meal in eucharist and the Christian washing in baptism name the meal and washing as something other than what is practiced in other communities and form us in their very structures.

It was in this regard that I turned to the work of Catherine Bell and her definition of ritual practice as situational, strategic, embedded in misrecognition, and able to reproduce or reconfigure the ordering of power in the world.[4] As I argued at the end of the Chapter 4, liturgical practices are further characterized by a particular relation to time and, in that relation, to particular forms of strategic action. Christian sacramental liturgical practices, as practices in this technical sense, work to manifest that which is past, to present or re-present that which is in and of the present, and to continue to develop or emerge in and from the future. The fullness of the law of prayer and of the law of belief requires each of these to be operative in some form.

Our prayer and sacrament are always about what God has done, what God is doing, and what God is yet to do in our world and in our lives.[5] As situational and strategic events of the present, we engage the past and the future, even as we reconstruct or reinterpret

---

[4] *Ritual Theory, Ritual Practice* (New York: Oxford University Press, 1992) 81–82.

[5] A corollary to this normative statement suggests that when our ritual actions and prayers are about something or someone else, about some other story, we must acknowledge that what we do is neither Christian sacrament nor about the practice of the *Christian* self. This is one of the risks, even deficiences I think, in recent proposals about so-called "contemporary worship" that intentionally exclude specifically Christian biblical and theological language.

the past and envision the future—if only as a "foretaste of the glory divine." What we discover in this interpretation of liturgical practices is an understanding that while "we do not know yet what we shall be," while our future is open and undefined, that future is conditioned by the past and present of our life together with God. It is in the context of this ongoing life that we begin to anticipate, in life and practice, this future of self and other.

In a less technical and more familiar sense, I have been speaking of liturgical catechesis as practice in the sense of a rehearsal for a future event and way of life. As a practice, our performance and practice of the liturgy looks toward the future of our life with God. What we discover in this rehearsal is that this life is neither a solitary life nor a life of private salvation. The rule of prayer, as transacted in liturgical sacramental practices, works to place in our bodies and minds, hearts and souls, a pattern of life together, with the world and for the world.

This patterning of life has two consequences. First, much as my own practice of scales at the piano develops a certain kind of strength and ability in my fingers as well as an ability to hear what I see printed on the page (and, in contrast, as my lack of practice hinders such development), so, too, our sacramental liturgical practice develops strengths and abilities for our relatedness to the world and to God. By this I mean that in this practice we develop in our bodies, minds, and hearts a readiness or disposition to "play" the song of God. Another way of saying this, I think, is that in these practices we are writing in and on the body a form of memory through which we recognize in sight, sound, and affect God's way in the world and by which we are disposed to act in accordance with this way.

The second consequence of this patterning of life is the development of a certain depth of experience and knowledge that only comes with repeated practice. I am cautious here, however, as I think about my own practice habits at the piano. It is all too easy to practice in a way that reinforces mistakes. That is, if I learn a piece of music incorrectly, my continued practice of the mistakes only reinforces them. Here I am dependent upon others to hear the mistakes, to offer correction, even to point to new terms of interpretation. Nevertheless, my repeated practice also permits me, over time, to learn more than the notes. I learn, finally, the music and come to interpret that music as I engage its tradition through my own performance. Yes, repetition and ritual breed familiarity. But it is just this familiarity that is required for our ability to take the music into the depths of our being.

In the ritual practice of the sacramental life, we come over time to take into ourselves, to make our own, the grammar and narrative of the Christian life, the grammar of God's Trinitarian relatedness and the narrative of God's life with us. It is in this sense that I speak of liturgical practice as a practice of the theonomous self, self patterned in relatedness to a relational God for the sake of the world. It is in this sense that I began to speak of the relationship between the law of prayer, the law of belief, and the law of living, the *lex vivendi.* Our practice of prayer and sacrament argues for a way of being and knowing in the world that is written in body and mind, in the whole of the person. As Leonardo Boff reminds us, "Being in relationship . . . exists only in practice, through being performed."[6]

There is a story about Abba Joseph of Panephysis and a visit to him by Abba Lot. Abba Lot said to Joseph, "'Abba, as far as I can I say my little office, I fast a little, I pray and meditate, I live in peace and as far as I can, I purify my thoughts. What else can I do?' Then the old man stood up and stretched his hands toward heaven. His fingers became like ten lamps of fire and he said to [Lot], 'If you will you can become all flame.'"[7]

We may never be able to turn our fingers to flames, but this is the direction of our work as a Christian people in the liturgical practice of the theonomous self: In coming to know and practice the pattern of God's relatedness, we are formed in that pattern. In being shaped in the image and likeness of God, our lives are transformed in glory. Is this not what it means to live a doxological (or perhaps *doxa*logical) life? This doxologically shaped life led me in the previous chapter to suggest a final variation on my definition of liturgical catechesis as a practice of the theonomous self: Liturgical catechesis, as a practice of the theonomous self, is oriented

[6] *Trinity and Society* (Maryknoll, N.Y.: Orbis Books, 1988) 129.
[7] *The Sayings of the Desert Fathers*, trans. Benedicta Ward (Kalamazoo, Mich.: Cistercian Publications, 1984) 103.

toward the reacquisition or development of the image and likeness of God in response to God's saving grace through participation in the divine life as made available in liturgy and sacrament.

My discussion has drawn primarily from the sacramental liturgical practices of baptism and eucharist. It may be helpful, therefore, in a Protestant ethos of suspicion or distrust of ritual practices, to explore this last variation through a more typically, though also increasingly contested, "Protestant" example: the practice of hymn singing.

HYMNING THE SELF BEFORE GOD

In the midst of the current divisions, skirmishes, and even battles about "traditional" and "contemporary" worship, it could appear to be either sheer boldness or outright foolishness to make any claims about the function of hymnody in the life and practice of Christian communities that reach beyond understandings of song as personal or communal expressions. We sing because it expresses who we are. Yet both sides of the traditional/contemporary debate do make claims that exceed those of mere expressiveness. We know, too, that if the issues were only that of expression, there would be no cause for the present debate. Whether "traditional" or "contemporary," both argue, at least implicitly, that the shape, context, and style of Christian song are normative and constitutive— normative in that they provide rules about personal and communal life in faith, and constitutive in that they provide a means through which persons come to faith and by which communities are nurtured in faith.

Regardless of which side one chooses in these conflicts, we know that Christian song is powerful. We also know that the singing of hymns is more than making music:

"The hymns that I have sung often and memorized are ones that I quote to myself in times of spiritual need or in times of rejoicing. I can remember the words, and if not the exact words, I can remember the spirit and the general message of the hymn. So hymns continue to minister to me just like the scripture does. Which [sic] is one good argument for repeating certain hymns in liturgy with some frequency, so people have a chance to recall them."[8]

[8] Interview elicited as part of the study "The Faith and Practices of Christian Congregations" (Thomas E. Frank, Candler School of Theology, project

Or, as Fred Pratt Green states in one of his well-known hymns:

How often, making music, we have found
a new dimension in the world of sound,
as worship moved us to a more profound
Alleluia![9]

And, in his preface to *A Collection of Hymns for the use of the People called Methodists* of 1780, John Wesley commends its hymns and the hymnal to the reader "as a means of raising or quickening the spirit of devotion, of confirming his [sic] faith, of enlivening his hope, and of kindling or increasing his love to God and man. When poetry thus keeps its place, as the handmaid of piety, it shall attain, not a poor perishable wreath, but a crown that fadeth not away."[10]

The poetry of which Wesley speaks is presented for the purpose of congregational song and personal devotion. His reserve about its place as the "handmaid of piety" echoes Augustine, who was himself of divided opinion about song in Christian worship. In the *Confessions*, Augustine remembers the hold that music exercised upon his spirit, finding in it not only the "pleasures of the ear" but a "sense of restful contentment" as well. He resisted pure emotional expressiveness, arguing that it was not the music but the words or "thoughts which give [it] life" that granted music a place of honor in Christian worship. Fluctuating "between the danger of pleasure and the experience of the beneficent effect," Augustine settled for the latter, permitting music in worship that "through the delights of the ear the weaker mind may rise up towards the devotion of worship."[11] John Wesley encourages a similar attitude in his "Directions for Singing":

"Above all sing spiritually. Have an eye to God in every word you sing. Aim at pleasing him more than yourself, or any other creature. In order to do this attend strictly to the sense of what you

---

director) on the reception and use of *The United Methodist Hymnal* undertaken by Don Saliers. Used by permission.

[9] "When in Our Music God Is Glorified," *The United Methodist Hymnal*, 68.

[10] *A Collection of Hymns for the use of the People called Methodists*, 75.

[11] *Confessions*, trans. Henry Chadwick (New York: Oxford University Press, 1991) 207–208 (Book X, chap. 33).

sing, and see that your heart is not carried away with the sounds, but offered to God continually; so shall your singing be such as the Lord will approve here, and reward you when he cometh in the clouds of heaven."[12]

THE HANDMAID OF PIETY, INDEED

Each of these examples suggests that the singing of a hymn is more than making music, more than a nice song filling dead space in a liturgy, more than an aesthetic act, more than an act of self-expression. It is also an act of pastoral care in times of need and rejoicing. It provides, or at least has the potential to provide, a dimension of depth in our worship of God. It has a place as "the handmaid of piety" and directs us to worship. It is all of these things, and more. As Don Saliers has argued, "To thank God, to praise God, to confess, to intercede—all these are ways of gesturing the self in and through words."[13] While Saliers's concern is to describe how we "gesture the self" in and through the words and actions of the liturgy, I want to explore how the singing of a hymn might be such a gesture. I also want to argue that this gesture of the self, while expressive of who we are as Christian people, in some way also norms and constitutes us as Christian people.

What does it mean to "hymn the self before God"? Rather than speaking about hymns in general, I propose one hymn, Charles Wesley's "O for a heart to praise my God,"[14] as the instantiation of a particular gesture. The 1780 version of this text reads:

O for a heart to praise my God,
A heart from sin set free!
A heart that always feels thy blood,
So freely spilt for me!
A heart resigned, submissive, meek,
My great Redeemer's throne,

---

[12] *The United Methodist Hymnal*, vii.

[13] "Liturgy and Ethics," in *Liturgy and the Moral Self*, ed. E. Byron Anderson and Bruce T. Morrill, S.J. (Collegeville, Minn.: The Liturgical Press, 1997) 19.

[14] *A Collection of Hymns for the use of the People called Methodists*, Hymn 334, pp. 490–491. This hymn first appeared in the Wesleys' collection *Hymns and Sacred Poems* of 1742. It has appeared with regularity in the major Methodist hymnals since then.

Where only Christ is heard to speak,
Where Jesus reigns alone.

O for a lowly, contrite heart[15]
Believing, true, and clean,
Which neither life nor death can part
From him that dwells within!

A heart in every thought renewed,
And full of love divine,
Perfect, and right, and pure, and good—
A copy, Lord, of thine!

[Thy tender heart is still the same,
And melts at human woe;
Jesu, for thee distressed I am—
I want thy love to know.

My heart, thou know'st, can never rest
Till thou create my peace,
Till, of my Eden repossessed,
From every sin I cease.

Fruit of thy gracious lips, on me
Bestow that peace unknown,
The hidden manna, and the tree
Of life, and the white stone.][16]

Thy nature, gracious Lord, impart;
Come quickly from above;
Write thy new name upon my heart,
Thy new, best name of love!

Four questions will guide this conversation: (1) What does this text say or do? (2) What does the context of the text do with or to the text? (3) How does the practice of this text become a gesture of the self before God? (4) How is the practice of singing a hymn a liturgical gesture of the Christian self?

1) What does this hymn say or do? As a devotional text, the hymn comes from Wesley as a form of self-expression, commentary

[15] The 1742, 1765, and twentieth-century versions read "A [or An] humble, lowly, contrite heart."

[16] All the North American Methodist hymnals of the past century omit these three stanzas.

and reflection on Psalm 51:10: "Create in me a clean heart, O God, and renew a right spirit within me." S T Kimbrough describes Wesley's work as biblical interpreter, in part, as re-enacting "the initial experience of Scripture," personalizing "the text so that the text becomes his own," and "transforming the imagery of Scripture into categories of contemporaneous experience."[17] While we do not have access to Wesley's state of mind or heart when he wrote this text, placing his hymns in chronological order does provide the closest text we have to a spiritual autobiography. As an expressive act, Wesley wrote this hymn some three years after his evangelical awakening. In the context of this awakening, it reflects Wesley's hope for a new heart as well as a new life.

The psalm itself is a statement of unwavering honesty about the depth of human sinfulness. The psalm verse to which Wesley responds (v. 10) follows a confession of sinfulness and a prayer for the forgiveness of this sin. Verse 10 begins a prayer for renewal only possible following forgiveness. This renewal leads the psalmist to end the psalm with an act of praise.[18] Rather than paraphrasing the psalm text or Christianizing it, as we find in English hymnwriters before Wesley (such as Thomas Sternhold, Nahum Tate, or Isaac Watts), Wesley appropriates David's experience of a ruptured relationship with God as his own, interprets that experience through the heart and mind of Christian faith, and sets out an expectation of the new and perfected life that comes from the healing of the relationship through the transformation of the heart.[19] The way in which Wesley states this expectation reflects his reliance on Matthew Henry's commentary. In Henry's comments on

[17] "Charles Wesley and Biblical Interpretation," in *Charles Wesley: Poet and Theologian*, ed. S T Kimbrough, Jr. (Nashville: Abingdon Press, Kingswood Books, 1992) 114, 118.

[18] Artur Weiser, *The Psalms* (Philadelphia: Westminster Press, 1952) 401–407.

[19] Teresa Berger writes, "For Charles Wesley, the creation of a new heart is the essence of the 'new creation.' Wesley's preference for this image of a new heart is a good example of his interiorization of the larger image of the new creation. Those hymns devoted to the theme of Christian perfection repeatedly offer prayers for a new heart as a precondition for the life of perfection. . . . The heart, which longs for re-creation, is to be a copy of the heart of Jesus, and the *imago Dei*, which is to be restored is the *imago Christi* . . . ." *Theology in Hymns?*, trans. Timothy E. Kimbrough (Nashville: Abingdon Press, Kingswood Books, 1995) 147–148.

verses 7-13 of the psalm, he names the concerns of the psalmist as seeking an assurance of pardon, an assurance of restoration to God's favor, and God's sanctifying grace that his nature, his heart, might be changed.[20]

Wesley's first four stanzas focus on the present imperfect character or heart of the individual Christian. The heart is not completely free from sin even as it is not solely the dwelling place or throne of Christ. It is a heart renewed but not yet perfect in thought and love. It is a heart aware of its imperfection and of what it yet requires to bring it to completion. The perfect heart will be "believing, true, and clean," "perfect, and right, and pure, and good," a heart fashioned in the *imago Christi.* However, it is not until the end of the fourth stanza that we discover that the hymn is not only a vehicle for the expression of the singer's self-awareness of imperfection but a prayer directed to Christ in the form of a comparison between the heart of the singer and that of Christ. The editorial decisions to delete stanzas 5-7 in later Methodist hymnals undercut this comparison.

At the end of the fourth stanza and in the succeeding stanzas we come to realize that the hymn is a petition, as is the psalm verse on which it builds. This petition, even as it expresses a certain self-awareness, enacts a relationship between God in Christ and the singer, thereby constituting the person in relationship with God. The petition also intends a transformation of that relationship, thereby indicating a set of norms for that relationship. The goal of the text, as petition, is named at the end of stanzas 5 and 8: "I want thy love to know" and "Write thy new name upon my heart,/ Thy new, best name of love!" The heart fashioned in the *imago Christi* is the heart enabled to praise God through an experience of the love

<hr>

[20] *Commentary on the Bible* (New York: Revell, 1935) 3:432–433. It is worth considering another influence on Wesley's language at this point. One of the concluding prayers in the Great Litany of the *Book of Common Prayer,* which John Wesley commended to the Methodists to read each Wednesday and Friday, reads: "O God, merciful Father, that despiseth not the sighing of a contrite heart, nor the desire of such as be sorrowful; mercifully assist our prayers that we make before thee, in all our troubles and adversities whensoever they oppress us . . . ." (The prayer text is that found in John Wesley's abbreviation of the *Book of Common Prayer* for the Methodist societies in North America, generally known as the "Sunday Service" of 1784.)

of God for the singer. The heart upon which the "name of love" is written is the heart brought to Christian perfection.

2) In answering the second question, "What does the context of the text do with or to the text?" we must acknowledge that there is more than one context shaping the reception of this hymn. The first is the context of Charles Wesley's work in the early years after his conversion of 1738. In reading his journal from this period, we find a man filled with evangelical fervor, traveling the countryside, preaching as often as five times a day, visiting and praying with the sick and imprisoned, in active conflict with "predestinarians," and successfully winning hearts and minds to the way of Jesus Christ. This was a time filled with new hope and new life for Wesley.

The hymn also has a particular theological context within the Methodist movement itself. Charles and John were in agreement upon the ideal of Christian perfection, but they were not of one mind on its attainability in this life. While John remained cautiously convinced that perfection was attainable in this life, Charles believed that it was only likely to be attained at the end of the Christian's life. He believed that while the Christian person longs for perfection of the heart throughout one's life, living is characterized less by the attainment of perfection than by an ongoing striving toward perfection.

This theological context provides the framework for the hymn's place within the 1780 hymnal itself.[21] One might expect a text petitioning Christ for "a heart to praise my God" to address the concerns of the "mourner convinced of sin" or the "mourner brought to new birth"—the concerns of those awakening in faith for the first time and the categories of the hymns in the early part of the hymnal. While this text does help with these concerns, its position in the hymnal functions as a resource for those presumably mature

[21] The Wesleys intended the hymnal to function as a theological document as well as a "manual for public worship and private devotion" for the Methodist people, what John Wesley called "a little body of experimental and practical divinity" (Berger, *Theology in Hymns?* 1). As editor, John Wesley gave the hymnal a specific theological shape, much as we find explicitly or implicitly in any contemporary hymnal. But he also gave it an experiential shape. For the Wesleys, this shape was determined by what they understood to be the pattern of the Christian life, from an initial exhortation to return to God to its culmination in the life of glory, a life that is simultaneously individual and communal.

Christians "groaning for full redemption." It is concerned with the ongoing growth of the Christian person toward and in perfection. This context of the hymn within the hymnal also positions it to address the teleology of life with God in perfect love. In this regard it echoes the final stanza of the familiar "Love divine, all loves excelling": "Finish, then, thy new creation; pure and spotless let us be."

There are two performative contexts, that of private devotion and that of corporate song, that also require our attention. It is from the former that the text seems to develop at the first. In his personal reflection on the psalm, Wesley has engaged the text as if it names his own experience. What we discover in his hymn is that this engagement is no longer an "as if"; it is a naming of Wesley's personal experience in and with God in Christ. As such, it becomes a personal petition for the ongoing transformation of Wesley's heart and a statement of personal relationship with God. The personal character of this hymn is clear throughout: "O for a heart to praise my God," "My great Redeemer's praise," "My heart, thou know'st, can never rest/Till thou create my peace." This personal devotion and experience were central to the Wesleys' conversion experiences and to the work of evangelical revival that followed from it. It was out of concern for the personal appropriation of this experience that the Wesleys engaged in their work.

The more difficult question, I think, is, What happens when this form of personal petition is sung corporately? Does its corporate performance make it any less personal? Here it is helpful to make a distinction between personal and private. What is personal is of and about me but not "owned" by me, whereas what is private is mine alone. By placing this hymn in the 1780 *Collection* and in the hymnals that preceded it, John and Charles Wesley offer a personal rather than private language and teleology of relatedness to individuals and a people "called Methodist." As the language of a people rather than a person, the hymn establishes a framework within which Methodist people join in the song of all creation as, together, it groans for full redemption. In this form it becomes a petition for a corporate heart with which to praise God. It takes the individual experience of a broken relationship with God, as described above, and claims that experience for the evangelical society. It claims for that society a vision of the new and perfected life that comes through the healing of the relationship by the transformation of the heart. It is the heart of the body of Christ yearning to be shaped in and united with the perfect love manifest in the "tender heart" of Jesus. It is the heart yearning in new life and new hope for the completion of God's sanctifying work.

Teresa Berger describes the expressive-constitutive work of doxology through hymnody this way:

"Doxology is the bearer of a very specific and unique worldview (or more concretely, of a particular interpretation of religious existence), which, in the final analysis, only has meaning for those who make doxological speech their own. Specifically, the doxological interpretation of existence has meaning for those who understand and commit themselves to 'a sacrifice of praise to God, that is, the fruit of lips that confess his name' (Heb. 13.15)."[22]

What was a personal expression of faith becomes a communal expression that also begins to constitute person and community. The singing of the hymn not only provides the means for person and community to express their faith but also proposes to them a way of meaning and being in the world. Singing the hymn commits us as persons and community to a vision of relatedness to God and one another no longer marked by rupture. Singing the hymn commits self and community to a stance of love and desire before God. It binds each one of us and the community with which we sing to the doxological life that seeks perfect praise and perfect love of God. In doing so, we have gone beyond self-expression. Our singing of the hymn results, in a fashion, in the hymn "singing" us, naming us, identifying us as people of faith.

We know that the act of singing identifies us as singers. But in singing a hymn, we identify ourselves also with a particular text and tune, even if only momentarily. To sing requires the full engagement of body and mind in a commitment to act. It engages us in an intention to form sound at a particular pitch and in a particular rhythm not otherwise defined by the habits of speech. In these acts we are reminded that we have something to do with a text and tune, with something printed on a page and something to be realized in performance. While we may read the text silently or listen

[22] *Theology in Hymns?* 162.

to someone else sing it, our performance of the hymn results in our apprehension of the hymn "being registered integrally, by body and mind together."[23] The images, themes, and claims of the text are realized not as text but as a "writing on the body" in performance. To the extent that the hymn is sung by a corporate body, it requires not only our engagement in mind and body but a bodily engagement that is simultaneously individual and communal. The strophic and rhythmic character of the hymn requires that if we are to sing, we must sing and breathe together. What is registered integrally is registered communally. As the images, themes, and claims of a hymn are appropriated through performance and repetition, the hymn begins, so to speak, to take on a life of its own and to have its way with us. Writing in body and mind, the hymn is no longer only the expressive statement "This is who I am" but a constituting statement, "This is who you are coming to be."

3) This leads to my third and fourth questions and, more specifically, to the central question of this chapter: How does the practice of this text, the singing of a hymn, become a gesture, a "practice" of the self before God?[24] As I have tried to suggest in the preceding paragraphs, the liturgical gesture of the self is more than a form of self-expression, more than a mode of private action by which the autonomous person stands in solitude, even if with a community, before God. As a practice by which persons express personal and communal faith, hymn singing physically and mentally situates the person in a context of relatedness to the whole of a community

---

[23] Frank Burch Brown, *Religious Aesthetics* (Princeton: Princeton University Press, 1989) 93.

[24] While I may be accused of a sleight of hand in equating *gesture* and *practice*, there is a meeting point for the two terms that justifies this. Generally we think of gestures as physical acts to assist in expressing a thought or emphasizing a speech act. Gestures also function as signs of intention or attitude. It is this latter usage which I believe Saliers intends and which suggests my use of practice. Here I want *practice* to function in two ways. First, in its more familiar form we speak about the rehearsal of something intended for future, more polished performance. Second, in the technical sense now shaped by the retrieval of an Aristotelian understanding of *praxis* and as developed by Rebecca Chopp (see p. 84, n.3) practices are "culturally constructed and individually instantiated" patterns of meaning and action. It is the "sign of intention or attitude" and the "individually instantiated pattern of meaning and action" that describe equal human actions.

whose voice is united in song and to God. In this the hymn offers an experience of relatedness that is ours to appropriate. At the same time it offers a language with which we may name and interpret that experience.

As I indicated above, our appropriation of this experience and its interpretation suggest that in singing a hymn we engage in a ritual practice that makes claims upon us individually and in community. That is, in at least a small way, the singing of the hymn helps us as Christian persons and communities to mark, contain, and direct the flow of our lives in relationship to God and the world. Here we need only recall the pastoral function of hymn singing described in the opening quote. We also know that ritual events variously reveal, convey, and enact the power and permanence of a group. They break the individual out of isolation and define the boundaries of the community in which we are situated. They attend to the human needs for the affirmation and maintenance of the values and beliefs that ground the unity of a group. Here we need only think of the power conveyed by the playing and singing of a national anthem. Judith Kubicki, in her discussion of music as ritual symbol, argues that such a symbol is "a mediation of recognition which evokes participation and allows an individual or a social group to orientate themselves, that is, to discover their identity and their place within their world."[25] Our hearing of a tune, repeatedly associated with texts and other events, recalls not only our physical act of singing but particular emotional states and experiences. It recalls in us an engagement of mind and heart with an event, a text, an image, a relationship. Its symbolic effectiveness, Kubicki argues, is not our rational apprehension of what we are doing, but the "insight and interaction" determined by participation.[26]

It is tempting, especially in contexts that treat tradition as that which is only of the past, to treat hymn singing as the dull repetition of past poetic, musical, and theological languages. But if our singing is a form of participative knowing through which we come to know ourselves and our place in the world, then our singing is a

[25] "The Role of Music as Ritual Symbol in Roman Catholic Liturgy," *Worship* 69:5 (September 1995) 431.
[26] Ibid., 437.

context in which past and present encounter each other, meaning and self-understanding are transformed, and tradition engages the future. We may understand ourselves to be only singing a hymn, but this ongoing practice results in the writing of a variety of poetic, musical, rhythmic, and theological languages on the body and in the mind and heart of the singer. We "are moved to a more profound alleluia"; we are moved to more perfect praise. As a ritual practice, the singing of the hymn expresses the faith of persons in community even as it defines the terms by which person and community are constituted. In singing and praying for a new heart with which to praise God, we begin that for which we ask.

It is relatively easy, perhaps even commonplace, to understand ritual practice as involving person and community in a statement of its past and present identity, the story of a people in a particular relationship. In this sense the singing of Wesley's hymn manifests and presents a confession of personal and communal identity in imperfect relationship with God, unable to fully praise God due to the binding power of sin. But if we are also beginning that for which we ask, if we are singing the hymn in the knowledge and expectation of God's transforming power, in the possibility of a transformed heart, then our gesture is about the future as much as it is about the past and present. In beginning that for which we ask, "a heart to praise my God," we begin to gesture ourselves into the future of our relationship with God.

The self that we sing in this hymn is a self living in expectation of the life that is yet to be, a self emerging in time and in relationship to God. As an act of petition—as is the psalm verse on which it builds—the hymn enacts an unfolding relationship between God in Christ and the singer and prays for the ongoing transformation of that relationship. Walter Brueggemann makes a similar argument: "Praise is not a response to a world already fixed and settled, but it is a responsive and obedient participation in a world yet to be decreed and in process of being decreed through this liturgical act."[27] Even as person and community name a present state in which the heart is not yet free, not yet resigned, submissive, or meek, not yet believing, true and clean, it names and

[27] *Israel's Praise: Doxology Against Idolatry and Ideology*, (Philadelphia: Fortress Press, 1988) 11.

209

begins a future in which this is the case, in which the love, peace, and nature of Christ are bestowed. In singing and petitioning for a heart with which to praise God, we open ourselves to and engage in the transformation of our heart because we are praising God. In our hymnic gesture we sing our future into being.

The practice of singing the future into being is not to suggest that our future as Christian people is unconditionally open, that there are no expectations for the shape of that future. Were unconditional openness the case, we would have no reason to sing. Our lives would be marked, to the extent that they could be, by aimless wandering or indifference to the condition of our future. The theological and experiential shape of the *Collection* of 1780, as does the Christian story, suggests that there is a normative horizon for that future that yields neither aimlessness nor indifference. As Brueggemann argues, "It is the act of praise, the corporate, regularized, intentional, verbalized, and enacted act of praise, through which the community of faith creates, orders, shapes, imagines, and patterns the world of God, the world of faith, the world of life, in which we are to act in joy and obedience."[28] The future that we sing into being is already the world of God, faith, and life. It is undetermined in that our participation shapes the future. But it is conditioned, it has direction. Our singing directs us toward relatedness to God and transformation by God, a direction that in turn invites concern and commitment.

In singing "for a heart to praise God," our expectation of a new and perfected life in Christ defines a normative horizon. The in-breaking future is a heart fashioned in the *imago Christi*, a heart that is right, pure, and good. Yet as a practice in which past, present, and future meet, the hymn becomes an instantiation of that for which it asks. For a moment we seem to transcend our present imperfection and are united in that "love divine" and "peace unknown." In our hymnic gesture we manifest our openness to God's future for us, practice our intention to act in and with God, and reveal "the reality of God's intention to act toward us in accordance with God's unfailing promise."[29] In this we are constituted in a particular vision and practice of the Christian life.

[28] Ibid., 25–26.
[29] Don Saliers, *Worship as Theology: Foretaste of Glory Divine* (Nashville: Abingdon Press, 1994) 78.

It is perhaps in this sense that we can speak about the liturgical practice of hymn singing as a gesture of ourselves by which we participate in the divine life of the Triune God. That is, our gesture not only identifies our stance before God but engages us in the life and practice of God. The openness we express permits God's work of liberation, healing, and transformation. Our expression permits our participation in God's constituting work of grace and normative future. In this vein John Thornburg suggests that hymns do more than remind us of God's work of grace:

"They do not simply act as reminders of God's grace and the people and circumstances in which God's grace was present. Hymns also provide saving moments by placing us face to face with the glories and blemishes of our inherited faith tradition. They push us into places we might not otherwise go."[30]

Our expressive gesture constitutes and defines a pattern of relatedness to God. We also find that, as this relationship develops, we develop an awareness of and ability to be in relationship to other persons and to the world. The conclusion to which we are led is that the practice of singing the hymn, while a gesture of the self, is also an instantiation of the rule of prayer determining not only belief but our life in the world as well. *Lex orandi, lex credendi, lex vivendi.*

Within the larger complex of liturgical sacramental practices defined by the rites of Christian initiation and the eucharist, Wesley's hymn provides a specific example, perhaps a "micro-practice," of the liturgical gesture of the self. In our hymnic gesture we practice what is already and not yet in our Christian lives. Already there is a pattern of relatedness in and with the Triune God. This prompts our song in the first place. What is not yet is the completion of our "being made perfect in love." This prompts the particular gesture of this song, the petition for "a heart to praise God." While our singing requires conscious action on our part, the transformation and participation in God that it enacts are less overtly conscious. It is simultaneously something done to us, with us, and by us in God's name. It is simultaneously a gesture of ourselves before God

[30] "Saved by Singing: Hymns as a Means of Grace," *The Hymn* 47:2 (April 1996) 7.

and God's constituting and normative action with us in and for the world. It is a way of writing God's way on our bodies and in our hearts and minds. Our sung prayer for a heart that is "a copy, Lord, of Thine!" is a way of cooperating with God's redeeming work to fulfill human identity in the image and likeness of God. It is a way of practicing ourselves in relationship with one another and with the relational God revealed to us in God's own practices of exodus, lawgiving, covenanting, incarnating, dying and rising, and inspiriting. With Wesley, we hymn ourselves before God:

Thy nature, gracious Lord impart;
Come quickly from above;
Write thy new name upon my heart,
Thy new, best name of love!

Bibliography

Allchin, A. M. "Our Life in Christ: In John Wesley and the Church Fathers." In *We Belong to One Another*. Ed. A. M. Allchin. London: Epworth Press, 1965.

Augustine, St. *Confessions*. Trans. Henry Chadwick. New York: Oxford University Press, 1991.

Austin, John. *How to Do Things with Words*. New York: Oxford University Press, 1962.

Baptism, Eucharist and Ministry. Geneva: World Council of Churches, 1982.

Bass, Dorothy, ed. *Practicing Our Faith*. San Francisco: Jossey-Bass, 1997.

Bauman, Richard. "Performance." In *Folklore, Cultural Performances, and Popular Entertainments*. Ed. Richard Bauman. New York: Oxford University Press, 1992.

Bell, Catherine. *Ritual: Perspectives and Dimensions*. New York: Oxford University Press, 1997.

_____. *Ritual Theory, Ritual Practice*. New York: Oxford University Press, 1992.

Berger, Teresa. *Theology in Hymns?* Trans. Timothy E. Kimbrough. Nashville: Abingdon Press, Kingswood Books, 1995.

Boff, Leonardo. *Trinity and Society*. Trans. Paul Burns. Maryknoll, N.Y.: Orbis Books, 1988.

Book of Common Worship. Louisville: Westminster/John Knox Press, 1990.

Briggs, Charles L. *Competence in Performance*. Philadelphia: University of Pennsylvania Press, 1988.

Browning, Robert L., and Roy A. Reed. *The Sacraments in Religious Education and Liturgy*. Birmingham: Religious Education Press, 1985.

Brueggemann, Walter. *Israel's Praise: Doxology Against Idolatry and Ideology*. Philadelphia: Fortress Press, 1988.

Bryant, Barry E. "Trinity and Hymnody: The Doctrine of the Trinity in the Hymns of Charles Wesley." *Wesleyan Theological Journal* 25:2 (Fall 1990) 64–73.

Burch Brown, Frank. *Religious Aesthetics*. Princeton: Princeton University Press, 1989.

_____. *Good Taste, Bad Taste, and Christian Taste*. New York: Oxford University Press, 2000.

Bynum, Caroline Walker. "Women's Stories, Women's Symbols: A Critique of Victor Turner's Theory of Liminality." In *Fragmentation and Redemption: Essays in Gender and the Human Body in Medieval Religion*. New York: Zone Books, 1991.

Campbell, Ted A. *John Wesley and Christian Antiquity*. Nashville: Abingdon Press, Kingswood Books, 1991.

Carr, Anne E. "The New Vision of Feminist Theology." In *Freeing Theology: The Essentials of Theology in a Feminist Perspective*. Ed. Catherine Mowry LaCugna, 5–29 . New York: HarperCollins Publishers, Inc., 1993.

Chopp, Rebecca. *Saving Work*. Philadelphia: Westminster/John Knox Press, 1995.

Church, Michael G. L. "The Law of Begging: Prosper at the End of the Day." *Worship* 73:5 (September 1999) 442–453.

Collins, Mary. *Worship: Renewal to Practice*. Washington: The Pastoral Press, 1987.

_____. "Principles of Feminist Liturgy." In *Women at Worship: Interpretations of North American Diversity*. Ed. Marjorie Proctor Smith and Janet Walton, 9–26. Louisville: Westminster/John Knox Press, 1993.

Companion to the Book of Services. Nashville: Abingdon Press, 1988.

Confessing the One Faith. Geneva: WCC Publications, 1991.

Connerton, Paul. *How Societies Remember*. New York: Cambridge University Press, 1989.

Constitution on the Sacred Liturgy. New York: Paulist Press, 1964.

Cunningham, David. *These Three Are One*. Malden, Mass.: Blackwell Publishers, 1998.

Dalmais, Irénée Henri. "Theology of the Liturgical Celebration." In *The Church at Prayer*. Vol. 1: *Principles of the Liturgy*. Ed. A. G. Martimort. Trans. Matthew J. O'Connell. Collegeville, Minn.: The Liturgical Press, 1987.

De Clerck, Paul. "'Lex orandi lex credendi.' Sens original et avatars historiques d'un adage equivoque." *Questions Liturgiques* 59 (1978) 193–212.

_____. "La prière universelle, expression de la foi." In *La liturgia expression de la foi*. Conference Saint-Serge, XXV Semaine d'études liturgiques. Ed. A. M. Triacca and A. Pistola, 129–146. Rome: Edizioni Liturgiche, 1979.

Dorrien, Gary. "The Origins of Postliberalism: A Third Way in Theology." *Christian Century* 118:20 (JULY 4–11, 2001) 16–21.

Douglas, Mary. *Natural Symbols: Explorations in Cosmology*. 2nd ed. New York: Pantheon Books, 1982.

Duffy, Regis A., ed. *Alternative Futures for Worship*. Vol. 1: *General Introduction*. Collegeville, Minn.: The Liturgical Press, 1987.

Dykstra, Craig. *Growing in the Life of Faith: Education and Christian Practices*. Louisville: Geneva Press, 1999.

Easum, William M. "What I Now See in Worship." http://www.easum.com/netresul /Easum/00-06.htm.

_____. *Dancing with Dinosaurs*. Nashville: Abingdon Press, 1993.

_____. *How to Reach Baby Boomers*. Nashville: Abingdon Press, 1991.

_____. "21st century Worship." http://www.easum.com./netresul/Easum/ 96-08.htm.

Erickson, Craig Douglas. "Liturgical Participation and the Renewal of the Church." *Worship* 59:3 (May 1985) 231–243.

Erikson, Erik. "Ontogeny of Ritualization." In *Psychoanalysis—A General Psychology*. Ed. Rudolph Loewenstein, Lottie Newman, Max Schur, and Albert Solnit, 601–621. New York: International Universities Press, 1966.

_____. *Toys and Reasons: Stages in the Ritualization of Experience*. New York: W. W. Norton, 1977.

_____. *The Life Cycle Completed*. New York: W. W. Norton, 1985.

Erny, Pierre. "Rites et éducation: Les grandes fonctions du rite." *Lumen Vitae* (1992/2) 159–173.

Faber, Heije. "The Meaning of Ritual in the Liturgy." In *Current Studies in Ritual*. Ed. Hans-Günter Heimbrock and H. Barbara Boudewijnse, 43–56. Amsterdam and Atlanta: Rodopi, 1990.

Fides, Paul. *Participating in God*. Louisville: Westminster John Knox Press, 2001.

Finney, Charles Grandison. *Lectures on Revival*. Minneapolis: Bethany House Publishing, 1988.

Ford, David F. *Self and Salvation: Being Transformed*. New York: Cambridge University Press, 1999.

Fowler, James W., and Sam Keen. *Life Maps*. Ed. Jerome W. Berryman. Waco, Tex.: Word, Inc., 1985.

Frost, Brian. *Living in Tension Between East and West*. London: New World Publications, 1984.

Gadamer, Hans-Georg. *Truth and Method*. 2nd ed. Trans. Joel Weinsheimer and Donald G. Marshall. New York: Continuum, 1993.

Geertz, Clifford. *The Interpretation of Cultures*. New York: Basic Books, 1973.

Gennep, Arnold van. *The Rites of Passage*. Trans. Monika B. Vizedom and Gabrielle L. Caffee. Introduction by Solon T. Kimball. Chicago: University of Chicago Press, 1960.

Grimes, Ronald L. "Infelicitous Performance and Ritual Criticism." In *Ritual Criticism*. Columbia, S.C.: University of South Carolina, 1990.

Handelman, Don. *Models and Mirrors*. Cambridge: Cambridge University Press, 1989.

Happel, Steven. "Speaking from Experience: Worship and the Social Sciences." In *Alternative Futures for Worship*. Vol. 2: *Baptism and Confirmation*. Ed. Mark Searle, 171–188. Collegeville, Minn.: The Liturgical Press, 1987.

Harakas, Stanley Samuel. *Toward Transfigured Life*. Minneapolis: Light and Life, 1983.

Harrison, Verna. "Perichoresis in the Greek Fathers." *St. Vladimir's Theological Quarterly* 35:1 (1991) 53–65.

Heim, S. Mark. "The Depth of the Riches: Trinity and Religious Ends." *Modern Theology* 17:1 (January 2001) 21–55.

Henry, Matthew. *Commentary on the Bible*. New York: Revell, 1935.

Hilkert, Mary Catherine. "Experience and Tradition—Can the Center Hold?" In *Freeing Theology: The Essentials of Theology in a Feminist Perspective*. Ed. Catherine Mowry LaCugna, 59–82. New York: HarperCollins Publishers, 1993.

Hütter, Reinhard. *Suffering Divine Things: Theology as Church Practice*. Trans. Doug Stott. Grand Rapids, Mich.: Wm. Eerdmans Publishing Co., 2000.

Irwin, Kevin W. *Context and Text: Method in Liturgical Theology*. Collegeville, Minn.: The Liturgical Press, Pueblo Books, 1994.

Jacobi, Jolande. *Complex/Archetype/Symbol in the Psychology of C. G. Jung*. Trans. Ralph Manheim. Princeton: Princeton University Press, 1971.

Jennings, Theodore W. "On Ritual Knowledge." *The Journal of Religion* 62:2 (1982) 111–127.

Johnson, Elizabeth. *She Who Is*. New York: Crossroad, 1993.

Johnson, Maxwell E. "Can We Avoid Relativism in Worship? Liturgical Norms in the Light of Contemporary Liturgical Scholarship." *Worship* 74:2 (March 2000) 135–155.

Jung, Carl G. "Transformation Symbolism in the Mass." In *Psyche and Symbol*. Ed. Violet S. De Laszlo. Trans. R. F. C. Hull. Princeton: Princeton University Press, 1991.

Kapferer, Bruce. *A Celebration of Demons: Exorcism and the Aesthetics of Healing in Sri Lanka*. Providence, R.I.: Berg Publishers Ltd. and Washington, D.C.: Smithsonian Institution Press, 1991.

Käsemann, Ernst. *Commentary on Romans*. Ed. and trans. Geoffrey W. Bromiley. Grand Rapids, Mich.: Wm. Eerdmanns Publishing Co., 1980.

Kavanagh, Aidan. *On Liturgical Theology*. New York: Pueblo Publishing Co., 1984.

Kegan, Robert. *The Evolving Self*. Cambridge, Mass.: Harvard University Press, 1982.

Kelleher, Margaret Mary. "Liturgy: An Ecclesial Act of Meaning." *Worship* 59:6 (November 1985) 482–497.

Keller, Catherine. *From a Broken Web: Separation, Sexism and Self*. Boston: Beacon Press, 1986.

Kenneson Philip D. "Worship Wars and Rumors of Worship Wars." *Reviews in Religion and Theology* (May 1996) 72–75.

Kilmartin, Edward. *Christian Liturgy: Theology and Practice.* Kansas City: Sheed and Ward, 1988.

Kimbrough, S T, Jr. "Charles Wesley and Biblical Interpretation." In *Charles Wesley: Poet and Theologian.* Ed. S T Kimbrough, Jr., 106–136. Nashville: Abingdon Press, Kingswood Books, 1992.

Knight, Henry H., III. *The Presence of God in the Christian Life: John Wesley and the Means of Grace.* Metuchen, N.J.: Scarecrow Press, 1992.

Kubicki, Judith Marie. "The Role of Music as Ritual Symbol in Roman Catholic Liturgy." *Worship* 69:5 (September 1995) 427–446.

LaCugna, Catherine Mowry. "The Baptismal Formula, Feminist Objections, and Trinitarian Theology." *Journal of Ecumenical Studies* 26:2 (Spring 1989) 235–250.

_____. "The Filioque Clause in Ecumenical Perspective." In *Spirit of God, Spirit of Christ: Ecumenical Reflections on the Filioque Controversy.* Faith and Order Paper 102. Ed. L. Vischer. Geneva: WCC Publications, 1981.

_____. *God for Us: The Trinity and Christian Life.* New York: HarperCollins, 1991.

Langer, Susanne. *Philosophy in a New Key.* New York: Mentor Books, 1942.

Lathrop, Gordon. *Holy Things: A Liturgical Theology.* Minneapolis: Fortress Press, 1993.

_____. *Holy People: A Liturgical Ecclesiology.* Minneapolis: Fortress Press, 1999.

Lindbeck, George. *The Nature of Doctrine.* Philadelphia: Westminster Press, 1984.

Lindström, Harald. *Wesley and Sanctification.* Stockholm: Almgvist and Wiksells Boktryckery A. B., 1946. Reprint, with a foreword by Timothy L. Smith. Wilmore, Ky.: Francis Asbury Publishing Co., 1980.

Lossky, Vladimir. *In the Image and Likeness of God.* Crestwood, N.Y.: St. Vladimir's Seminary Press, 1985.

MacIntyre, Alisdair. *After Virtue.* Notre Dame: University of Notre Dame Press, 1984.

Macmurray, John. *Persons in Relation.* London: Faber and Faber, 1961.

_____. *The Self as Agent.* London: Faber and Faber, 1957.

Maddox, Randy. "John Wesley and Eastern Orthodoxy: Influences, Convergences and Differences." *Asbury Journal* 45 (1990) 29–53.

_____. *Responsible Grace.* Nashville: Abingdon Press, Kingswood Books, 1994.

Mantzaridis, Georgios I. *The Deification of Man.* Crestwood, N.Y.: St. Vladimir's Seminary Press, 1984.

Marshall, Bruce D. "Why Bother with the Church?" *The Christian Century* 113 (January 24, 1996) 74–76.

_____. *Trinity and Truth.* New York: Cambridge University Press, 1999.

Mead, George Herbert. *Mind, Self, and Society.* Ed. Charles W. Morris. Chicago: University of Chicago Press, 1934.

_____. *Philosophy of the Act.* Ed. Charles W. Morris. Chicago: University of Chicago Press, 1938.

_____. *The Philosophy of the Present*. Ed. Arthur E. Murphy. Chicago: University of Chicago Press, 1932.

Meeks, M. Douglas, ed. *Trinity, Community, and Power: Mapping Trajectories in Wesleyan Theology*. Nashville: Abingdon Press, Kingswood Books, 2000.

Methodist Service Book, The. Peterborough, Eng.: Methodist Publishing House, 1975.

Methodist Worship Book, The. Peterborough, England: Methodist Publishing House, 1999.

Metz, Johann. *Faith in History and Society: Toward a Fundamental Practical Theology*. Trans. David Smith. New York: The Seabury Press, 1980.

_____. *Followers of Christ: The Religious Life and the Church*. Trans. Thomas Linton. New York: Paulist Press, 1978.

Meyendorff, John. *Byzantine Theology*. New York: Fordham University Press, 1974.

Moltmann, Jürgen. *History and the Triune God: Contributions to Trinitarian Theology*. Trans. John Bowden. New York: Crossroad, 1991.

_____. *The Spirit of Life: A Universal Affirmation*. Trans. Margaret Kohl. Minneapolis: Fortress Press, 1992

_____. *The Trinity and the Kingdom*. Trans. Margaret Kohl. Minneapolis: Fortress Press, 1993.

A Monk of the Eastern Church (Lev Gillet). *Orthodox Spirituality*. London: SPCK, 1945.

Moran, Gabriel. *Religious Education Development*. Minneapolis: Winston Press, 1983.

Morrill, Bruce T. *Anamnesis as Dangerous Memory: Political and Liturgical Theology in Dialogue*. Collegeville, Minn.: Liturgical Press, Pueblo Books, 2000.

Morrill, Bruce T., ed. *Bodies of Worship: Explorations in Theory and Practice*. Collegeville, Minn.: The Liturgical Press, 1999.

Myerhoff, Barbara. "Rites of Passage: Process and Paradox." In *Celebration: Studies in Festivity and Ritual*. Ed. Victor Turner, 109–135. Washington: Smithsonian Institution Press, 1982.

Neibuhr, H. Richard. *The Responsible Self*. New York: Harper and Row, 1963.

Novak, David. "Theonomous Ethics: A Defense and a Critique of Tillich." *Soundings* 69 (Winter 1986) 436–463.

Oden, Thomas. *John Wesley's Scriptural Christianity*. Grand Rapids: Zondervan, 1994.

Ostdiek, Gilbert. *Catechesis for Liturgy*. Washington: The Pastoral Press, 1986.

Ottati, Douglas. "Being Trinitarian: The Shape of Saving Faith." *Christian Century* 112 (November 8, 1995) 1044–1047.

Outler, Albert. *John Wesley*. New York: Oxford University Press, 1964.

_____. "John Wesley: Folk Theologian." In *The Wesleyan Theological Heritage*. Ed. Thomas C. Oden and Leicester R. Longdon, 111–124. Grand Rapids, Mich.: Zondervan, 1991.

_____. "John Wesley's Interest in the Early Fathers of the Church." In *The Wesleyan Theological Heritage*. Ed. Thomas C. Oden and Leicester R. Longdon, 97–110. Grand Rapids, Mich.: Zondervan, 1991.

Peters, Ted. *God as Trinity: Relationality and Temporality in Divine Life*. Louisville: Westminster/John Knox, 1993.

Pfatteicher, Philip H. *The School of the Church: Worship and Christian Formation*. Valley Forge, Pa.: Trinity Press International, 1995.

Philibert, Paul J. "Readiness for Ritual: Psychological Aspects of Maturity in Christian Celebration." In *Alternative Futures for Worship*. Vol. 1: *General Introduction*. Ed. Regis A. Duffy, 35–121. Collegeville, Minn.: The Liturgical Press, 1987.

Power, David. *Unsearchable Riches: The Symbolic Nature of the Liturgy*. New York: Pueblo Publishing Co., 1984.

Procter-Smith, Marjorie. *In Her Own Rite: Constructing Feminist Liturgical Tradition*. Nashville: Abingdon Press, 1990.

_____. *Praying with Our Eyes Open*. Nashville: Abingdon Press, 1995.

Rahner, Karl. *The Trinity*. New York: Herder and Herder, 1970.

Ricoeur, Paul. "The Model of the Text: Meaningful Action Considered as a Text." *Social Research* 38 (Autumn 1971) 529–562.

Rodriguez, Richard. *Hunger for Memory*. New York: Bantam Books, 1982.

Roebben, Bert. "'Do We Still Have Faith in Young People?' A West-European Answer to the Evangelization of Young People in a Post-Modern World." *Religious Education* 90 (1995) 327–345.

Runyon, Theodore. *Wesleyan Resources for Ecumenical Theology*. J. D. Northey Lectures, 1993. Candler School of Theology, Emory University, Atlanta, Ga.

Ruth, Lester. "Lex Agendi, Lex Orandi: Toward an Understanding of Seeker Services as a New Kind of Liturgy." *Worship* 70 (September 1996) 386–405.

Saliers, Don E. "Liturgy and Ethics: Some New Beginnings." *Journal of Religious Ethics* 7 (1979) 173–189. Reprinted in E. Byron Anderson and Bruce T. Morrill, S.J., eds., *Liturgy and the Moral Self*. Collegeville, Minn.: The Liturgical Press, 1997.

_____. *The Soul in Paraphrase: Prayer and the Religious Affections*. New York: Seabury Press, 1980.

_____. *Worship as Theology: Foretaste of Glory Divine*. Nashville: Abingdon Press, 1994.

The Sayings of the Desert Fathers. Trans. Benedicta Ward. Kalamazoo, Mich.: Cistercian Publications, 1984.

Schaller, Joseph J. "Performative Language Theory: An Exercise in the Analysis of Ritual." *Worship* 62 (September 1988) 415–432.

Schmemann, Alexander. *Liturgy and Tradition*. Ed. Thomas Fisch. Crestwood, N.Y.: St. Vladimir's Seminary Press, 1990.

Searle, John. *Speech Acts: An Essay in the Philosophy of Language*. Cambridge, Mass.: Cambridge University Press, 1969.

Searle, Mark. "New Task, New Methods: The Emergence of Pastoral Liturgical Studies." *Worship* 57 (July 1983) 291–308.

Senn, Frank. "'Worship Alive': An Analysis and Critique of 'Alternative Worship.'" *Worship* 69 (May 1995) 194–224.

Stephanopoulos, Robert G. "The Orthodox Doctrine of Theosis." In *The New Man*. Ed. John Meyendorff and Joseph McLelland, 149–161. New Brunswick, N.J.: Agora Books, 1973.

Tambiah, Stanley. "A Performative Approach to Ritual." *Proceedings of the British Academy* 65 (1979) 113–169.

Teilhard de Chardin, Pierre. *The Divine Milieu*. New York: Harper and Row, 1968.

Thomas, J. Mark. "Theonomous Social Ethics: Paul Tillich's Neoclassical Interpretation of Justice." In *Being and Doing: Paul Tillich as Ethicist*. Ed. John J. Casey, 109–123. Macon, Ga.: Mercer University Press, 1987.

Thornburg, John. "Saved by Singing: Hymns as a Means of Grace." *The Hymn* 47 (April 1996) 7–11.

Tillich, Paul. *The Protestant Era*. Trans. James Luther Adams. Chicago: University of Chicago Press, 1948.

_____. *Systematic Theology:* I. Chicago: University of Chicago Press, 1951.

Timpe, Randie. "Ritualizations and Ritualisms in Religious Development: A Psychosocial Perspective." *Journal of Psychology and Theology* 11 (1983) 311–317.

Tracy, David. *The Analogical Imagination*. New York: Crossroad Publishing Co., 1981.

_____. *Plurality and Ambiguity*. San Francisco: Harper and Row, 1987.

Tucker, Karen Westerfield. *American Methodist Worship*. New York: Oxford University Press, 2001.

_____. "Sunday Worship in the Parish: Observations." In *The Sunday Service of the Methodists: Twentieth-Century Worship in Worldwide Methodism*. Ed. Karen Westerfield Tucker, 323–332. Nashville: Abingdon Press, Kingswood Books, 1996.

Turner, Victor. *The Anthropology of Performance*. New York: PAJ Publications, 1987.

_____. *Dramas, Fields, and Metaphors: Symbolic Action in Human Society*. Ithaca, N.Y.: Cornell University Press, 1974.

_____. *The Ritual Process: Structure and Anti-Structure*. Ithaca, N.Y.: Cornell University Press, 1977.

_____. "Ritual, Tribal and Catholic." *Worship* 50 (November 1976) 504–526.

United Methodist Hymnal, The. Nashville: The United Methodist Publishing House, 1989.

Vincie, Catherine. "The Cry for Justice and the Eucharist." *Worship* 68 (May 1994) 194–210.

_____. "Rethinking Initiation Rituals: Do Women and Men Do It the Same Way?" *Proceedings of the North American Academy of Liturgy* (1995) 145–170.

Wainwright, Geoffrey. *Doxology: The Praise of God in Worship, Doctrine and Life*. New York: Oxford University Press, 1980.

_____. *Eucharist and Eschatology*. New York: Oxford University Press, 1981.

_____. *Worship with One Accord: Where Liturgy and Ecumenism Embrace*. New York: Oxford University Press, 1998.

Walton, Janet. *Feminist Liturgy: A Matter of Justice*. Collegeville, Minn.: The Liturgical Press, 2000.

_____. "The Missing Element of Women's Experience." In *The Changing Face of Jewish and Christian Worship in North America*. Ed. Paul F. Bradshaw and Lawrence A. Hoffman, 199–217. Notre Dame: University of Notre Dame Press, 1991.

Warren, Michael. "Speaking and Learning in the Local Church: A Look at the Material Conditions." *Worship* 69 (January 1995) 41.

Weiser, Artur. *The Psalms*. Philadelphia: Westminster Press, 1952.

Wesley, Charles. *Gloria Patri, Etc., or Hymns to the Trinity*. London, 1746.

Wesley, John. *The Sunday Service of the Methodists in North America*. Introduction, notes and commentary by James F. White. Cleveland, Ohio: OSL Publications, 1991.

_____. *The Works of John Wesley*. Vol. 1: *Sermons*. Ed. Albert Outler. Nashville: Abingdon Press, 1984.

_____. *The Works of John Wesley*. Vol. 2: *Sermons*. Ed. Albert Outler. Nashville: Abingdon Press, 1984.

_____. *The Works of John Wesley*. Vol. 7: *A Collection of Hymns for the use of the People called Methodists*. Ed. Franz Hildebrandt and Oliver A. Beckerlegge. Oxford: Clarendon Press; New York: Oxford University Press, 1983.

_____. *The Works of John Wesley*. Vol. 11. Ed. Thomas Jackson. London: Wesleyan Book Room, 1871.

_____. *The Works of John Wesley*. Vol. 12. Ed. Thomas Jackson. London: Wesleyan Methodist Book Room, 1871.

_____. *The Works of John Wesley*. Vol. 14. Ed. Thomas Jackson. London: Wesleyan Book Room, 1871.

_____. *The Works of John Wesley*. Vol. 18: *Journals and Diaries I (1735–1738)*. Ed. W. Reginald Ward and Richard P. Heitzenrater. Nashville: Abingdon Press, 1988.

_____. "Thoughts on Christian Perfection." In *John Wesley*. Ed. Albert Outler. New York: Oxford University Press, 1964.

White, James. *Protestant Worship*. Louisville: Westminster/John Knox Press, 1989.

Worgul, George S., Jr. *From Magic to Metaphor*. New York: Paulist Press, 1980.

Wuthnow, Robert. *After Heaven: Spirituality in America Since the 1950s*. Berkeley: University of California Press, 1998.

Zimmerman Joyce Ann. *Liturgy and Hermeneutics*. Collegeville, Minn.: The Liturgical Press, 1999.

Zizioulas, John D. *Being As Communion: Studies in Personhood and the Church*. Crestwood, N.Y.: St. Vladimir's Seminary Press, 1993.

Index

formation, 56–58, 59, 194

Gadamer, Hans-Georg, 102, 105–106
Geertz, Clifford, 65 n. 16
Gen-X, 14, 16
gesture 125, 126; gesture of self, 200, 201, 207–210
grammar 31, 56, 116–123; Trinitarian, 132, 143–144, 150, 156, 162–166, 188–189, 192, 197

Handelman, Don, 55 n. 51, 65–66 n. 16
Hilkert, Mary Catherine, 52
hospitality, 9–10, 17–18, 20–22
hymn-singing, 152, 198–212

identity, Christian, 2, 13, 35–36, 57, 79–80
image and likeness, 176–179, 181
inscribing and incorporating practices, 78–79
instrumental action, 106, 108
internal good, 102–105
Irwin, Kevin, 27–28, 99–100

Jennings, Theodore, 75, 80–81
Johnson, Maxwell, 44, 46, 57

Kapferer, Bruce, 90–94, 96–98, 106, 112
Kavanagh, Aidan, 26, 40, 93, 156
Kegan, Robert, 124, 129–132, 146, 150
Keller, Catherine, 147–148 n. 88
Kilmartin, Edward, 27
Knight, Henry H., 4–5, 184, 185

LaCugna, Catherine, 114, 133–134, 136–137, 140–142, 144, 148–150
Langer, Suzanne, 102 n. 59
Lathrop, Gordon, 20 n. 25, 44–45, 57, 166 n. 27
lex orandi lex credendi, 24–29, 49, 108, 193–194, 196–197, 211
Lindbeck, George, 117–123, 144, 151

liturgical catechesis, 4, 109–112, 113–114, 167–168, 188–190, 192–198
liturgical participation, 39–40, 57–58, 178, 192, 194–195, 208, 210–211
liturgical practice, 23–24, 28–29, 34, 40, 46, 54–58, 114, 115, 149–150, 174, 179, 188, 192–197
liturgical reform/renewal, 33, 37, 39–40, 45, 47, 52
liturgy and ethics, 27–28

MacMurray, John, 93, 124, 126–130, 140, 145–146
Maddox, Randy, 5–6
Marshall, Bruce D., 105 n. 71
McIntyre, Alisdair, 102–105
Mead, George Herbert, 106–108, 124–126, 128–132, 144, 146
means of grace, vii–viii, 2, 4–6, 152, 175, 178, 180, 183–185, 188
Methodist, United, 1, 28, 33, 121, 160–164, 172; British, 160–162, 164, 172
Metz, Johann Baptist, 187
Moltmann, Jürgen, 133–140, 142–144, 146, 148
mystagogy, 168

Neibuhr, H. Richard, 147–148 n. 88

ordo, 44–46, 57–58
orthodoxia, 24, 29, 56–58
Ottati, Douglas, 132–133
Outler, Albert, 182 n. 29, 186 n. 39

perfection, 180–189, 204–205
perichoresis, 138, 142–149, 186
practice, 29, 91, 114, 165, 179, 194–196, 210; definitions of, 29 n. 41, 84, 103
practicing ourselves, 83, 169, 178, 184, 188, 189–190, 193, 207
praise worship, 47–48

224